NINE MONTHS
FOR A LIFETIME

DUSTIN ELKIN

To Jennie…

Table of Contents

Chapter 1
First Kiss

I was in between clients and standing in the break room of the salon, drinking stale black coffee. I didn't care what it tasted like. I needed the caffeine to get me through the rest of my shift. My phone rang in my pocket, so I pulled it out to see who was calling. It was a local number with a 480 area code, but I didn't have the number saved, so I ignored the call, then finished my coffee fast, like a well drink at a dive bar. The faster you drink it, the less you have to taste it, but it'll get you feeling the way you want.

My phone rang again, and it was the same number. I thought to myself, "These guys selling extended warranties on cars don't give up." I ignored this call as well. Then I got a text message from the number.

"It's Jennie, nerd! Answer your phone."

Jennie Sadusky. I forgot I had made plans to make tacos with Jennie tonight. We had been messaging each other on Facebook Messenger for a few months. I posted a picture on Facebook last week of some tacos I had made, and Jennie messaged me asking if I'd show her my secrets to making tacos since I'm half Mexican. Jennie was divorced and living back at her parents' house—the same house she grew up in—only now with her three kids: Sophie, 12; Noah, 10; and Max, 6; just a few blocks from where I lived.

Jennie had gone through a bad divorce five years ago. Her husband had repeatedly cheated on her, and after the last girl, Jennie finally had enough and left him. For work, Jennie tutored kids after school. For a time, she was a special needs teacher but had stepped away from that. Jennie helped out at the house by paying the electric bill, buying groceries, and cooking. That's why she asked me how to make tacos.

Anyone who is lucky had a Jennie Sadusky in their lives growing up.

I grew up across the street from Jennie in the '90s in Gilbert, AZ, in the neighborhood of Val Vista Lakes. VVL, as we called it, was a master-planned community built in the 1980s. It had three man-made lakes in the middle of the Phoenix desert. It was like an oasis with palm trees, green grass, and water. Pontoon boats lined the backyards of lake houses, with ducks that never had to fly south for the winter. The Arizona desert heat would hit your face, but your eyes made you think you were in Southern California.

Jennie was blonde, beautiful, popular, smart, and funny. I had first seen her the day my family moved into our new house. I was 15 years old and fell in love immediately, like most 15-year-olds do. She had blond pigtails, braces, jean shorts with high white socks, and brown leather three-hole Doc Martens on the day I first saw her. Jennie had the most beautiful light blue eyes with big cheekbones. When she smiled, the cheekbones would rise and highlight her eyes.

Her parents had placed a portable basketball hoop by their mailbox, and you could play on it from the street. When I wanted to see Jennie, I would walk across the street with a basketball and start shooting hoops. Her bedroom was above the garage, and she'd see me playing on her hoop and come out to shoot with me. She wasn't any good, and I couldn't call her for double dribbling because it was her basketball hoop.

Sometimes, I'd go over and start shooting hoops to get her attention. But sometimes, when the door opened, her younger brother Matt came out, so I'd play with him. All the kids on the street played basketball at the Sadusky basketball hoop.

Jennie and I were one grade apart. When I went to 9th grade at Highland High School, she went into 8th grade at Greenfield Jr. High School. That year, I made the varsity soccer and track teams as a freshman. I even got a letterman jacket. Jennie kept getting prettier. Dating a girl a year younger than you who was in junior high was social suicide—and kind of creepy—so I thought I'd ask her out when she got to high school. I waited too long.

Jennie showed up on the first day of high school, and all the upperclassmen guys had their eyes on her. A letterman jacket can't compete with a car, even if it was their parents' car. She quickly stopped riding the bus with me and started getting rides from boys with cars. She went to prom in her freshman year—the only freshman to get asked. I soon found myself in the friend zone—a zone I never wanted or chose to be in. I was in a teenage love purgatory, and there I'd stay for 25 years, until one day I posted a picture on Facebook of some tacos I had made.

I got another text message from Jennie: "Call me back."

I had told her the week before that I was off work at nine on Saturday night. If she wanted to come over, I'd make some tacos and show her how I do it. She told me nine was too late to eat, and I never heard back. I figured she wasn't interested. Then I got the phone call. I didn't have her number saved because I had never had her number. We messaged on social media from time to time over the years. She had my phone number because I gave it to her the week before.

I called Jennie back from the salon's back room. She answered and said, "Are we still making tacos tonight at nine?"

"Of course," I said, even though I didn't have anything to make tacos with at my house.

"What's your address?"

I gave Jennie my address. And then she asked, "Can I bring anything?"

"No, I have everything." I didn't.

"Hurry up, I don't have all night, and I'm hungry."

"Don't be bossy, we're not shooting hoops in your parents' front yard."

"I wasn't bossy! That was like 25 years ago, Dustin."

"Ok, I'll see you tonight, Jennie," and I hung up.

I got through the rest of my shift and managed to finish my last haircut 20 minutes early. On my way home to Val Vista, I rushed to the Fry's grocery store and hurried through the parking lot, grabbing a shopping cart that someone had left near my car. I hurried to grab cheese, cilantro, onions, jalapeños, garlic, lemons, limes, and tomatoes. Then, I headed to the meat department to get skirt steak. On the way to the alcohol, I picked up some small flour tortillas. Once in the alcohol section, I picked up a six-pack of Corona, then a bottle of white wine and red wine. I hadn't seen Jennie in years and didn't know what she liked, so I got both. I paid for my groceries and texted her that I was leaving work as I got to my car.

I pulled up to my house, and Jennie was already there, sitting in her gray Jeep Cherokee. I parked in my driveway, grabbed the groceries from my back seat, and started walking to my front door. Jennie got out of her car and walked to my front door, but ran into some overgrown tree branches hanging near my entry from the mesquite tree in my front yard.

She pushed them out of her way and said, "You need to trim your tree."

"Still bossy," I said.

"Bossy is just a cute way of calling someone bitchy."

"Well, I haven't seen you in a while. I was going to try and wait an hour before I called you a bitch."

"Nice to see you're still a dick, Dustin."

"I prefer to be called an asshole."

"Well, I haven't seen you in a while, Dustin. I was going to wait an hour."

Jennie smiled, and I unlocked the door and let her in first. Then I put the groceries on the island in my kitchen. She laughed as she walked around the house, giving herself a tour, and looked at my bachelor pad and the four-foot-tall Stormtrooper I had in my entryway. I also had a pinball machine in my kitchen and a slot machine in my living room next to a bar with a kegerator. An oversized framed poster of Johnny Cash flipping the bird was the centerpiece of my living room.

"Your house is a man cave!" she said.

"The garage is a full arcade with a pool table, Golden Tee, Cruis'n USA, NBA Jam, Mortal Kombat, Tekken, NFL Blitz, and two more pinball machines." I smiled like it would impress her, but Jennie just rolled her eyes and said, "Boys."

I opened a bottle of Corona with my Bic lighter and handed it to her.

"A beer for the homecoming queen?"

"Runner-up," Jennie replied.

"Isn't that a cute way of saying second place? I have to take a shower real quick to get the hair off me," I said as my dog Chichi came running out to say hi.

Chichi is an old girl chihuahua who only likes me. My nephew Kaden found her a few years ago, trying to cross a busy intersection. He asked me if she could stay at my house until he found the owner because his dogs tried to eat her. After a few days, I gave her a name, and she was mine—or I was hers.

Jennie went to pet Chichi, but I warned her, "She bites everyone!"

While in the shower, I heard a scream followed by a bark. Chichi strikes again.

I got out of the shower and put on my clothes, then came into the living room where Jennie was holding Chichi, with a paper towel around her finger showing blood.

"She likes you," I said and laughed as I walked into the kitchen and started separating the groceries.

Jennie sat across the island from me as I prepared the food. I opened myself a beer, then started chopping the onions. And we started to talk and catch up.

"So, you're not with Jeffrey anymore?" I asked.

"Uhhhh, no! What happened with you and Rachel?"

Social media makes it so you might not talk to someone for years, but they know everything.

"Ya, she broke up with me for calling her my ex-girlfriend's name by mistake one too many times."

"Shut up, that was for real?"

"Ya. I asked Rachel for a beer, but I said 'Lauren.' She got so mad at me, I said, 'It's not my fault your names both have the same number of syllables.'"

"You did not!"

"I did. Then I asked Siri what's my problem with women, and she said,

'This is Alexa.'"

Jennie laughed and spilled her beer, then asked, "Can I help you? I came to learn, not to have you make dinner for me."

I handed her my knife from across the island.

"Come on over here," I said.

She walked over and shook her empty beer, so I got her another. I handed her some cilantro, and we both started chopping. Then our elbows touched, and I looked at her. She was wearing a black dress that stopped just above the knees, and her tiny feet were in black flip-flops. I looked up and saw her blond hair in a bun and those big cheekbones that led into her light blue eyes. I handed her some more cilantro. As we chopped, our bodies leaned into each other until our legs tangled, and we laughed and talked as we continued to cut the tomatoes and onions, then squeezed the lemons and limes into a bowl that had the skirt steak.

Then we were finished, and I didn't want this moment to end. I grabbed a bottle of red wine and said, "Wine?"

"That's what I really like," she said.

I didn't open it. I put it in my black Herschel backpack, along with my favorite Batman blanket, a wine opener, and two glasses. Then I told Jennie, "Let's go!"

"Go where?" she asked.

"To the lake to have a drink. It's too nice out to stay inside."

Jennie agreed and followed me out...

The lake was only a block away, so we walked with our beers in our hands. We got to the lake, and I laid out the Batman blanket on the green grass, and Jennie sat on it. We had a million-dollar view of the lake surrounded by the million-dollar houses that were built on the lakefront property. My house was far from a million-dollar home, but still, these were my neighbors. I put our empty beers in the trash can by the sidewalk, opened the wine, and poured two glasses. We sat staring at the sky and the million-dollar homes on the lake.

"You're scoring brownie points. I come to the lake by myself all the time and stare at the sky and the water with a glass of wine."

"I do too. It's funny that we never ran into each other."

"I go to a different spot closer to my house."

"Hey, that's the Big Dipper," I said, pointing to the only constellation I know.

"That's what she said," she said.

We laughed and leaned on each other, getting closer with every laugh. I rested my left arm on her right leg and was building up the courage to kiss her. I had kissed many girls in my life, but this time I was nervous. What if I was reading this wrong? What if I'm still just the boy across the street? What if...

Then Jennie kissed me. I wasn't ready! Her lips hit mine, and I froze.

"I'm sorry," she said.

"No, I wasn't ready. I need a do-over."

Then I kissed Jennie again, and it was perfect. We locked lips, gently, and I held the back of her head with my left hand as we glided to the blanket, with my right hand grabbing her waist.

I heard a voice in my head, "It's over, you're going to marry her." We kept kissing and rolling on the blanket, our flip-flops scattered around the grass, and the wine knocked over.

"We should go back to your house," she said.

Barefoot, I picked up the Batman blanket and stuffed it into my backpack, then looked around for our flip-flops. After I found them, I helped Jennie up and threw the empty bottle of wine into the trash can. We started walking back to my house down Key Biscayne Way, holding hands and smiling. I thought to myself, I'm going to marry you.

Then Jennie said, "Everyone is going to freak out when they find out."

It was like she was saying we were together. If any other girl ever said that after a first kiss, I would have run! But I just gripped her hand tighter and said, "I know, right?"

We talked the whole way home, and I opened the door to my house for her. I followed her into my bedroom, and we picked up where we left off at the lake—until Jennie stopped me and said, "What happened to my tacos?"

"The carne asada needs to marinate overnight, so I could cook it for you tomorrow?"

"Tomorrow? So, this is a two-night date?"

"Is it a date?" I asked.

"No, you have to take me out for it to be a date."

I kept kissing her, and she said, "Don't you have to teach Sunday school tomorrow?"

I laughed and said, "Ya, I do."

Then I looked at my phone: it was after one in the morning.

We lay there for several more minutes, and I started to fall asleep with her in my arms. Jennie got up and out of the bed, and I woke up.

"Stay in bed. Go to sleep. I'll see you tomorrow. Call me after church. I want my tacos," she said.

I got up anyway to walk Jennie to the door, then kept walking her to her car. She clicked her key to unlock the door. I opened the door for her. We had one more kiss, then I watched her car drive away. After she had turned around the corner, I threw my arms in the air and said out loud, "I just made out with Jennie Sadusky! And she's coming back tomorrow for more." I walked inside my house and locked my door, then went to my bedside, kneeled, and said my prayers. It was a short prayer... simply, "Thank you, Lord." I then fell asleep with Jennie on my mind and Chichi on my chest.

Chapter 2
Sweet Child of Mine

After church that morning, Jennie texted me that she'd be over later that night after she put the kids to bed at her parents'. It was noon, so I picked up a six-pack of Coors Light and went to meet my brother at the Val Vista Lakes Clubhouse. He lived two blocks from me, in a condo across the street from the Clubhouse. We grew up in Val Vista Lakes and, as adults, moved back because of our love for the Clubhouse. The main reason for our love for the Clubhouse was that it had a beach pool lagoon with sand that sat next to one of the three man-made lakes and made us feel like we were in California. A waterfall flowed behind the pool, and there was a sand volleyball court that was hardly used but looked good in the background. There was a Jr. Olympic-size pool and a jacuzzi, two large cabanas that provided shade, several tennis courts, and the clubhouse itself had two indoor racquetball courts, a small gym, and a large ballroom for big events like weddings.

I walked in and was greeted by one of my best friends, Chad, who had worked there for 25 years. He started in high school and never left. He even graduated from ASU but kept his job at the Clubhouse after graduation. He was two years older than me. When I was 16, he used to kick me out of the club all the time—but it was always my fault. One time, someone left the tennis ball machine out on the courts, so I angled it up by putting a couple of bricks under it and aimed it at the street, turned it on. It's all fun and games until you hit a Mercedes. Chad knew it was me because I went to the street to see what cars I'd hit, and he caught me laughing. Another time, I filled the pockets of my swimsuit with soap from the hand dispenser in the men's restroom, then got in the jacuzzi and had my own foam party. The adults in the jacuzzi didn't enjoy my enthusiasm for fun, and I got kicked out again. But eventually, Chad and I went from foes to friends. We started hanging out at the local dive bar, Crabby Don's, in our 20s and bonded over draft beers and sports—mostly baseball.

"Hey Chad," I said as I walked in with my towel over my left shoulder and the six-pack in my right hand.

"You suck," he said. He was still salty after my Dodgers had recently swept his Diamondbacks in a series.

"Don't get mad. We're good and you suck."

"You bought the team, and the 2020 World Series doesn't count."

"They bought a team. I bought a Bellinger jersey."

"Same thing. You support them," Chad said.

"The Diamondbacks bought the 2001 World Series, my man. Grow up. Maybe you and some fans can start a GoFundMe. Better yet, start a 401k. Then in 30, maybe 40 years, you guys can save up enough money to buy some decent talent." I liked the Diamondbacks, but I grew up going to Dodgers games in L.A., at Chavez Ravine, with my dad and brother before we moved to Arizona. Also, I loved a chance to talk trash.

"Do you know why they named the Arizona baseball team after a rattlesnake?" I asked Chad.

"Why?"

"Because you hardly ever see them in October."

"Your brother and dad are at the beach pool."

"Thank you, princess," I said as I blew him a sarcastic kiss.

"I hate you," he said, while trying not to laugh.

When I got to the beach pool, my dad and brother were already throwing a frisbee, and I put my beers in my brother's cooler. We made small talk like, "What's up, how's it going?" I couldn't truthfully answer them. I wanted to tell them, "I think I'm dating Jennie Sadusky, and she is coming over tonight, and I love her and I'm going to marry her, and we're going to get a Live

Laugh Love sign in our house and take family pictures in the desert." But instead, I said, "Nothing."

We found shade by the pool under a tree in the 110-degree Arizona heat and cracked open some beers, then walked into the pool on and off to try and stay cool. A few more friends we knew showed up with more beer. We drank until we ran out, then I went home to wait for Jennie. I fell asleep on my couch with the sun still up.

My phone rang and woke me. It was Jennie. I answered.

"Hello."

"Hey, the kids are in bed and my parents are watching them. I'm coming over."

"Awesome, see you soon."

I jumped in the shower to wake up and change. Jennie was at my house as soon as I got dressed. She walked in and we kissed.

She said, "Where are my tacos?" Jennie was holding a Tupperware of guacamole she had made.

"Let's cook them." The meat was still in the refrigerator.

She thrust the guacamole into my chest and said, "They're not ready?"

"I was waiting for you."

She saw the unopened white wine on my counter from the night before, so I said, "Have a glass of wine and I'll cook for you."

I poured her a glass, and she sat as I cooked the carne asada on the stove. Most people do it on a grill, but I found cooking it in a pan kept more of the flavor, like cooking a filet in butter in a pan. We dipped tortilla chips into the guacamole she had made as we talked about our days. Her glass was half full, so I poured her some more wine. I was drinking Pepsi.

I put the meat on the cutting board to cool down. Then we started kissing again. Eyes closed, but we managed to stumble into my bedroom and onto my bed. I took my shirt off, then hers.

Then she said, "How was church?"

"Great," I said, as I kept kissing her.

"What were they talking about?"

"Not abstinence."

She pushed me away lightly and said, "Really, what did they talk about?"

I told her, "Honestly, I don't know because I couldn't stop thinking about you the whole time."

"So you were thinking about this? Us having sex? At church?"

"No, I was thinking about you at the bus stop 25 years ago and how I wanted you then."

"We should wait," Jennie said.

"Ok."

"Just ok?"

"Yes, ma'am."

"Don't call me that," she said, and gently hit me. "We should wait…"

I told her, "I've been waiting 25 years. I have no problem waiting a little while longer."

Jennie liked my answer and started rubbing my back, caressing it with strokes up and down, sometimes in a circular pattern. Soon, I was off to sleep.

I woke up alone and immediately looked for my phone.

I had a text from Jennie that read: "Hey, you fell asleep, and I didn't want to wake you. I'll call you tomorrow." So I rolled over and went back to sleep.

I woke up in the morning alone. I felt like being productive on my day off, so I went to the gym and worked out. When I got home, I decided to clean. A good deep clean. I moved the furniture and swept, then mopped. Cleaned the two bathrooms in my house, including the showers. Then I made my bed and dusted my room. Finally, I made it to my office. Sounds professional, but it was just a place to display my vintage action figures and toys. I had a salon chair in the office with a mirror, and I'd do haircuts there for extra money.

I came across a green mask that was a replica from the Jim Carrey movie

The Mask. I tried to put it on Chichi, but she ran, so I put it on myself, then looked in the mirror and said, "Ssssmokin'!" There was a knock at my door. I thought, "Who knocks and doesn't text first?" I figured it was Mormon missionaries, Jehovah's Witnesses, or someone trying to get my pest control business. I left the mask on and answered the door without looking.

It was Jennie.

"Hey, nerd," she said with a grin on her face. She was wearing large black sunglasses. She walked into my house and put her sunglasses on top of her head. I took the mask off and said, "Hey." Then she gave me a hug.

I looked down at my phone—no missed texts from her.

"I hope you don't mind that I just stopped by. I was in the neighborhood tutoring a kid and was passing by, so I thought I'd stop by."

"You live in the neighborhood," I laughed.

"I was thinking about you." Then she paused, took a big smell of my house, and looked around. I thought she was impressed that I cleaned.

"Are you covering up a murder scene? It's so clean and smells like bleach."

"I mopped with bleach."

"Use Fabuloso. It smells great."

"So, you stopped by to give me cleaning tips?"

"No, I missed you."

"I missed you too."

Then we kissed, and kissed, and kissed some more until we found ourselves back in my room.

"I thought we were going to wait?" she said.

"Now I've been waiting 25 years plus a day to lose my virginity to you," I replied.

"You are not a virgin. Far from it!" She laughed.

"Those other girls were practice," I insisted.

"Never mention other girls!" she said, leaning in to kiss me again.

I nodded my head, and that was the first time we made love. On a Monday afternoon in late August.

The next day, I went to work at the salon. I texted Jennie after every client, and she texted back. We were like two high school kids falling in love. We didn't see each other that night—she needed to stay home with the kids—but we continued to text late into the night.

The next day, I woke up to a text from her: "Have you told your friends?"

I replied, "No, I don't think they'd believe me."

I went to work and continued to text her between clients. She wanted me to come over to her house that night to watch a movie after work. I couldn't go because I had plans to spend the night at my dad's house so I could take him to the airport at five the next morning. We texted late into the night again. I told her I was driving to California after work to visit my grandmother and would be back on Monday.

My grandpa—or Pappy Earl, as we called him—had passed away earlier that year from cancer. I wanted to visit my Grandma Bonnie. I missed my Pappy Earl so much, and I could only imagine how my grandma felt. Their house was the only place that ever felt like home. They bought their house in Baldwin Park in 1959, raised four kids there, and never moved. It was the only house in my life that was always there. It was home to all of us.

I got off work that day at 2 p.m. and stopped by my house to get my bag and Chichi. Then the two of us drove to California, only hitting a little light traffic outside Phoenix in Glendale. The six-hour drive went by in the blink of an eye because I was talking to Jennie the whole time on the phone, with the exception of a few spots with no service and when she had to go do mom things.

I stopped 10 miles before my grandma's house at The Hat. "World Famous Pastramis," the sign read out front—and they were. I grew up eating there, and the first bite was like a taste bud time machine taking me back to my childhood, remembering my parents, my brother, and me here on Friday nights—and how we always wanted more. Not that there wasn't enough food to eat, but the taste left you wanting more. It reminded me of kissing Jennie—wanting more—so I sent her a picture of my sandwich.

She responded with a picture of the food she cooked for her family. It was a salmon filet marinated with orange juice. I remembered then that I had told her a shortcut to marinating the meat that first night we were making tacos was to just add Sunny D instead of fresh lemons and limes. I laughed because I had never tried it on salmon. It didn't sound good, at least not compared to my pastrami from The Hat.

I arrived at my grandma's house around 10 p.m., and she was waiting for me. We hugged and she showed me to my room, which was the same room my dad and Uncle Darrell shared years before. There were two twin beds in the room and a small nightstand. I removed my shoes and belt, then lay in the bed with my jeans still on. Chichi was tucked comfortably against my back in the bed. At my house, I slept in a queen bed, but this twin felt the same because Chichi always slept so close to me that often I found myself almost hanging off the bed.

I awoke in the morning to the smell of fresh coffee, and I walked barefoot to the kitchen, passing several pictures of my younger cousin Marshall in his Marine uniform. He had passed away 15 years before from cancer while on active duty. His memory was still alive in my grandparents' house. I poured my coffee and stared at the two folded American flags over the fireplace mantle. One for Marshall and one for my Pappy Earl, who served in the Navy. There was another picture of my cousin Goober, Marshall's little brother. He was in uniform as well—only he was in the Navy. He was the pride of our family. He graduated from the Naval Academy and was an officer in the Navy, currently serving in France at the American embassy. The first one in our family to graduate college.

I sat at the table with my grandma, and she asked, "What are your plans?"

"I'd like to see a Dodgers game. Would you like to go?"

"I'm too old. I can't walk in the stadium, plus the traffic, D."

D—she always called me D.

I asked my uncle Kevin, who was waking up. He still lived there. He was in his 50s and never left home.

"No, the traffic, Dustin."

I texted my aunt Cindy, who lived nearby, to see if she and her husband wanted to go. She replied, "No, the traffic," and invited me over to watch the game with her and her husband, my uncle Ray.

I decided I was going alone and told my grandma, "If you don't mind, I'll go by myself. I haven't been to Dodger Stadium since I was 13."

"Of course not, D. Please go. Have fun."

So I went on my phone and purchased one upper deck ticket.

Then my grandma said, "I have to show you something, D."

I followed her to the living room and saw my Pappy Earl's 1960s Schwinn that she had restored.

"Take it for a ride, D," she said.

I looked for Chichi, and she was out back, infatuated with these moving rocks. Chichi had never seen a turtle before. So, I took my Pap's Schwinn for a ride downtown. I rode for 20 minutes before I was tired. Lucky for me, I accidentally stopped outside King Taco. I walked inside and ordered two carne asada tacos and a large horchata. I took a picture of my food with my phone and sent it to Jennie.

She replied, "Not fair!"

After I ate, I rode around town for an hour, then ended up back at my grandparents'. My uncle was in the garage in his man cave watching horse racing. He worked for years in the stables at Santa Anita. I parked the bike back inside the house and went to lie on the couch in the living room to rest. This house always made me feel welcome and loved. I soon fell asleep looking at a wall that had a picture of my Pappy Earl on the beach in Malibu, walking in from the surf shirtless, his old-man abs still showing while carrying his yellow Mach 7 boogie board and fins.

My grandma woke me up, saying, "D, you're going to miss the game." I showered and put on my Cody Bellinger jersey, then left for the game with Grandma Bonnie letting me know she was going to watch it on TV to see if she saw me.

I pulled out of the driveway and made a left, then called Jennie from the car. I had the Bluetooth on, listening to directions to the stadium while trying to talk to Jennie in the car. It didn't last long before I said, "Babe, I'm going to have to call you back." The traffic was a nightmare, and driving the L.A. freeways was nothing like it was in Phoenix. You can't use your blinkers in L.A.—if you do, people speed up to not let you in. You just have to turn and cut someone off. After 30 minutes on the freeway in stop-and-go traffic, my exit came up on the right. I cut off a Tesla to make my turn, and for no reason at all, it made me smile.

There was almost no traffic driving through the streets of the L.A. ghetto. Old concrete buildings decorated with graffiti and small old homes that looked like something the big bad wolf from *The Three Little Pigs* could blow over with a huff and a puff. Yet, they managed to survive the countless earthquakes, fires, and mudslides. Before turning up the hill to Chavez Ravine, there was a Black man selling tall cans of beer for $7 apiece out of a red cooler with wheels.

He yelled, "$7 from me, $15 in the stadium!"

My window was rolled down because the weather in L.A. in August was so nice compared to Phoenix. I pulled a $10 bill from my wallet and hung it out the window.

The man approached my car and said, "What it be?"

"Coors Light."

"Just one?"

"Yeah, buddy."

He took my ten-dollar bill, handed me the beer, then went to his pocket to make change.

I said, "We're good. You keep it."

He smiled and said, "Go Dodgers!"

The light changed, and I turned to drive up the hill to Dodger Stadium. Immediately, it didn't seem like I was in the city anymore. I was surrounded by trees and bushes growing off the side of the hill, with dried leaves scattered on the dirt ground. I drove up to a Mexican woman in a Dodger-blue shirt and badge. She was checking parking passes. I pulled out my phone, and she scanned it.

As I pulled away, she said, "Go Dodgers."

I shouted back, "Go Dodgers."

The road continued uphill. Then I turned left, and there it was: Dodger Stadium. One of the last great MLB stadiums still standing. Wrigley Field, Fenway Park, and Dodger Stadium. I don't count Yankee Stadium. That's not the house that Ruth built.

The stadium sits between the Los Angeles hills and the downtown L.A. skyline. Behind the skyline lies the Pacific Ocean. It's where the ghetto meets the rich. I drank my beer in my Scion XB and enjoyed the view of the downtown skyline as my car faced west. I finished my beer and walked north to the stadium.

A fan high-fived me, noticing my jersey, and said, "Yeah, Bellinger!" I got the jersey not because Cody was a Dodger, but because he grew up in Chandler, AZ, and played baseball at Hamilton High School. His Chandler Little League team went to the Little League World Series.

I responded, "MVP."

I walked alone into the stadium and immediately got a beer. It was my first beer in Dodger Stadium. The last time I was there, I was a kid. The beer was $19 but said it came with a souvenir cup. The cup was a plastic cup with the Dodger logo—the same one they give you at any gas station for a soda.

My seat was in the upper deck, so I took the elevator up. The seat was so high I got dizzy looking down at the field. I took a picture with my phone and sent it to Jennie. She responded with, "Eat a Dodger Dog for me." I sent the same picture to my friend Chad, and he responded, "Tell me you didn't pay money to sit that high?"

It wasn't the seat I paid for, but I took a seat high above the first baseline in a section that was empty, so I was alone. Baseball is a slow game but also calming. I watched, enjoyed the sound of the crack of the bat, my Dodger Dog, and a $19 beer with a souvenir cup. The Dodgers were getting beat by the Rockies, but I stayed till the bottom of the 9th, then speed-walked to my car to beat traffic. Dodger game traffic is legendary. I was surprised no one was leaving.

Then I got to my car and heard the boom. Fireworks erupted behind me and lit up the sky like the 4th of July. I was unaware that at Friday night home games they let fans onto the field after the game to enjoy a fireworks show.

I called Jennie and told her how I beat traffic.

She said, "You always stay for the fireworks, Dustin!"

Then she said, "They even let you on the field!"

I messed up. But I got home to Grandma Bonnie's before 12 a.m., and she was waiting for me with Chichi on her lap.

I walked in, and she said, "Did you go on the field to see the fireworks?"

I woke up the next day and had coffee with Grandma Bonnie, then I drove back to L.A. to pick up my mom for a day at the beach in Malibu. I met my mom in the parking garage of her apartment in downtown L.A. and loaded my car with her beach necessities, then headed to the PCH to make our way to Leo Carrillo. I wanted to tell my mom about Jennie, but it had barely been a week, so I kept it to myself.

At the beach, I boogie boarded while my mom sat in a beach chair. I hiked the cliffs alone and took pictures, then sent them to Jennie. She wanted me to take her there. I told Jennie my family goes camping here every summer, so I'd bring her next summer.

After the beach, I drove my mom to Neptune's Net for dinner. I had fish and chips and was getting tired, so I drove her home. I walked her inside, told her I loved her, then drove back to my grandma's because I had told her I would go to church with her in the morning.

We went to church, and when we got home my Pappy Earl's truck was still parked on the street. I grabbed the keys from the kitchen and opened the truck door. It was a 1995 Chevy Silverado. The green paint had sun damage, but the interior was in great condition. I sat in the driver's seat and remembered being 15 when my Pap got the truck. Since I was turning 16 the next year, I asked him if I could have it. He laughed out loud and said, "In your dreams, Dusty." He was the only one who called me Dusty, and I liked it.

I noticed a card tucked in the windshield wiper. I got out of the truck and grabbed it. There was a phone number asking how much for the truck. I took it into the house and showed it to my grandma.

"Yeah, people keep wanting to buy the truck."

"If you're selling it, I'll buy it."

"Why do you need two cars, D?"

"I don't need two cars; I just want Pap's truck. He drove that truck to Malibu every year, and I want to keep driving it there."

"Then it's yours. I was hoping someone in the family would want it."

"How much?"

"No, D, it's yours."

I was so excited I had to tell Jennie, so I called her.

"My grandma just gave me my Pap's '95 Chevy Silverado!"

"Why do you need two cars?"

The fireworks at Dodger Stadium and the truck—Jennie and my grandma had the same thing to say about them. I loved it.

"I don't. When I was 15, I wanted two things: my Pap's truck and this hot blonde that lived across the street from me. Now I have them both!"

"Do you?" Jennie said.

"I have to call you back." I hung up.

I had tickets to a Guns N' Roses show for the next night. I forgot I had invited my ex-girlfriend Rachel to go two days before Jennie and I made tacos. I bought the tickets a month before, thinking I'd find a date. But as the concert got closer, I had no date, so I asked Rachel if she'd go with me. Free ticket if she drove and paid for parking. She told me yes, but she wanted to check with her boss if she could get the next morning off.

I hadn't talked to her since. So technically, it was never a yes, right? I walked into the house and texted Rachel, "Hey, I never heard back from you about the show, so I asked Lethan to go."

Lethan was one of my best friends and the owner of the salon I worked at. It was a lie, but it sounded better than "Hey, I'm sorry I called you Lauren. I found the love of my life and I want to take her. Hope things are well." I sent the text and threw my phone on the couch, then went outside to smoke a cigarette. I thought, *If she is mad, she can just have the two tickets.* I wanted to see Jennie more than Guns N' Roses.

I finished my cigarette and went inside to check my phone. There was a message from Racheal. It read, "No problem. I don't think it's a good idea if we are seen out together with each other." I was off the hook! So I called Jennie.

"Hey, can you get a babysitter tomorrow night?"

"Why?"

"I have two cheap seats to Guns N' Roses."

"You just got them?"

"No, I've had them."

"And you're just telling me?"

"I want to start things with you always telling the truth. I was supposed to take Rachel. I asked her two days before we hung out, and once we kissed, you were all I've been thinking about. And I forgot I was going to take her. I told her I'm taking Lethan, but I'm really taking you."

"So, you're starting off with telling me the truth while lying to someone?"

"I'll just give the tickets to her then. Can we go do something else?"

"Hell no, we are going to see Guns N' Roses!"

Jennie asked her mom to watch the kids, and she agreed. I was so excited; I stood in the front yard talking to Jennie on the phone. We talked about the band and how long we had loved them, and that this was the first time seeing them for both of us. I apologized for the nosebleed seats, but she said, "It doesn't matter where we are, as long as we are there."

I don't know what came over me, but I felt like everything was on my side. So, I asked, "Do you want to go to Jerome with me in a couple weeks?"

She said, "Yes."

I felt like a pitcher throwing a perfect game—bottom of the 9th, nothing can stop you now.

I went on my phone and booked a room for the Jerome Grand Hotel.

Jerome, AZ, is a small town on the side of the mountain that overlooks Sedona and the Verde Valley and happens to be haunted. It also has great food and good wine.

I talked to Jennie for another hour on the phone before my phone started to die. So, we said goodnight. I walked to my room and lay on the bed for a minute until I heard Chichi trying to get up. I picked my little dog up, gave her some rubs, and drifted off to sleep.

I awoke again to the smell of coffee and walked barefoot out to the kitchen, with my grandma sitting at the kitchen table. She was upset, but not with me.

"Your dad is selling his house in Gilbert to move to Montana with his wife."

My dad had remarried, and his wife had a house in Montana. The two of them were snowbirds. They lived in Arizona in the winter and escaped the Phoenix heat by spending summers at his wife's house in Montana.

I was shocked. I had given my dad a ride to the airport just a few days ago, and he said he was thinking about it—not doing it.

I was angry he didn't tell me when I drove him to the airport. Then I remembered my concert tickets with Rachel. Sometimes you lie not to hurt someone. So, Grandma Bonnie and I had several cups of coffee and talked. I thanked her for the truck, and we talked about what I would do with it. But mostly we just enjoyed each other's company.

I was happy to be silent with her. When she was quiet, she was thinking— and she looked beautiful. Her long gray hair and deep brown eyes, thinking about a lifetime.

I told her I had the concert to get to, but I'd be back for the truck soon. She tried to feed me, but I told her I had to go to In-N-Out. I invited her, but she refused. So I hugged my uncle Kevin and kissed Grandma Bonnie, then drove away looking in the rearview mirror to see the house and my grandma until they faded away.

I drove to the In-N-Out off Francisquito Ave in Baldwin Park. It was the very first In-N-Out and special to me. My grandparents always took my brother and my cousins to this one. In-N-Out was the pride of Baldwin Park because it all started here.

I ordered a Double-Double Animal Style cheeseburger, fries, and a pink lemonade. I sat in my car and ate my cheeseburger over my fries, so they caught everything that fell from the burger. Extra cheese, sauce, grilled onions, and meat gathered on top of my fries, making Animal Style fries.

The legend of "Animal Style" goes back to the late 1960s, when the hippies used to smoke marijuana and get stoned. This caused them to get the munchies, and they'd ask for extra everything on the burger to cure their stoner appetite on a budget.

I got on the freeway and headed back to Arizona to pick up Jennie for the Guns N' Roses concert. I was on the road by 11:30, so I figured I'd be home by six. I'd shower and change, then pick her up around seven.

I called her on the road, and we talked until outside Palm Springs, when there was no more cell service. When I had service again, I called Jennie. She asked what I was wearing to the show. I said I didn't know. But that was a lie. I was going to wear my black high-top Doc Martens with ripped jeans, my CBGB shirt, and a black Dodgers hat.

She went through 20 possible outfits, and each one sounded great.

I reminded her we had cheap seats, that they were up top, and we'd have to walk a lot—not to mention the parking and walking to the show. She said she knew and that she was just excited to go out. I was too.

I got home, showered and changed, then texted her that I was coming to get her. Surprisingly, she said she was ready. So I drove the three blocks to her house and pulled into my old neighborhood of Runaway Bay.

I found Jennie lying in her grass with her youngest son, Max, playing with toys in the yard. Her daughter, Sophie, was hitting a volleyball to herself in the driveway, so I parked on the street.

I got out of my car and waved while walking up to Jennie, holding out my hand to help her up. She was wearing tight blue jeans, a black top, and black stilettos that looked amazing with her outfit—but were uncomfortable too.

"Are you going to be okay in those shoes?" I asked her.

"They're really comfortable," she said.

I gave her a hug and whispered in her ear, "I thought we weren't going to lie?"

"I'm not," she said, and pushed me away.

Max was standing between us now, holding a toy.

"Is that a Pikachu?" I asked.

"Yeah, you know Pokémon?" he said, excitedly.

"Yeah, but I like Squirtle more."

"He's cool too, but Pikachu is my favorite." Max gave his toy a hug.

I asked, "Is it okay if I take your mom out tonight?"

Max looked at his mom and smiled before responding, "I guess."

I put my fist out, and Max gave me knuckles. I turned to Sophie, who was hitting the ball to herself, and I said, "Pass." She hit the ball to me. I hit it back, and we started a volley before I eventually dropped it.

"My bad," I said. "We should all go play at the clubhouse sometime?"

Sophie got really excited and said, "For real?"

"Yeah, we can go this weekend. I go every Sunday." I looked at Jennie and said, "We should go."

Jennie gave the two kids a hug and a kiss goodbye, then told them, "Tell Noah I said goodbye."

"Noah?"

"My son."

"I forgot there were three."

Noah was the middle child.

"He didn't want to come outside to meet you. He's in his room drawing."

"Meet me? So this was a setup?"

"You date me, you date the whole gang," she said.

"So, we're dating?" I laughed.

"Let's see how tonight goes," she said, with a smile.

I opened the door to my car for her and walked around to the driver's side. I looked across the street to the house I grew up in and thought to myself, *You just picked up Jennie Sadusky to take to a Guns N' Roses concert! How awesome.*

I drove to the end of the block, put my car in park, and kissed Jennie. She kissed back and said, "I really missed you."

"Yeah, I missed you," I replied.

We drove to the concert, but not before we stopped at the QT gas station for some tall boys to drink in the parking lot. Thirty minutes later, we were in downtown Phoenix. I pulled into a below-ground parking lot and paid $20 cash to the parking attendant.

We tried to drink the beers as fast as we could and got about halfway done, then started to walk to the elevator, drinking as we walked through the parking lot. We took the elevator up to ground level, finished our beers, and threw them away in the Subway shop's trash can. I picked her up and spun her around one time before saying, "Guns N' Roses." I put her down, and she high-fived me. Then we speed-walked to the show.

I held Jennie's hand with my right hand and pulled up our tickets on my phone with my left hand. I found them just as we got to the security check-in. We emptied our pockets and walked through the metal detector without it going off, then put our belongings back in our pockets and took the escalator up to our seats.

We could hear the opening act playing. The son of Eddie Van Halen was playing with his band, VH Mammoth. We walked straight to the beer line. Within a minute, Jennie was friends with the two women behind us. They complimented her shoes. And a minute later, she was friends with the woman in front of us as well. This woman was with her husband, so I struck up small talk with him. They had their 12-year-old son with them. I told Jennie, "Next time we bring your kids." I could tell by the smile on her face that she liked that.

I went to pay for the beers, but Jennie tried to pay. I stopped her and paid, saying, "I got it, babe."

"Well, you got the tickets and paid for parking," she said.

"Well, I've been wanting to take you out since we were kids. Unlike in high school, now I have some money."

We kissed, then noticed there was no music. We rushed to our seats because the opening band was done. It was time for Slash, Axl, and Duff. We found our seats and sat down, still holding hands. It wasn't long before the lights went out. Then there was an intro followed by their song *It's So Easy.* We stopped holding hands and stood up, waving our hands in the air.

The music filled the air and entered everyone in the building's bodies as we were all taken back to our youth—a time of MTV, FM radio, cassette tapes, and CDs. Guns N' Roses delivered.

An hour into their set, Jennie and I went to get another beer. The line was much shorter, and we were back in our seats within 10 minutes.

Two people were in our seats when we got back. They played dumb, like they were in the right seats, then Jennie stepped in.

"These aren't your seats—you know that!" Jennie looked at the people we were sitting next to and said, "Hello, remember us?" She looked back at the seat stealers and said, "Just go away." Jennie waved her hand, and they went away.

The band played for three hours! Every song you wanted to hear—*Sweet Child O' Mine, Welcome to the Jungle, Mr. Brownstone, You Could Be Mine*—as well as some long guitar solos by Slash. My generation's Jimi Hendrix. Slash controlled the stage like a lead singer, but instead of words and a microphone, he used guitar chords and his Gibson Les Paul guitar.

Jennie pulled on my shirt for my attention and said, "Don't be mad."

"I'm not," I told her.

"I have to pee," she said.

"Okay, let's go."

"The show is almost over. Maybe we just beat the traffic?"

"The encore is *Paradise City.* I love that song. But not as much as I hate traffic. Let's go," I said.

I walked with Jennie to the restroom. I had to use it too. Then we left the arena and walked onto the almost empty streets of downtown Phoenix. Jennie was walking funny. I looked at her feet. They were bleeding a little.

I pointed at her feet and said, "Babe."

"Shut up," she shot back at me.

"Let's get home, babe," I said, taking her by the hand to cross the street.

We walked to the elevator of our parking garage and got on with two other couples. They got off a level before us, but not before the two women in the group said to Jennie, "I love your shoes." After they were gone, Jennie took her stilettos off, looked at me, and said, "Worth it," as she walked to my car barefoot through the downtown Phoenix parking garage.

I opened the door for her and asked, "Do you want to get some wine and go sit by the lake?"

"Sounds perfect." She then connected her phone to my car stereo's Bluetooth and played the Guns N' Roses song *Paradise City.*

I stopped back at the QT gas station and went in alone, leaving Jennie in the car with it still running. I grabbed a bottle of cheap white wine with a twist-off top, since we didn't have a corkscrew. I asked the clerk for two plastic water cups that were free. I paid, went back to the car, handed Jennie the bag, and drove to the lake.

A different spot this time than our first night at the lake. This was her favorite spot. She would come up here to clear her head or just enjoy the view of nice homes with pontoon boats docked in their backyards. I knew the spot well because it was the closest spot to the neighborhood where we grew up. I fished there with my best friends as a kid. We caught catfish and carp and always threw them back because we didn't want to clean or eat them.

We had no blanket, so we sat on the grass and leaned on each other, toasting our clear plastic cups of $10 gas station wine.

Jennie was silent, so I asked if she was okay. She told me she was "Perfect." I enjoyed the silence with her, rubbing her back with my left arm and occasionally kissing her. We finished the bottle, and then I drove us back to my house, only a few blocks away.

We walked into my house, sat on the couch, and immediately started kissing—until she stopped us by saying, "Is that a Nintendo?"

"Yes," I said.

"For real?" she asked.

"Yeah, it's a mini Nintendo with 24 old-school games," I told her.

"Does it have Donkey Kong?"

I took my arm away from Jennie and walked to the video game console. I turned it on, looked back at her, and said, "Oh, yeah."

We played Donkey Kong and Excitebike while I poured more wine from my bar. Eventually, it was two in the morning, and she said she had to go home. The kids would be up in a few hours. I turned off the TV and suggested I walk her home since I was now drunk and couldn't drive. She smiled and grabbed her purse, then we walked to the door.

I opened it for her, and after that, I kept it open for Chichi, who came walking out like a princess with her head held high.

The three of us walked, and I was the only one with shoes on. Jennie had not put her shoes on since the concert.

We walked down the street and into the park, Chichi without her leash the whole time. Jennie asked me, "Won't she run away?"

"Dogs are like people. If you treat them well and give them some cheese, they usually stick around."

Chichi was a stray who liked walking without a leash, so I would walk her that way late at night.

We held hands as we walked and talked down the streets of our childhood, with tall, overgrown trees and cracks on the sidewalk. The fifteen-minute walk was over too fast, and I found myself standing in Jennie's driveway. We kissed and said goodnight. I stood in the driveway until I heard the door lock, then looked up to Jennie's room over the garage and saw her light turn on. I started to walk away but looked back at her window one more time.

I was reminded of a time in high school when I was a sophomore and Jennie was a freshman. It was a Friday night, and I was drinking some beers in the park with friends. I walked home around midnight and saw that Jennie's bedroom light was on. I stood in the driveway and yelled to the window, "Jennie! Jennie!" She came to the window holding a cordless phone to her ear, saw me, smiled, and said, "Dustin?"

I didn't have a plan, so I mooned her. Dropped my JNCO jeans, showed her my bare ass, and mooned her.

She yelled, "Dustin!"

I hurried home across the street, almost tripping over my way-too-baggy jeans.

I called to Chichi, who was sniffing the grass, and the two of us walked home.

Chapter 3
You Are Like Costco

I woke up the next day smiling, then remembered I had work. I showered, changed, and headed to the salon. I received a text from Jennie as I pulled into the salon parking lot. It said, "Thank you for last night, I had so much fun!"

I replied, "How are your feet?" I called and told Jennie that I was walking into work and I'd call her later. I had a full day of clients and would be busy.

I managed to get a fifteen-minute lunch, so I walked to the Trader Joe's next to the salon to get something to eat. I walked straight to the cheese section. The store had an amazing cheese called Unexpected Cheddar. It was cheddar cheese with parmesan, and it crusted and broke apart as you sliced it. Next to the cheese were some individually wrapped bags of pizza dough.

I called Jennie, and when she answered I asked, "Do you and your kids want to come over on Thursday for dinner to make homemade pizza? It's the only day I'm off early and thought they'd have fun playing in my arcade."

Jennie laughed and said, "I told them about your man cave arcade, and they asked when they can see it!"

"So, you're talking about me to the kids?" I asked.

"They asked about the concert," she told me.

"And you replied that Dustin has an arcade in his garage?"

Jennie laughed and said, "Well, I was impressed."

"So, you and the kids on Thursday?" I asked again.

"Yes. But what are you doing tonight?" Jennie responded.

"I'm off at 9," I told her.

"Ugh, so late?" she said.

"Do you want to come over?" I asked.

"I guess, but you better have wine," she said.

The alcohol section just happened to be next to where I was standing, so I grabbed a bottle of white wine for her and red wine for me, then said, "Of course."

Work went by fast. I was quiet with my clients. I usually talk a lot, but I was thinking about Jennie. I couldn't stop thinking about her, not even for a minute—and I tried.

I called Jennie when I got off to let her know I was on my way home. She told her parents she was going to my house but stayed there until the kids were all asleep.

Jennie came to my house around 9:30 and told me, "It would be a lot easier if you still lived across the street."

My parents divorced 13 years ago. I loved that house.

"I'm like three blocks away, babe."

We kissed, made love, and played Donkey Kong and Super Mario Brothers until she went home.

The next day, I went to work. I checked my phone after every client for a text from Jennie. There was always a text.

One text I asked, "Why do you still have your ex-husband's last name?"

"It's just easier with the kids in school that we all have the same last name, but I do need to change it. That, and it's a big hassle to go do it at the Social Security office."

"What if you changed it, then had to change it again?" I asked.

"That's what I was thinking," she replied.

I knew I wanted to marry her. I think I'd known since I was fifteen, when I hid her brother Matt's bike in a house that was still being built. I did it just for fun, but Jennie knocked on my parents' door and I answered it. She said, "Where's my brother's bike?" I walked her to the house next door and into the master bedroom, where I had hidden the bike in the closet. There was this awkward moment where I wanted to kiss her in the kitchen, and I felt she wanted to kiss me, but we just kept talking about the house we were in. I watched her walk the bike back home across the street. I knew I wanted her. I knew I wanted to be close to her as much as I could. Being close to her made me feel like I was on fire.

That night, Jennie stayed home with the kids. I felt lonely even though I had Chichi. I missed Jennie being by my side. So, I rubbed Chichi's chest and under her leg until I fell asleep.

I woke up the next morning, and it was Thursday. I was going to see Jennie that night. I got through work and made it home. Of course, she was there with the kids waiting for me—Max, Sophie, and now Noah.

I let them in and then immediately showed them the garage. The man cave garage with a pool table and all the arcade games. Their eyes got big as they walked through the man cave, touching everything. They were even happier when I said, "No quarters, it's all free!"

Jennie and I walked into the kitchen to start preparing the dough, but soon found ourselves kissing, neglecting the food. That was interrupted by Max coming into the kitchen saying, "Sophie and Noah are being mean."

I lifted Max onto the counter and asked, "Do you want to make the first pizza?"

"Yes," Max replied.

Max and I started rolling the dough. I let him do most of the work. He said he was done and what he had made was something that looked like a volcano. It was a giant biscuit of red marinara and mozzarella cheese.

The other two kids came in from the garage, and it was their turn to make a pizza. I rolled the dough for them because I wanted a good pizza. Noah and Sophie decorated their pizzas competitively with only cheese and tried to beat each other with the best pizza.

After the pizzas were done, all three kids asked me which one was my favorite pizza. All three kids looked at me for approval, and Jennie looked at me like, "How do you answer that?"

"Do you guys want to walk to Handel's and get ice cream?" I asked.

"Can we take Chichi?" Noah asked.

"Yes," I said. "But get the leash—we have to walk on Guadalupe."

So the five of us walked to get ice cream. The kids took turns holding the leash, and Jennie and I held hands until we were on Guadalupe. Then Max broke Jennie and my hands to hold both of our hands together, so it was the three of us. Max was a very little kid, and Jennie and I swung him as we walked down the street. I looked back behind me, and Noah had Chichi on the leash as Sophie walked near him. The two of them looked at the three of us and giggled.

I picked up Chichi, and the six of us walked into the ice cream shop.

"Would your dog like a pup cup?" a woman behind the counter asked.

Chichi barked.

"That's a yes, please," I said.

"Chichi can talk?" Max asked me.

"Yes, but only I understand her," I teased.

"Oh," Max said.

The kids ordered their flavors of ice cream, followed by Jennie and me. I ordered chocolate peanut butter with brownies. We sat outside and enjoyed our ice cream in the September Arizona heat. The ice cream melted faster than we ate it and ran quickly from our cones onto our hands.

"I'm full, I don't want it anymore," Max said.

"You have to fini—" I cut Jennie off.

"Chichi will finish it," I said.

Max smiled and took a knee, then fed Chichi the strawberry ice cream cone. She finished the whole thing, even after finishing her own pup cup.

We walked home. Then Jennie drove the kids home and told me to stay up because she'd be back over after the kids were asleep. So I left the front door unlocked. She arrived back after 10 and climbed into my bed. I was almost asleep.

She kissed me and held me tight and said, "Go to sleep, babe," and I did.

I woke up in the morning and reached for Jennie, but I was alone. She had come to sleep with me for a couple of hours, then went back home before the kids woke up.

I went to work again that morning and texted Jennie between every client. We made plans to go to the clubhouse on Sunday to swim with the kids. She came over Friday and Saturday night after the kids were asleep and safe with her parents.

"You do need to spend the night at my house eventually," Jennie said.

I agreed by nodding my head, then went in for a kiss.

"But not tonight," I said.

Sunday afternoon came, and she met me at the Val Vista Lakes clubhouse with the kids. My brother, Justin, was there. The kids met him, and they all laughed.

Max said, "Your parents named you Dustin and Justin?"

I laughed.

My parents had named my younger brother Justin. My name was supposed to be Justin, but my mother changed her mind in the end and named me Dustin, after the Hollywood actor Dustin Hoffman.

My brother and I were a year and a half apart, so when she found out she was pregnant a second time, she already knew his name. He was Justin. But my brother was born a preemie, almost two months early, on December 23rd, when he was supposed to be born in February, close to my birthday on the 19th.

My parents hadn't picked a middle name for Justin. Mine was Earl, named after Pappy Earl. They thought they still had plenty of time to pick a middle name.

After my brother was born, he was taken to a different hospital in an ambulance with my father to a preemie ward. My mother, after just giving birth, stayed at the hospital until they released her.

The guys driving the ambulance let my father know he hadn't picked a middle name yet. My father, being very quick-witted, said, "How about Nuther?" The driver of the ambulance said it out loud, "Justin Nuther Elkin?" The ambulance erupted with laughter, and my father filled in his middle name on his birth certificate.

He was Justin Nuther Elkin.

My mother was less than thrilled when she got to the hospital and found out what her husband had named their second son. They tried to change it but couldn't.

I tormented my brother about his name when we were young. I would sing a song to him my uncle Kevin came up with, and it went, "Justin Nuther peanut butter, want another peanut butter cookie."

My parents said they would pay the money to legally change his name when he was thirteen. Justin thought he got to pick his name. It was the 1980s, so he chose Justin 'Michael Jackson' Elkin. I didn't think that was fair, so I wanted to change my name to Dustin 'Mr. T' Elkin!

Neither of us got what we wanted, and eventually his middle name was changed to Randle—my father's first name.

Jennie went to talk to Justin in the sand under an umbrella, and I went to hit the volleyball with Sophie while Max swam—or more like floated—and Noah sat on a beach chair, not wanting to have fun until I hit the volleyball at him. Then he joined us in the pool. Jennie swam to me in the pool, and I left the kids to meet her.

"Your brother doesn't know we are dating?" she asked.

"I haven't told anyone yet. Have you?" I replied.

"I told Mary. She approves."

Mary was one of Jennie's three best friends since 7th grade. They were Mary, Margo, and Ashley. These four were the Mount Rushmore of popular girls when we were in high school, and they were still best friends twenty-five years later.

I looked to the beach and saw my brother grinning and told Jennie, "He knows now."

"Poor Justin, dealing with his ex," Jennie said.

"That's what you guys talked about?" I asked.

"Well, yeah," she replied.

My brother had found out a year earlier that he had a son who was seven years old with a girl he had seen for a week eight years prior. She had contacted him a year ago and let him know he had a son. Justin went to her house to take a paternity test, and Jaxson ran out to see him. Justin sent me a picture of the kid. I thought it was a picture of my brother when he was seven, but it was my new nephew, Jaxson.

I told Justin to save the money on the paternity test; there was no question the kid was his. But Justin did the test anyway. Immediately after, he started dating Jaxson's mom again. They moved in together right away, and it looked like the start of a true love story—but ended with them hating each other.

My brother had to deal with her, but she also had to deal with him, which is not easy. He's my brother. I love him, but sometimes I hate him. We are brothers—Dustin and Justin. Brothers fight. Sometimes I might not like him, but I still love him the most out of all my friends. He was born the day before Christmas Eve, so that year Christmas was canceled because we had a new baby boy. My mother would tell me he was my Christmas present. I would have liked some Star Wars action figures instead.

The kids hit the volleyball at the two of us. We all started hitting the ball to each other. My brother waved from the sand, picked up his cooler, and went to his condo across the street.

We kept playing. The snacks Jennie brought for the kids soon ran out, and they wanted to go home. The sun was still high overhead, and I walked them to Jennie's car. She invited me over, but I was still nervous about seeing her parents.

I didn't know why I was nervous. They were always nice to me when I lived across the street from them on Anchor Drive, but I wasn't sleeping with their daughter then.

Then I remembered her dad. That was why I never asked Jennie out in high school. He was a big man who worked out a lot and had a flat top for a haircut. He was always seen in our neighborhood walking their big dog around the block. I thought of him as Herman Munster walking their dragon Spot—and how I had to get through them to get to Marilyn.

I didn't go over that night, but Jennie came over the next day while the kids were at school. It was a Monday and my day off, so I took her to lunch at Pei Wei Asian Kitchen near my house at Dana Park.

We had lunch, and we opened too many fortune cookies until we found some fortunes we liked. Jennie's fortune said, "Love is in the air." Mine still said something dumb: "Look how far you've come." I didn't like it, so I made up my own fortune.

"What does your fortune say?" Jennie asked.

"You will marry your old neighbor from high school," I told her.

Jennie looked at me with squinted eyes and said, "No it doesn't. Let me see." Then she tried to take it from me, but I crumbled it up and threw it into the restaurant.

I smiled like I had won, but you never really win against Jennie. She threw some broken fortune cookies at me. Then Jennie stopped herself and said, "We're making a mess. We should stop."

"It's fine. I'll leave a tip," I said and threw some broken cookies back at her.

"You should always leave a tip, Dustin."

"No, one person took our order at the cash register, then another brought the food out. We had to get our own chopsticks and refills on soda. Do you tip at Taco Bell? But I will leave a tip for the busser, because you are messy."

We got another soda refill before we walked out, and I held the door open for her.

"So you made up your own fortune," she said.

"I wouldn't say I made it up. I think I'm going to marry you," I told her.

We stopped walking, and she smiled and said, "You know I come with three kids?"

"Yeah, you're kind of like Costco. I went to get one thing and left with four things I didn't know I needed," I said, smiling at her.

Jennie kissed me. Then we got in my car and drove back to my house, where we sat on the couch with the TV on but kept talking. She had to leave to get the kids and then had some students to tutor.

She asked if I'd come over to her house tonight. Without hesitating, I said, "Yes."

I laid around my house for a few hours and played some games in my man cave, waiting for her to text me that she was home. The text came around seven and said she was putting Max in a bath and I could come over whenever.

I showered and brushed my teeth, then brushed them a second time. I didn't know why I was so nervous.

I put some cheese in Chichi's food bowl, then left while she was distracted. The drive only took a couple minutes, but I waited in my car for another five when I got to her house. I texted Jennie I was there. She told me to just come in, and that the door was open. So I did.

But I waited at the door for a minute, looking at my phone. I was buying time, hoping she would open it. She did not, so I opened the door and immediately two large dogs started barking at me.

Her dad was sitting at the dining room table on his laptop doing work. He was a professor at ASU in the business department. He looked up and saw me, and I waved as I tried to silence two dogs with strong petting. All he said was, "I heard you were back around."

I didn't know how to respond, and thank God I didn't have to, because just then Jennie came down the stairs and grabbed me by the arm and led me upstairs to her room.

This was my first time ever going in her room. I had looked at the window to her room a thousand times growing up but had never been inside. Jennie had been to my house lots of times. Usually, when my parents went out of town, I'd throw a party, and she always came.

One night, when I was 21, my parents were out of town and I threw a party. I had a chance to hook up with Jennie that night, but I had just started seeing a girl, and Jennie was drunk. Really drunk. She told me she'd hook up with me if I gave her some beef jerky. So, I put her on the couch and got her some water. She ended up leaving with another guy that night.

But there I was, twenty years later, being led into her room. I sat on the bed and heard a yell. I had sat on Max, who was under the blanket on his tablet. Max poked his head out and said, "Hey, Dustin!"

The boys' room was next to Jennie's room. Noah heard and came in to say hi and asked, "What are you doing here?"

"I came to watch a movie with your mom," I told him.

"Cool. Can we go back to your house this week? I want to play pool."

"Yeah, buddy. Say when."

Jennie interrupted the boys and me and said, "Bedtime is in 20 minutes. Go brush your teeth."

"So what are we watching tonight?" I asked.

Labyrinth?

"I haven't seen that since I was a kid!" I was excited and told Jennie, "You remind me of the babe."

She replied, "What babe?"

"The babe with the power."

"What power?"

We were saying the lines to the song in *Labyrinth*, "Magic Dance," by David Bowie. The boys were still in the room.

Noah said, "You guys are weird," and left with his brother to brush their teeth. Sophie was downstairs in her room on her phone doing 7th-grade girl things.

Jennie tucked the boys in, and we got comfortable on her bed. It was a queen bed tucked in the corner of the room, and the TV was on her dresser to the left of her closet. The closet doors were slightly pushed out because of

40

the amount of clothes she had in there. There was a computer to the right of the door that was on an L-shaped desk that reached the bed and was used as a nightstand as well.

I held Jennie and kissed her forehead as we watched the movie. It was over before we knew it. She asked me if I wanted to watch another movie, and I said, "Yes."

She asked, "Is *The Notebook* okay?" She looked at me like I was going to say no—only what she didn't know was that I loved that movie! I'd watch anything with Ryan Gosling. He's great. I've loved him since *Remember the Titans* when he was an absolute liability at cornerback.

"I'm going to write a book one day. That is my destiny. Will you read it to me when I'm old and can't remember?" she asked.

"Well, if you can't remember, I'll just read you *The Notebook* and tell you that was us," I told her.

She playfully punched me. "No, read me my story!"

"How about I read you *The Princess Bride*?"

Jennie rolled her eyes, got a drink of water, and said, "I'm going to write a book."

"As you wish."

Jennie was a great writer. She graduated from ASU, and you could tell she could write just by reading her Facebook posts.

"Well, what is it going to be about?" I asked her.

"I don't know yet, but I'm going to do it," she said.

"I believe you," I told her, pulling her close.

"What's your destiny, Dustin?" she asked me.

"I don't know. I thought I was destined to be alone—then you came into my life to make tacos," and I gave her another kiss.

We watched the movie, then tried to go to sleep. But I wasn't tired, so Jennie put the sound of the ocean on her phone.

"That stuff doesn't work," I told her.

My shirt was off, and Jennie started rubbing my back. She was like a snake charmer; I was out cold.

I woke up and it was still dark. I looked at my phone and it was almost 5 a.m. I kissed Jennie on the forehead and put on my shirt and shoes. She woke up.

"Where are you going?" she asked, still groggy from sleep.

"Home. I have to go to the gym," I told her quietly.

"You do?" she said.

"Yes." I kissed her on the lips and said, "I'll call you later. Now go back to sleep."

She did, and I let myself out by walking very slowly down the stairs— and even slower as I walked past her parents' room. Instead of breaking in, I was like a burglar breaking out. I didn't want her dad to catch me.

I shut the door and walked across the street to my house. I got to the driveway before I remembered I didn't live there anymore. Then I turned to my car on the street and got behind the wheel. I started it, trying not to make noise, then drove home.

I changed and went to the gym. I didn't want to, but I didn't want to be a liar, so I went.

I lied about the fortune cookie, but that was just a white lie.

Chapter 4

I Love You

I continued going over to the Sadusky house to spend the night, always sneaking out in the early morning, and Jennie would come to mine. We lived so close to each other it made it perfect.

That weekend I told my nephews Jaxson, eight years old, and Bryer, nine years old, that I'd take them to the D-backs game. I had three nephews; the third was Kaden, who was 18 and living in Flagstaff with his girlfriend. Kaden was brother to Jaxson and Bryer, but Jaxson and Bryer had no blood relationship. I wasn't even Bryer's blood uncle. Kaden's mom was Dana, who we went to school with and was Jared's sister. Jared was one of my best friends. Justin and Dana dated in high school then had Kaden right after they graduated. They broke up eventually, and Dana got married to another guy we went to high school with named Ron. It was just easier to tell the boys I'm Uncle D. We did lots of fun things with each other—especially baseball games. The boys both played Little League and looked forward to Diamondbacks games with me.

I picked up my nephews for the game and grabbed a Little Caesar Hot and Ready pizza to eat on the way. We got to the ballpark, which was much different than Chavez Ravine. Chase Field was more like watching a baseball game in an indoor mall. It has a retractable roof that they close in the summer months because of the heat. Even though I had just fed the boys, they wanted hot dogs as soon as we walked in. You can't go to a baseball game and not get a hot dog. So, we got hot dogs and sodas, then hiked to the cheap seats. The seats were not high enough for the boys, so we walked to the very top. It was so high I felt like I was hiking Camelback Mountain.

Once we sat down, they wanted to explore. There was no one around us for 50 rows, so I let them go, and I watched the game. I enjoyed my hot dog and soda and the beauty of the ballpark. I could sit in a ballpark every day and listen to the crack of the bat.

The boys came back and said they were bored, so I took them to the batting cages in the park. Chase Field has a batting cage in left field in the kids' zone for fans to take a swing. After the cages, it was time for a souvenir, so the boys each picked out a mini bat. Then I saw a D-backs keychain, so I got that for Jennie.

On the way home, I stopped at a Home Depot and had a Diamondbacks key to my house made for Jennie. I texted Jennie that I had gotten her a souvenir and was dropping it off. The boys were both in the back seat, and I pulled up to Jennie's house. She came out alone. I had the passenger window down. I had the keychain between my knuckles, with the key hidden in my palm.

She came to the door and waved to the boys in the back, and I said, "Hey, I got you this."

Jennie took the keychain and pulled it out of my grasp, then saw the key. "A key?" she asked.

"Come over anytime, even if I'm not home. I don't have anything to hide—snoop all you like."

"Oh, I will!" she said.

"I'm going to take these guys home, then meet you later," I told her.

"Ok," she said.

I dropped the boys off and drove home. Jennie's car was parked outside my house when I got there. I walked in, and Jennie was waiting on the couch with Chichi. She got up and brought me a beer, then kissed me and said, "Thank you. My parents said they'd watch the kids tonight."

I asked if she was hungry and looked in my fridge. She said, "Kinda."

I pulled out the one ribeye steak I had and turned on the stove. I seasoned it with salt and pepper, placed a pan on the stove, and threw a stick of butter into it. Then I started chopping fresh garlic. I had half an onion, so I diced that into little pieces and threw them into the pan as well. The sound of the sizzle got Chichi and Jennie's attention, and they walked into the kitchen to see what was happening.

"I like when you cook," she said.

"I like to cook. Babe, can you get a bottle of red wine from under the bar?" Then I put the steak in the pan.

"What are you making for a side?" she asked.

"Babe, it's a 12 oz ribeye—we're good," I told her.

Jennie had me open the bottle of wine. Then I handed it back to her, and she poured two glasses. I flipped the steak and asked, "Medium rare okay?"

"Is there any other way?"

I wanted to say "I love you," but held back. I had already said I wanted to marry her, but hadn't said I love you… It had only been a few weeks. I skipped over "I love you" and went straight to "I want to marry you." I did love her. I always had. I wanted it to be perfect when I said it. But saying "I love you" the first time is never perfect. It's usually awkward.

After five minutes, I flipped the ribeye a third time and added shredded cheddar cheese on top of the steak, then covered the pan with a plate to melt the cheese faster. When the cheese was melted, I slid the steak from the pan onto an old wooden cutting board that used to be my parents'. I sliced up the steak in long strips, then transferred it to a plate and garnished it with some salsa I had made a few days before. I brought it to the coffee table and sat on the couch where Jennie was waiting with our wine.

"Where did you learn to cook this?" She looked impressed.

"I waited tables at a steakhouse when I was going to beauty school and used to smoke weed with the Mexican cooks all the time. Sometimes they let me help cook. They served this there and called it Southwestern Ribeye. Pretty much anything you put salsa on becomes Southwestern."

"That ain't Pace Picante salsa. Where'd you get it? New York City?" Jennie said.

I answered her, "Get a rope."

Jennie was referencing the salsa commercials from the '90s. I loved it.

She took the first bite. "I love it," she said.

I took a bite and said, "I love it too."

"Do you?" she asked.

"Yes."

"What else do you love?"

I looked around the room and said, "I love lamp."

"*Anchorman*! You are quoting *Anchorman*! Are you just looking around the room, Brick?"

I laughed and loved that she knew the movie I was talking about.

We finished dinner and went outside to have a smoke. Jennie noticed my firepit in the back.

"Almost firepit season," she said.

"I love fires in the back. A few more weeks and it should be cool enough," I said.

"You love lots of things, don't you?" she said.

"Yes."

"But what do you love the most?"

"Jesus," I answered, and Jennie got closer to me.

"And then?" she prodded.

"Chichi," I told her.

"I love you," Jennie said, looking into my eyes and grabbing my hands.

I replied with, "I know." It was a reference to *Star Wars*—Han Solo telling Leia after she said, "I love you." I couldn't resist!

Jennie jabbed me in my stomach, laughing, and said, "Say you love me, jerk!"

"I love you. I always have," I told her, seriously.

"See? That wasn't so hard." Then she gave me a little kiss, grabbed my hand, and led me into the bedroom.

"You're not going to hit me some more, are you?" I asked.

"Oh, I'ma hit it," she said with a smile.

"I love you!" I told her.

That night in bed, Jennie said, "So you tell a girl you are going to marry her before you tell her you love her?"

"I *am* going to marry you," I insisted.

"You have to ask, you know," she told me.

I felt so strange in that moment. Like I was 13, going for my first kiss. I was scared. Then the room turned green. Everything was green. I smelled green, and I tasted green. I cannot explain it. I rolled on top of her and took her right hand with my right hand, and my left hand held me up.

"Will you marry me?"

"Okay," Jennie said.

"Okay?" I said, a bit indignantly.

"You have to ask with a ring, dummy. And do it in a cute way. I've never really been asked in a special way," she told me.

"Okay. I thought you meant to ask right now." I laid back down and said, "Well, what kind of ring?"

"Nothing fancy. I don't even want a diamond. I want an opal."

"Opal?" I said. I had no idea what an opal was.

Chapter 5

Jerome

It was mid-September, and Jennie and I were getting ready to go on our trip to Jerome. Jennie had given me something from her dad. It was a key to their house. She told me her dad said for me to lock the door when I left for the gym in the morning. By now I had learned her parents' names: Brian and Linda. It may sound strange that I didn't know their names, but they were always Mr. and Mrs. Sadusky to me, or Jennie's mom and dad. I got their names once 25 years ago, but never used them, so I forgot. I'm bad with names.

On Sunday, September 19th, I drove to Jennie's house after church to pick her up. I already had my bag packed and in the car. I left food for Chichi and had my brother, Justin, coming over to my house to check on her while I was gone for the night.

I walked into the house with a bag. Jennie had several bags at the bottom of the staircase. I saw her walking down the stairs smiling, and I said, "Three bags, babe? We're only going for one night?"

"I've never been there, so I didn't know what to bring," she replied.

Her mother, Linda, was downstairs, and I said hi. Then Max came from around the corner and saw my bag and asked, "What's in the bag?"

I put the bag on the ground and said, "Open it, dude."

Max ran to the bag and pulled out a brand-new Kenner Ghostbuster blaster that shot foam darts.

"WOOOO," Max said.

"I'm taking your mom ghost hunting, so we need it for protection, but when we get back, it's yours."

Max's eyes got tight like Dirty Harry, and he said, "Promise it's mine?"

"I promise." He handed it back to me.

I talked to Noah and Sophie while Jennie ran around finishing getting ready, and they were excited about the trip for us. They liked seeing their mom happy. I told them we'd be home by the time they got home from school tomorrow and would have souvenirs for them. It was a little after 11 a.m., so we went to the car with the kids and Linda following. I was carrying Jennie's three bags, and I put them in the back of my car. Jennie kissed the kids and her mom. I waved, and we left.

I pulled into the QT gas station to fill up on gas and get some sodas and snacks. Jennie grabbed some Slim Jims. She told me it's not a road trip without beef jerky. I remembered what she told me she'd do to me twenty years ago for beef jerky. So, I paid for it.

We got on the 60 freeway and headed west, then got on the 17 and drove north. Jennie controlled the radio with her phone. We listened to Sublime, Slightly Stoopid, Dirty Heads, Jack Johnson, and some Wu-Tang Clan. Halfway there, I made a pit stop at Rock Springs in Gold Canyon because Jennie had to pee. This place has the best pies in the world, but we didn't get one because I already planned on stopping there on the way back. There was a small shop there that had hot sauce, some fresh produce, and snacks. It also has what claims to be "the best beef jerky." So, Jennie picked out some jerky, and I grabbed some wasabi peas. Jennie also picked up one tomato.

"One tomato?" I asked.

"Mary loves tomatoes. She eats them like apples," she said.

"Let's get it on the way back. I don't think it will last the trip."

We were back on the road and about an hour from Jerome when Jennie told me, "Please don't be mad at me?"

"Ok, for what?"

"You just can't get mad!"

"What?"

"I think I'm going to start my period."

The timing was perfect, and there was a highway sign coming up. I've seen it a hundred times. And I pointed at it for Jennie to see. "That's your new nickname then." The road sign read "Bloody Basin."

"No, Dustin, that's a horrible nickname!"

I just laughed and said, "Babe, we're going to stay in a haunted hotel, and it's going to end up looking like that elevator scene in *The Shining*."

Jennie whined and said, "It's not fair."

"What's not fair?"

"Guys don't have to deal with this."

"Oh, I have to deal with this."

Jennie playfully pouted and said, "In junior high, I had not used a tampon yet, and Margo had to tell me how to use them. I was in the shower, and Margo was outside it looking away, trying to give directions on how to insert the tampon."

I was laughing hysterically! And I told her, "Sounds like extreme team building."

Then Jennie went on and said, "When I was in junior high, I had a young new male P.E. teacher. At the end of every month, he had us run a mile. I didn't want to run the mile, so I told him I couldn't because I was on my period and my tampon would fall out. My young male P.E. teacher said of course, and he excused me from class. Eventually, I let the P.E. teacher know that when girls hang out a lot, their periods sync up. By the end of the year, no one had to run the mile."

"Not all heroes wear capes," I said.

"No, we wear Tampax," she replied, laughing.

I pulled off the 17 for our exit to Jerome and headed west. We drove through Camp Verde, Cottonwood, then Clarkdale, where we stopped at a gas station for a six-pack of beer and headed up the two-lane road to Jerome. Pulling into the town, it looked like a town out of a Stephen King movie. The town sits on the side of a mountain, one mile up, looking down on Sedona.

The houses hang off the sides of cliffs, and the buildings were built as far back as the 1920s. There's one road in and one road out—until you go a few times and learn that there is a back road that goes to Prescott. We pulled off the street onto a dirt one-lane street named Cleopatra St. and drove up to the Jerome Grand Hotel.

The hotel was built in the 1920s as a hospital for the town. It was built by the Phelps Dodge Mining Company for its workers. In its heyday, the town had 15,000 people living in it and was full of miners, hookers, and gamblers. Jerome was known in the Old West as "the most wicked city in America." Corruption, murder, hookers, and thieves. Now the town has a population of over 400 people. Most of them work at or own the shops in town.

I parked, and we got out of the car.

"This looks like the *Shining* hotel, Dustin."

"Not yet, Bloody Basin."

"Stop!" Jennie told me.

I grabbed my bag and two of hers. Jennie took the smaller third bag. I checked us in, and since I knew the manager, Bob, it was a fast check-in. Jennie noticed I knew Bob and told me, "I forgot you got engaged here. Please don't ask me here!"

"I'm not! I love this town. I come here a few times a year, and Bob has been here since before I started coming. You know, I come here by myself a lot too!"

"I know."

"I love the people and the views. Let's go to our room, babe. I want to share this place with you."

"You mean show?"

"No, I mean share."

Bob handed me the key, and we walked to the old original Otis elevator. It has a gate you have to open first, then open the door by hand. We walked in. I put my key in the keyhole and selected the third floor. The elevator shook, Jennie grabbed me, and the elevator went up. We got to our floor, and I took my key out and opened the door, then the gate, and let Jennie out first.

"Dustin, it smells like the Haunted Mansion at Disneyland."

"Yeah, but this is real."

"Dustin!! Why did I agree to come here?"

"For adventure and wine, babe."

"Where's the wine?"

"We have to walk to the town. There are like five tasting rooms and three bars."

I opened the door to our room and walked in first, then held the door for Jennie. She entered, then dropped her bag and said, "This looks like something out of *The Great Gatsby*!"

"You like it?"

"I love it!" She walked around the room that had one bathroom to the left, which had a shower and sink. To the right was a table with two chairs, and then the queen bed just to the right of the door. There was a second bathroom with a toilet and sink in the far-right corner of the room. As you walked in, there were two French doors straight ahead that opened to the balcony, and the view was of the mountain that was carved out almost a hundred years ago to build this building. You could almost touch the mountain.

"It really is perfect, Dustin."

I handed Jennie a small box from my bag. "Open it?"

She did and pulled out a wine cup with a lid that read, "You're my Lobster."

"From *Friends*?" she asked, referencing the TV show.

"Yeah, I feel like we have a Chandler and Monica thing going on. Our friends don't know we're dating. I always thought I was more of a Joey."

"I love it. Now let's go get some wine to test it."

I handed Jennie one of the beers. "Hang on. I need to get ice first." I took the bucket and left the room to get ice. I came back and put the beers in the bucket, then told Jennie, "Let's go."

"But I'm not done."

"It's okay. You can drink while we walk."

"It's like Las Vegas here?"

"Kind of. More like card counting in Vegas. You can do it, just don't get caught."

Jennie looked worried, so I told her, "We'll throw the beers away in the lobby."

I went into my bag and took out a ghost meter.

"What's that?" Jennie asked.

"A ghost meter. It picks up electromagnetic waves." I put the meter next to the light socket, and it went off. "Electricity will make it go off. It detects energy. You leave it in a stationary place to see if anything passes."

"Nerd," Jennie called me, and I placed the ghost meter on the table.

We left the room and took the Otis elevator down to the lobby, finished our beers, and threw them away. I stopped at my car and took out a THC gummy that we split, then we walked down the dirt road to the shops, holding hands and enjoying the bird's-eye view of Sedona.

We walked down some long stairs that opened onto the street. Our first stop was Caduceus Cellars. Jennie had a white Chupacabra, and I had a red. We sat in the window seat and tried to talk, but we had a bartender that wouldn't leave our table. He was trying to entertain us, but we didn't need him—we entertained ourselves. To get him to go away, I asked for a bottle of white and red Chupacabra to go. We finished our glasses of wine and left for the bar a few doors down, the Spirit Room.

The bartender there made us leave our bottles outside. So we only had a shot of Jameson, then we went to the bar across the street, Paul and Jerry's. This place let us bring in our bottles, so we had a few shots and beers. Paul and Jerry's also happened to sell beer to go, so I got us another six-pack. We left and walked down the street and went in and out of shops, Jennie holding the wine and me holding the beer in a brown bag.

We walked into a jewelry shop. I thought maybe we could find an opal ring. The woman working wasn't friendly and told us she only sold silver.

We walked out.

"That lady looked like someone ordered Morticia Addams off of WISH!" I said.

Laughing, Jennie said, "You nailed it."

We ended up at another wine tasting room and each ordered a glass and sat at a couch by the window. We leaned in on each other and kissed. We didn't talk much, just enjoyed the people watching and looking at each other. I ordered another two bottles of white to go, and I carried those. It was only 4 p.m. Jennie asked if we could go back to the room to rest, so I took her hand and led her out.

We made one stop at the Jerome Christmas store.

"It's September? You want to buy Christmas ornaments?" Jennie asked.

"I want to buy one Christmas ornament with you every time we come to Jerome. When we are old, we will have a Christmas tree full of vacation memories."

"I like that," Jennie said, and she picked out a Christmas jalapeño.

I picked up an ornament that had an old Santa that looked like my Pappy Earl. I was going to mail it to Grandma Bonnie.

I paid for our ornaments, and we walked up the street until we got back to the stairs.

Jennie looked up the stairs like it was Mount Everest. "Babe, we have to go up there?"

"Come on, babe, let's do it!" I encouraged her.

We made it up the stairs, and she saw the dirt road up Cleopatra St. to the hotel.

"Another climb?"

"We're halfway there." I took the bag she had with the bottles and said, "We can do it."

Halfway up, I suggested we walk backwards because it would be easier, so we did. After many whines, groans, and a few *ughs*, we were back at the hotel and got on the Otis elevator. Jennie said she was sorry for complaining and thankful for the elevator.

We got in the Otis elevator and took it to our floor. Then we went to our room. I opened the French doors to our balcony, and the room was lit by the sunlight. I opened a bottle of white wine and walked out onto our patio. Jennie followed me, and I poured two glasses. We sat and enjoyed the good weather and good wine. Jennie played music from her phone. The first song was by Jack Johnson, *Always Better When We're Together.* She rested her foot on my thigh, and we relaxed. When the bottle of wine started to get empty, I said, "Let's walk back to the bar." Jennie got up from her chair. I thought she was ready to go. She said, "Wait," and walked inside. So I waited.

Jennie came out to the patio a few minutes later wearing light pink, almost peach-colored lingerie. She was barefoot and holding a beer for me.

"Or we can stay in?" she said.

"Stay in, please."

Jennie sat on my lap and handed me my beer, then took her glass of wine off the table to take a drink. The two of us sat there like that for a while, talking and kissing, with only the mountain watching us. We walked inside our room through the French doors and took a seat at the small table. I opened a bottle of red wine that I poured for both of us. We sat and drank and talked about everything—from who we had our first kiss with to our last relationship. We finished the bottle of wine, then switched from the table to the bed and lay down. Jennie lay her head on my chest while dressed in romantic lingerie, and the two of us took a nap with the wind ricocheting off the mountain and coming through the French doors.

We woke up, and Jennie joined me on the patio wearing the lingerie, and I opened another bottle, this time white. We drank, laughed, and kissed. The room was so secluded because of the mountain, and we felt like we were the only two people in the world. I loved her so much. It was getting late, and we needed to eat dinner. I wanted to go to the Haunted Hamburger for dinner. It was back down the dirt road. Jennie looked happy now, sitting inside the room at the table, and I didn't want to tell her we were walking again. So, I put my shoes on and told Jennie to change for dinner, and I'd be right back.

"Where are you going?" she asked.

"Downstairs to the restaurant to see if I can make a reservation."

"Don't leave me."

"If I don't get a reservation, we have to walk back down to town."

"GO!"

"Get ready!"

I took the Otis elevator down to the second floor of the hotel, where The Asylum restaurant was located. It is a 4.5-star restaurant. I didn't plan on spending that much for dinner, but I felt drawn to stay in the hotel. The restaurant was slow—only four tables were being used. We were lucky it was Sunday night. There was a table open by the window that had a view of the Verde Valley. The hostess greeted me, and I asked for that table.

She asked, "For one?"

"No, my wife is in the room getting ready." *My wife,* I'd said.

"What time?"

I looked at my phone, and it was almost 6:30. "7:30?" I said.

"Okay. We close at 9."

"Then 7," and I handed her a twenty-dollar bill from my pocket and said thank you. The restaurant was slow, and we were going to be the last table. I wanted her to know I would take care of them.

I went back to the room to shower. I felt I needed to shower for a nice meal. Jennie was doing her hair when I got out of the shower. I threw on jeans, a pair of Air Jordans, and a Dixxon flannel. Jennie switched from the lingerie she was wearing earlier to a black dress, her hair curled in beach waves, and she had brown flip-flops on. We each grabbed a beer for the Otis elevator ride and left the room.

We got into the Otis elevator and hit the button for the second floor. The elevator would not move. So I hit the button harder. Nothing.

Jennie walked to the elevator door, opened it, and said, "You have to shut the gate." She shut the gate, and I hit the second-floor button. Then the elevator moved. Jennie smiled at me, and we toasted our beers.

We exited the elevator and finished our beers. Then I took our empties and threw them away in the trash can, and we walked into The Asylum restaurant. There were only two tables occupied with customers now. The hostess greeted us and said, "Dustin, I have your table ready." She led us to the table with the view.

I pulled the seat closest to the window out for Jennie, and she sat. I started walking around to the other side of the table so I could look at her, and she stopped me and said, "Sit next to me." Then she pulled the seat out for me. So I sat down. Our waiter was there as soon as I was seated.

"Something to drink or an appetizer to start you off?" he said.

"Two Bloody Marys, please." The waiter nodded and left to get our drinks.

I told Jennie, "This place makes the best Bloody Mary."

We were his only customers, so the drinks came back fast. He dropped them off with some bread and menus, then left us alone. The Bloody Marys had large slices of bacon in them in place of celery. Jennie went straight for the olives.

"It's an appetizer and a drink," I said.

"I love it."

We looked over the menu, but I already knew what we wanted before we walked in. The waiter came back to our table to see if we were ready to order. Jennie was not. So I said, "We'll split the king crab legs, please, with an extra salad and a bottle of white wine."

"Which wine, sir?" he said.

"You pick, but please nothing that costs more than our meal." The waiter smiled and took our menus.

"How'd you know what I wanted? That's my favorite," Jennie asked.

"Who doesn't love crab legs?"

We finished our Bloody Marys, and the waiter came back with the wine. He opened the bottle and poured a small amount into my glass, then had me test it. I did. Then I nodded that I approved, and he filled our glasses, then walked away.

Sarcastically, Jennie said, "You're so fancy."

"No, it's just like when I have to take a car to a mechanic—I pretend like I know what is going on, but I really have no idea and end up with a huge bill."

Jennie laughed. Then we grabbed the crayons on the table. The table was covered in white paper for us to draw on, so we started playing tic-tac-toe. After several cat games and our attempts to draw Stussy S's, our salad came out. So we put the crayons down and picked up our salad forks and ate.

We ate, but stopped and noticed the moon that hung high in the sky with the thousands of stars that looked like white Christmas lights, and the cool air blew in from the open window. We were the only people in the restaurant now. I reached into my pocket for my phone to take a picture, but it wasn't there. I told Jennie, "I left my phone in the room."

"Good," she said. I looked at her, confused, then she said, "We don't need a picture. It would never be as beautiful as this. We just need us."

She was right. She stared at the moonlit sky as I stared at her. The moment was broken up by our server coming with our meal, which was almost as pretty as the sky: the steamed king crab legs with garlic mashed potatoes. He placed the plate between us, then put two empty plates in front of us and said, "Please enjoy. Do you need anything else?"

"No, it's perfect," I said, and he bowed and walked away.

I closed my eyes to pray silently, and Jennie noticed and took my hand and closed her eyes. I opened my eyes and kissed her on the cheek and said, pointing to the crab legs, "After you, babe." Jennie grabbed a crab leg, and I did after her. Then we snapped into them, mine spraying onto my flannel.

"Somebody needs a bib," she said and took her napkin off her lap to wipe my flannel.

"Thank you."

We used our plates to put the empty crab legs on and used our spoons to eat the garlic mashed potatoes from the main plate. We didn't talk. We just ate. Soon the food was almost gone, with only one crab leg left.

I pushed the plate to Jennie and said, "It's yours." Jennie took it.

The waiter came back and asked us, "Dessert?"

"Yes, we will have two shots of Jameson and the check, sir." He bowed and left.

"Did you want dessert?" I asked.

"Shots for dessert sounds perfect." Jennie laughed very loud and said, "We are the only ones here! We need to go."

"We will, after the shots."

The waiter came back with the shots and the check that he left in front of me, but Jennie tried to grab it. I took the check. She asked, "Please let me pay?"

"No way. I'm not going back to the friend zone ever again."

Jennie smiled, and we took our shots. Then I placed my debit card on top of the check without looking at the bill, and the waiter came to take care of it. We stared at the night sky with my arms around her and her hands holding my knee. We started kissing, and the kissing was broken up by the waiter saying, "Thank you for coming to The Asylum."

I tipped him well, then grabbed the bottle of wine that was two-thirds done, and we walked back to the elevator. I stopped to use the restroom, and when I came out, the bottle was empty. I looked at Jennie, and she said, "Oops, it's gone." Then she started kissing me aggressively as we fell into the old Otis elevator, and we were only held up from falling by the back wall. I went back to close the gate and shut the door, then went back to kissing Jennie. We arrived at our floor and left the elevator without shutting the gate and stumbled into our room. I kicked my shoes off as we were kissing, then picked Jennie up and threw her onto the bed. She had a seductive look to her. And just then, the ghost meter went off! Jennie jumped off the bed excitedly and screamed, "Ghost!" Then she stood up and grabbed the ghost meter and followed the beeps to the door.

I lay on the bed with my shirt off. "No babe, come back. Let the ghost watch."

She was standing barefoot at the door and yelled, "Come on."

I grabbed the last bottle of white Chupacabra and my flannel, opened the wine, then met Jennie at the door. The ghost meter was beeping quickly. We walked barefoot through the hotel chasing beeps. The ghost meter would stop, then we would run to another spot where it would go off again. We walked and ran up and down the five floors of the hotel, drinking the wine straight from the bottle. It felt like we were kids chasing the unknown. Our fun was stopped by a woman coming out of her room to yell at us to "Be quiet." Jennie told her to "Shut up, we are ghosts." Jennie and I laughed at the woman, then ran back to the room like kids that got caught out after curfew.

We got back into our room, and Jennie went to the bed. I put the ghost meter away, and the empty bottle of wine I placed on the table. When I turned around, Jennie was sleeping. I moved her to get her under the blankets, then got in bed and held her, and I fell asleep.

I woke up around seven in the morning, and Jennie's eyes were shut, her mouth open, and one word came out: "Coffee."

So, I put my jeans and flannel back on. I didn't bother buttoning it or putting on shoes and walked down to the hotel lobby. I skipped the Otis elevator and took the stairs. The hotel offered its guests free coffee, bagels, and danishes. The bagels were the kind from the grocery store that came in a plastic bag with a zip tie. Jennie's parents, being from New York, made Jennie a bagel snob, so I knew she'd hate them, but I got her one anyway and toasted it. There was a stack of brown cafeteria trays, so I took one and began to fill it up with as much free stuff as I could: two bagels, two cups of coffee, two bottles of water, two orange juices, an apple, a banana, and three danishes (they were packaged, so I knew I'd eat them later). A couple was getting onto the Otis elevator, and they waited for me to get in. Then they asked me, "What floor?"

The man looked at my tray, then at me with my bare feet and unbuttoned flannel, and asked, "Rough, right?"

"The best night—but, yeah, rough morning," I said.

When we got to my floor, the man opened the door and gate for me, and I told him thanks. Then I went to my room. I left it open a crack on purpose so I could push the door open because I knew my hands would be full. Jennie was still in bed and heard me come in. She sounded like a zombie demanding brains—only she said, "Coffee."

"Get up, sunshine," I told her and walked to the balcony through the French doors and placed the tray on the table outside, then brought Jennie back her coffee in bed. She reached for it, and I pulled it away.

"Get up. Come outside." And I walked away with her coffee.

"What time is it?" she moaned.

Looking at my phone, I said, "7:30."

"Are you psycho? Check-out isn't until 11!"

"I can never sleep in this hotel. It wakes me up every time around 7 a.m. no matter what I did the night before."

"The ghost wants you out," she said.

"Maybe, but I paid for the room until 11 a.m., so I'm staying. I got you a shitty bagel—come out here with me."

Jennie got out of bed and walked out to the balcony with the white hotel blanket wrapped around her and took a seat with me. She grabbed her coffee and the bagel. She took a bite of the bagel, then sipped her coffee and said, "Thank you, babe."

"You're welcome. Sorry they only had the grocery store bagels."

Jennie smiled and said, "They're fine."

We finished our coffee and most of the bagels. No one touched the apple and banana. Then I walked back into the room and jumped in bed.

"You're going back to bed?" Jennie asked.

"I'm not going to sleep. Come over here and bring the blanket back!" I said.

Jennie came back to bed, and we spent the next two hours lying in bed with the balcony doors open and cool morning breezes blowing into the room. Around 10 a.m. I got out of bed and jumped in the shower. I got out of the shower and put on my swimming shorts. Jennie was still in bed, so I pulled the blankets off of her and left them on the floor.

"Get up, we're going to Sedona."

"I know, five more minutes, Dustin."

"Okay, but we have to be out of the room in 30 minutes."

Jennie got out of bed and showered, then put on her swimsuit and a white sundress over it. Then we packed and cleaned up the room the best we could. On our way out, Jennie grabbed the empty bottle of white Chupacabra wine and put it in her purse. Then she looked at me as I was wondering why she put trash in her purse and said, "A souvenir."

We left the room and waited for the Otis elevator. I pulled out my phone and tried to take a selfie of us, and Jennie turned her head and said, "I look horrible. Don't take a picture, Dustin." I did anyway as her head was turned and said, "You look beautiful."

We checked out of the hotel and loaded our things into the back of the car. Jennie stopped to look at the view and said, "It is really pretty here."

"Wait until you see Slide Rock."

We drove down through the town of Jerome with the windows down and then down the hill. I'd look in the rearview mirror, seeing the Jerome Grand getting smaller, then looked forward and saw the red rocks of Sedona getting bigger. We drove through Camp Verde and then Cornville before coming to downtown Sedona, where we stopped at the gas station for gas, a six-pack of beer in cans, and some energy drinks.

We pulled into Slide Rock State Park. There was no line because it was a Monday. I had a small cooler that held the six beers. I packed our one towel in my backpack along with the danishes from the hotel. We walked holding hands through the old apple orchard and down the rock stairs to the creek, where there were lots of people enjoying the water. We walked as far back as we could and passed people jumping from the rocks and sliding down the creek. The creek was called Slide Rock because of the smooth rocks that, through thousands of years of water running over them, had created a natural waterslide. The stone sides were very slippery. We found a shallow area and started to cross.

"Hold my hand," I told her, and we stepped into the very cold water.

"It's freezing," she said as she almost fell, then took my hand.

We took baby steps crossing the creek, almost falling several times. We reached the other side, and I put the cooler down and my backpack and took off my shirt, then jumped into the small pool of water. It was freezing, but I knew this was the only way to get in.

"Come in," I yelled to Jennie. But she took little steps getting in.

"It's so cold, babe!"

"You'll get used to it faster if you just get in."

So Jennie made the jump and submerged her whole body into the creek. When her head emerged, she said, "It's freezing—I hate you!"

I grabbed Jennie and held her, trying to warm her up by rubbing her back. After a minute, she was fine, and I grabbed us two beers. We sat in the water and watched other people try to cross where we had. They all fell. We started to warn people that it's slippery, but no one listened to us. Another couple had joined us to watch the people fall. Jennie became friends with them immediately. We gave them some of our beers. They were tourists from Seattle, and the man had a joint, so I took a hit. Jennie passed. I had another beer, then floated on my stomach to the slides.

"Where are you going, babe?" Jennie asked.

"To slide. Come with me."

"Nope, I'm good here," she said.

So I went down the rocks by myself, going under the water a few times and twisting and turning until the creek spit me out into a clear pool where kids were cliff-jumping and a couple of trout were wading. I walked back to Jennie.

"You nerd," she said.

I smiled and jumped back in the water with Jennie. Jennie brought me an energy drink. "No more beer. You have to drive."

"Are you hungry yet?" I asked.

"Starving," she said.

So I drank my Monster energy drink in the water as Jennie dried off with our one towel. Then I got out of the water and dried off with the damp towel.

We packed our things, then walked slowly across the creek so we wouldn't fall, and made our way back to the parking lot.

"It really is beautiful here, Dustin."

"So are you. Now let's go eat."

We drove through Oak Creek and back to downtown Sedona, where we parked and walked to the Oaxaca Mexican restaurant. The restaurant has multiple levels, and you have to walk upstairs to get to the entrance. There was a foreign couple ahead of us in the line. The man was asking the hostess if they had a vegan or non-meat menu.

"No meat? I'll take his meat, don't waste it. I'll take all the meat," Jennie said quietly to me.

"Stop, I think he heard you." And the man looked back at us, and we looked at our phones to ignore his look.

We were seated in a room decorated in Spanish tile, green plants, and huge windows to see the views of Sedona. The busboy brought us water, chips, and salsa, and then the waiter came to drop off the menus. He asked if we wanted anything else to drink. We looked at each other and shook our heads, then I told the waiter, "The water is fine for now." Jennie looked through the menu, but I already knew what I wanted.

The waiter came back to take our orders, and Jennie ordered first.

"I'll have the cactus tacos."

"And for you, señor?" the waiter asked.

"I'll have the cheese enchilada and beef taco combo." Then we handed him our menus.

We finished our chips, and the busboy brought us more and refilled our waters. We had small talk, and Jennie said, "We've done so much in the last twenty-four hours, babe! I love you!"

"I love you too."

"Don't say 'I love you too,' just say 'I love you.' I hate the 'too' after 'I love you.' It sounds like someone only says it because you said it first."

"Okay, I love you," I said.

"I love you."

"I love you more."

"You can't say you love me more! That's not fair!" she said.

"But I do. Do you love me more too?"

"I hate you."

To break up our argument, the waiter arrived at our table with the food. Perfect timing. The food looked amazing, and the waiter said, "Be careful— hot plates." The sign of good Mexican food. Hot plates. It meant the cheese was melted onto the beans because the plates were put in the oven. I closed my eyes to pray, but Jennie was too excited and already started eating. She saw I was praying, then stopped.

"Keep eating. It's okay—I prayed for the two of us. How are your tacos?"

"So good," she said and kept eating. After a couple more bites, she opened the taco to look inside.

"Everything okay?" I asked.

"Babe, there is no meat in this!"

"Really?"

Jennie opened the other taco and showed me there was no meat in that one either. So I walked over to the hostess stand and grabbed a menu to bring back to the table. I sat down and read what was in Jennie's cactus tacos. I laughed and handed her the menu and said, "Read."

Jennie then looked at me with sadness in her eyes and said, "They're vegetarian tacos, Dustin."

I pointed to the foreign couple. "I'll take all the meat."

"Ask the waiter for meat," she said.

"No way. It's not his fault you didn't read what was in your tacos."

The waiter came back and asked if everything was okay. I pointed to Jennie, and she smiled and said nothing. So I asked for the check. He had it on him and placed it on the table. I reached for my wallet, but Jennie grabbed the check.

"This one's on me," she said, and I didn't argue.

When the waiter came back with Jennie's card, he asked if Jennie wanted a to-go bag. The tacos were barely touched. I stepped in and told him no and that we had to drive back to Phoenix. So we walked back to the car, and I teased Jennie about her tacos. We drove back through Camp Verde and onto the 17 Highway, only stopping in Rock Springs, where I left the car running and ran in to get a strawberry rhubarb pie. Then we were back on the road, and next stop: Anchor Dr.

After an hour drive, we got to Jennie's parents' house, and Max greeted us at the door.

"Do you have my Ghostbusters gun?"

I pulled it out of a bag and handed it to him. He smiled, then ran away to shoot things.

Jennie's parents met us in the kitchen, and we talked about the trip. Then I brought out the pie. Noah and Sophie came downstairs to say hi, and I remembered I didn't get them souvenirs.

"I didn't see anything cool I thought you would like, so I thought you might just like some money?"

I pulled out two twenty-dollar bills from my wallet and said, "Is cash okay?" They took the money and said thanks, then asked if we saw any ghosts, and Jennie told them about the ghost meter and how we chased beeps all night trying to find one. The kids were excited and said they wanted to go next time.

I said goodbye and drove home to my house to see Chichi. I took her for a walk, then fed her and laid on my couch and turned on the TV. I got a text from Jennie: "I miss you."

So I texted back, "I'm coming over."

"Yay," she replied.

I grabbed a handful of shredded cheese and placed it in Chichi's dog food bowl as an offering. Then I snuck out the front door and drove to Jennie's house to spend the night.

Chapter 6

Ice Blocking

Thursday came, and I had told Jennie I would take the kids out to do something when they got out of school since I was off at 2 p.m., and she had a couple of students to tutor. I told Jennie to text me when she was home, and the kids and I would come get her for dinner.

I picked up the kids around 3:30 at their grandparents' house and took them to downtown Gilbert. There was a retro arcade named Level One that I wanted to take them to. The arcade is also a bar, but they let you bring kids in until 7 p.m. Max noticed none of the games gave tickets. He looked confused.

"You don't win anything, Max, you just play," I told him.

"This is just like your garage. Why didn't we just go there?" Noah asked.

"Because this place has more games!" I said.

The arcade had ten pinball machines, Pac-Man and Ms. Pac-Man, Mortal Kombat 1, 2, and 3, Street Fighter II, NBA Jam, NFL Blitz, Rampage, Tetris, Donkey Kong—just to name a few. '90s grunge rock played in the background, along with the noise from all the games, and coins being dropped into machines sounded like we were in the Hard Rock Casino. I walked over to the token machine and put in a twenty-dollar bill, then placed a cup below to catch the coins like an old slot machine. I handed the cup to Sophie and said, "Go."

They did. Then Max came back to me. "Where do you put these?" He was holding a token. Max was only six, and his whole life arcade games had been paid with a card.

"Max, you put it in the slot," I showed him.

"Oh, that's cool."

Then he started playing, and he put another token in the next slot for me.

"Come on, play me," Max said.

I joined Max on Rampage. He was a werewolf, and I was a giant lizard. We destroyed skyscrapers and ate people. We were having fun. Sophie and Noah were not too far away on the pinball machines, so after a couple of losses Max and I joined them. The four of us all went to play the Teenage Mutant Ninja Turtles game because it is the only four-player game there. After we beat two bosses, we went to play Big Buck Hunter. I sat out and let the boys play since it's only two players, and me and Sophie played Mortal Kombat. I have that game in my garage, so I let Sophie win. We continued throwing tokens into slots until the cup was empty, and then we walked across the street to Rocket Fizz.

Rocket Fizz is a unique candy shop with hard-to-find candies and one-of-a-kind sodas. They have anything you could think of. Max picked up a Kit Kat.

"No, Max, get something fun," I told him.

"How many things do we get?" Noah asked.

"Two each," I said, and they scattered.

I walked around looking at the candies of my youth—Bazooka Joe bubble gum, Abba-Zaba bars, wax soda with different colored juice inside, and candy cigarettes. I picked up a Rocky Road candy bar. It was my Pappy Earl's favorite. I took the candy bar to the counter to pay and called for the kids. They each had three items, and I said that was fine. Noah was mad Max copied him on his choices. They had all picked Japanese candy since they were into anime.

"It's okay. Little brothers always copy. Get used to it," I told him.

"Yeah, Noah, and you copied me," Sophie said.

"You see?" I smiled and reached for my wallet to pay.

"Anything else?" the teenage girl working the counter asked.

Then I noticed behind the register they had stink bombs. They were the good ones—made of glass and came in a small box of three.

"I'll take one of those," I said, and pointed to the stink bombs.

"What are you going to do with those?" Noah asked.

"I don't know yet, but it's good to have them."

We left the store, and I handed the kids the bag of treats as we walked to the car.

"Where are we going now?" they all asked.

"To get dinner," I said.

"Do we have to wait to eat these?" Max asked.

"I won't tell if you don't tell." We drove to Fry's grocery store as the kids ate their candy in the car. It was a short five-minute drive to the store. By the time we arrived, their candy was gone, with only wrappers on my car floor.

We got into the store, and I grabbed a cart. Then Max jumped on the side, holding on like a fireman.

"What are we getting?" Sophie asked.

"What does your mom like?"

"Whole chickens," Noah said.

"I think you mean rotisserie, but okay." I pushed the cart toward the front, where they kept them around dinnertime, and grabbed two. "What else?"

"Mom loves cheese," Sophie said.

"Okay, who can find it?" I asked the kids, and they took off, and I followed them like hound dogs on the hunt.

Sophie found it and picked a sharp cheddar. Max picked up some Swiss cheese that was the shape of a slice of cake and said, "I think a mouse ate this one—it has holes?"

"No, that's how it comes," Sophie said.

"What else?" I asked.

"Bread. Mom likes bread," Noah said.

The bread happened to be close to us, so I picked up two French bread rolls.

"What do you guys like to drink?"

They all said water.

"That's boring. Try again."

"Lemonade?" Max asked.

"Now you're talking." We grabbed some Minute Maid lemonade in cans and bottles of water, then went to pay. Jennie texted that she was home. I told her we were on our way. After I paid for our groceries, we walked to the car and we all got in.

"One more stop," I said.

"Where?" they asked.

"Water and ice."

"Why?" Noah asked.

"You'll see."

We got to the Water and Ice store. I left the kids in the car with it running. I went in and grabbed two ten-pound blocks of ice and put them in the back, then drove to get Jennie. I walked into her house to get paper plates and knives.

"Where are the kids?" Jennie asked.

"In the car waiting. Come on."

"I'm hungry."

"It's in the car."

"Where are we going?"

"Freestone Park." I kissed Jennie, then grabbed her hand and led her to the car.

"Come on, Mom," Max shouted from the back seat.

"We're having a picnic," Noah said.

I opened the door for Jennie, and she asked, "What are we eating?"

"Chicken, cheese, and bread," Max said.

"My favorite," Jennie smiled.

"They picked it out," I said.

The park was a mile away, so we were there quickly. We got out of the car, and I carried the food and drinks to the top of a small hill that overlooked the miniature train track that rode around a small lake. I left Jennie with the food and kids and went back to get the ice blocks.

I came back to the top of the hill with the two ten-pound ice blocks. Jennie was cutting the bread, chicken, and cheese on a paper plate on a park bench.

"What are those for?" Sophie asked.

"It's called ice blocking. Come on."

"Seriously, Dustin?" Jennie said, smiling.

"You cut, we slide."

"Yeah! We slide! How do we do it?" Max asked.

I gave one block to Sophie and took Max on the other block.

"You don't have three?" Noah said.

"No, we can share."

I put a towel on the ice block, then put Max on the block.

"Just hold on." Then I gave Max a push, and he went down the hill—well, halfway down before he fell off. I thought he was going to cry, but he didn't. He stood up and said, "That's awesome! Can I do it again?"

Sophie got on her block and slid, and Noah came and got Max's block, carried it to the top, and slid down the hill.

"Take turns!" I told them and walked back up the hill to see Jennie. She had a mouth full of bread with cheese and chicken in each hand.

"This really is your favorite?"

"It is." Jennie then fed me some of the cheese from her hand.

The two of us ate, and the kids slid down the hill with minimal fighting. The kids would come up to Jennie and me, take a bite of something, then run back to the ice blocks. We were having a great time. Then Max asked, "Are you going to try, Dustin?"

"Yeah, Dustin?" said the other two kids.

I looked at Jennie and put my sunglasses on and said, "I'll be back."

"Okay, Arnold."

I'm much larger than the kids, and my butt barely fits on the ice block. I told Noah, "When I lift my legs, push me."

"Ok."

I lifted my legs, and Noah pushed me, but I didn't go anywhere.

Sophie came over to push too, then I went down the hill. It felt faster than I remembered it being, and the block started to shake under me. I tried to hold on to nothing. I was thrown about a third of the way down. I got up, and the kids cheered and Jennie clapped.

"Do it again, Dustin!" Max shouted.

I shook my head. "I'm going to eat with your mom."

I carried the ice block up the hill and placed it on the ground for Max. Without any words, he got on and went down the hill. I walked over to Jennie and sat next to her.

"You're just a big kid, aren't you?"

"I don't want to grow up, I'm a Toys R Us kid."

"You're so dumb! But thank you, the kids are having so much fun."

"And you?"

"Anytime I don't have to make dinner, I'm having fun."

"I like to cook, so you're in for the time of your life."

Chapter 7

Friday Night Lights

The next night was Friday night, and we went to a Highland High School football game. It was a special game to honor Marquis Cooper. We went to high school with him. He made it to the NFL but tragically lost his life in a fishing accident off the coast of Florida.

Sophie didn't come because she had plans with her friends. Sophie was in seventh grade and too cool for us on a Friday night. We picked up my nephew Jaxson to take her place. Jennie, Noah, Max, Jaxson, and I went to the game.

Jennie had changed her Facebook status to being in a relationship with me earlier that day. My phone was going off with texts from friends asking, "Is this real?" They thought it was a joke. They thought no way Jennie Sadusky and Dustin Elkin were dating. The two people who grew up across the street from each other in high school were dating. Even my best friends asked. I didn't tell them because I didn't care. I was infatuated with Jennie. She was all that I cared about, and she had all of my time and attention. I didn't even have time to say I was in love with Jennie Sadusky to my best friends. I didn't have time. I was too busy telling Jennie I loved her, and I told her constantly. Time? There is never enough time.

The school parking lot was full, so we parked in the visitor parking lot and had to walk across the campus to the football field. Jennie and I held hands and reminisced about our time at Highland as the boys ran wild, saying, "Go Hawks!"—our school mascot. I paid for our tickets at the one entrance that took debit cards; the rest required a scan code. Jennie and I walked in holding hands. It had been over twenty years since I was at a Highland football game with Jennie, only this time I was her boyfriend.

We walked in and went straight to the snack stand. The kids all picked out snacks—pretzels, popcorn, sodas, and candy. Jennie and I got Diet Cokes in the can. We walked the back way under the bleachers, and the kids were way out in front of us. Then Jennie stopped, kissed me, and said, "Want to make out under the bleachers?" So we did until we heard the word "Mom." We stopped kissing and went to the kids, then walked up the bleacher stairs on the south side of the stadium and found seats. I sat down, and Jennie stepped into the row in front of me and sat down. The boys sat in my row, then Jennie leaned back between my legs and grabbed my hand. I felt like I was back in high school with the prettiest girl at the game.

The boys lasted five minutes until they were bored and wanted to get their faces painted. I gave them a ten-dollar bill, and they ran to get their faces painted. You feel safe at a high school football game. Security is everywhere, and the main security guard, Valu, was a massive, friendly Polynesian who worked at the school when Jennie and I went there.

I held Jennie, and she leaned back into my legs more with every squeeze I gave her. Our team was winning, and we cheered and yelled! A lot of kids started sitting around us—all of them on their phones facing away from the field. I complained to Jennie.

"They're not even watching the game," I said.

"Did we when we were their age?"

I looked around and said, "Babe, we are in the student section."

Jennie laughed so loud she dropped her Diet Coke and said, "I didn't realize it until now—we walked right back to where we used to sit in high school." Then she pointed to all the adults in the middle.

"Should we move?" she asked.

"No, we were here first. In the '90s, this was ours."

Jennie picked up her dropped Diet Coke and raised it for a cheers, then said, "Damn straight."

We held our ground long enough for the boys to come back with their faces painted. Jaxson handed me change, and I told him, "No, you are supposed to tip." So they ran back to leave a tip. When they got back to us, they wanted another snack.

"Wait till after the halftime show," I said.

"Why?" all three boys said.

"Just wait."

And the boys did.

At halftime, the marching band came out like an army ready to conquer. Their uniforms were pristine. Their faces were serious. The crowd was silent. Then the drums hit, and the flags followed, waving in the air along with the horns blasting. They had our attention. Then they started moving while playing, and the boys were intrigued. The Highland band is one of the best in the country, and the boys knew they were seeing something special. The band continued to play with the horn section taking center stage and blew us away. When the band stopped, the crowd roared in excitement. The band exited the field.

The football team came back onto the field with high energy, jumping and screaming while pointing to the stands.

"You guys want snacks now?" I asked.

"No, we want to win!" Jaxson said.

Jennie squeezed me lightly, and the second half started. Three minutes into the third quarter, Max asked, "Can we get snacks?"

I handed them a ten-dollar bill and told them to hurry.

They ran from their bleacher seats and left Jennie and me alone.

"I really love you," Jennie said.

"I really love you—" then paused and said, "as well?"

"No, I just love you, babe."

"Ok, I really love you." Then Jennie laid back in my lap, and we watched the rest of the game. Highland won. Jennie loved going to the football games when we were in high school. It was never about the game. It was about being with your friends, and with Jennie laying between my legs, I was with my best friend.

We threw the stink bombs I had gotten at the candy store into the student section as we left. Dusty McAwesome.

Chapter 8
Van Gogh

For the rest of the week, I was thinking, *How am I going to ask Jennie to marry me?* I ordered her a gold band ring with an opal stone from an internet site Jennie showed me called Local Eclectic and was waiting for it to come in the mail. I thought maybe I could get us into the Highland High School homecoming dance and ask her there? Or maybe I would ask her at our old bus stop? Then I thought maybe I'd ask Jennie to marry me on the street on Anchor Dr., in between the two houses we grew up in. Nothing felt right.

I came home from work on a Wednesday night and had two packages waiting for me. One was the ring, and the other a green Dixxon short-sleeve dress shirt I had ordered and forgotten about. Then Jennie called.

"Hey baby," she said.

"Just walkin' in the door."

"Long day?"

"Always."

"Max fell asleep in my bed, and I wasn't sure if I should move him. I didn't know if you were coming over tonight?"

"Let Max sleep with his momma. I'm not even tired yet. I need to unwind. I'll be watching TV for a few hours."

"Have a beer for me."

"I'll have two for you."

"I'm so excited for tomorrow!" she said.

"Tomorrow?" I forgot I got us tickets for the Van Gogh experience on Thursday. Jennie's mom had gone a few weeks before and told Jennie how much she loved it. Jennie looked really excited as she told me how her mom explained the Van Gogh experience to her, so I took the hint and got us tickets.

"You forgot?" Jennie asked.

"No, I'm stoked. Van Gogh liked to party. Dude partied so hard he cut his ear off."

"I'm going to bed. Have fun watching TV. I love you."

"I love you. Goodnight."

"Goodnight."

I hung up and looked at the ring and green shirt. Then I remembered that night I asked her to marry me in my bed and how I saw green, felt green, tasted green. I looked at the green Dixxon shirt and knew now I was going to ask Jennie to marry me at the Van Gogh experience. I just didn't know how. I decided to do it the way I did most things in my life and wing it.

The next day was Thursday, and I was off work at 2 p.m. I was unusually quiet at work, but in my head I was loud. I was thinking, *How do I ask?*

After work, I went to pick up Jennie's birthday present—a used Burton snowboard I found on Facebook Marketplace. I had already gotten her some Blenders goggles to go with it. I came home and cut a friend's hair for some extra cash, then showered and put on my new green Dixxon and went to pick up Jennie at five. I pulled up to the house, and Jennie came running out so fast I barely got out of my car. She kissed me and said, "I made you this," then handed me a yellow used paintbrush that she had painted on. It said "D+J 9-30-21." Jennie had put the date on the brush with our initials. I walked Jennie around the car and opened the door for her.

We drove to a speakeasy bar called The White Rabbit. Fate was on my side, but I still needed some liquid encouragement.

We pulled into a parking lot in Downtown Gilbert a quarter after five.

"The Van Gogh experience starts at seven, Dustin."

"I know, just one drink. We have time. Besides, this place is cool."

Jennie gave me her half-smirk smile and agreed to go.

The bar was underground, and you needed a password to get in. I told Jennie the password was "didgeridoo." That wasn't the password, but I always thought it was a fun word to say. *Didgeridoo.* There was no line, as it was early on Thursday. But still, the bouncer stopped us and asked for the password.

Excited, Jennie said, "Didgeridoo."

"Excuse me?" the bouncer asked.

"Didgeridoo," Jennie said again.

I laughed and stepped in, then said, "Isn't it pretty to think so."

The bouncer opened the red rope, and we walked down the concrete steps to the bar.

"You lied to me."

"No, I teased you. There's a difference."

I opened the door for Jennie, and we walked through a narrow hallway that led to a dead end.

"There's no door, Dustin?"

"Of course there is. You just have to find it. I can do it for you if you like?"

"No, I can do it."

Jennie walked around the narrow hallway and examined everything. Then after a minute, she asked, "What's the name of this place?"

"The White Rabbit," I said.

Then Jennie walked to the end wall, saw a silver rabbit in a bookcase, and pulled it. The door opened, and she turned to me and said, "You're not getting me twice in one night."

A hostess wearing a black dress greeted us and sat us at a small booth near the bar and walked away. Jennie looked around the bar. There were no TVs and no music. It was very dark, with many framed pictures decorating the walls. Our waitress showed up with water for the two of us and menus. I took the water but gave her back the menus.

"I'll have an Old Fashioned with Bulleit."

"Rye or bourbon?" she asked.

"Bourbon, please. And for you, babe?" I pointed at Jennie.

"Vodka martini, dirty, please."

The waitress walked away, and Jennie said, "Thanks for putting me on the spot, Dustin."

"It's a drink, not a math problem. What do you want? I'm just happy you didn't say vodka Red Bull."

"This place is too nice for that. So I was thinking of ways you could ask me to marry you?"

"You were?"

"Maybe you show up to my house and stand in the driveway with a boom box like John Cusack in *Say Anything*? Or have the Highland band come into my living room—Isn't your friend's kid a drummer in the band?"

"Or how about I toilet paper your house like I did in high school and leave a sign that says 'I think you are the shit—will you marry me?'"

"I forgot you TP'd my house."

Then Jennie kept going on about different ways I could ask her to marry her. Each one got more elaborate. This was broken up by the waitress coming back with our drinks. She handed me my Old Fashioned and Jennie her dirty martini. Jennie ate the olives first, and I sipped my drink, then told the waitress, "This is a great Old Fashioned. Easy to make but easy to mess up. You have a good bartender."

"He's a mixologist, not a bartender," the waitress said.

"Oh, I cut hair," I said.

"Oh, you're a hairdresser?" the waitress asked.

"No, a cosmetologist. I can make my job sound fancy too."

The waitress gave a fake smile and walked away.

"Do you like to piss people off, Dustin?"

"*Sooo* much."

Jennie smiled and sipped her drink. We finished our drinks and had one more. Jennie kept telling me different ways I could ask her to marry her. I had the ring in the left pocket of my shirt, over my heart. The ring was pounding in my pocket like Frodo Baggins in *Lord of the Rings*. The precious.

"It doesn't have to be a big ring, babe—something small and cute," Jennie said.

"I need to go to the bathroom, babe."

I put my debit card on the table and told Jennie to ask for the check—we needed to go—then walked to the restroom. The restroom had an old-style toilet like the one in *The Godfather* movie, with the tank above the seat anchored to the wall. I looked at myself in the mirror and splashed water from the running sink on my face. Then I looked at myself and said, "You are going to ask Jennie Sadusky to marry you, and she is going to say yes." Then I high-fived myself in the mirror and went back to the table with Jennie.

Jennie was eating her olives from the second drink. I picked up the receipt, signed it with a tip, then finished my drink and told Jennie, "Let's Van Gogh."

"I hate you," she said, trying her hardest not to laugh at my dad joke, then slammed her martini.

We got in my car and drove thirty minutes to Scottsdale, listening to Sublime. I circled the venue twice before finding a parking spot, then we walked a block to the Van Gogh Experience. We took an escalator down from street level, and it took several minutes for me to find the tickets on my phone. We had to wear masks because the 2020 pandemic protocol was still in effect there. We put them on, then took them off once we were in. Jennie walked straight to a room that had Van Gogh's letters he wrote to his brother, and I walked straight to the restroom to pee. When I came out, Jennie was still reading.

"He was such a good writer," Jennie said.

"I thought he was a painter?"

"He was, but in his words you can see his anger. He wrote to his brother in detail how much he hated his waiter."

"The original Yelp?"

"Thank you for bringing me here, babe."

I kissed her, and we walked holding hands into the show. We found seats in the second room on the floor in a circle that was drawn on the ground. We sat like kindergarteners, legs crossed, waiting for story time. Then the show started, and the room went dark and lit up in green. I reached into my shirt pocket and pulled out the ring. I took Jennie's left hand and slipped the ring on her wedding finger.

"Will you marry me?"

Jennie looked at the ring, confused, then smiled. I had caught her off guard.

"Say it again," she said.

So much louder, I said, "WILL YOU MARRY ME?"

"Yes."

Then Jennie kissed me so hard I almost fell back. We kissed for minutes with our eyes closed while we heard a woman sing in Italian. When I opened my eyes, the room was green. The ceiling and all the walls had Van Gogh's art. It was like we were in one of his paintings. A couple in front of us started taking selfies with their phones, and other couples took pictures of each other. But there was one couple that sat alone on a bench. They were older and still in love. They embraced each other and stared at the walls of Van Gogh's art. Jennie pointed at the couple taking pictures and then at the old couple on the bench.

"Can we be like them?"

I was pulling my phone out to take a selfie.

"Of course, babe." And I put the phone back into my pocket without her seeing me.

We sat there holding each other tight, and we were no longer two people but one. We didn't talk; we just listened to the music we couldn't understand the words to but still understood what they were saying to our hearts. The room lit up with all of Van Gogh's art, and it felt like a child's dream—not real, but beautiful.

After about an hour, the show ended, and we were the last ones to stand up. We walked around looking at the art projected onto the walls, then made our way out to the lobby where they sold souvenirs. I saw a teddy bear coated with sunflowers instead of fur.

"Can I get you that as a souvenir?"

Jennie showed me her left hand with the ring on.

"I already have my souvenir, babe. Besides, it'd be a lot cooler if the bear only had one ear."

She was right. We walked to the car and drove back to Gilbert, then stopped at McDonald's because neither of us had eaten. Jennie started to eat as I drove, and she handed me my Big Mac.

"I love you, baby," Jennie said. Then she fed me some fries and looked at her ring, then said, "I'm lovin' it. Ba da ba ba ba."

Chapter 9

The Baseball Card

J ennie and I were engaged on September 30th, exactly one month after our first date to the Guns N' Roses concert on August 30th. Things had moved so fast we hadn't even told our parents yet.

Jennie's dad, Brian, was a big baseball fan. Being from New York, he was a Yankees fan. I decided to get him a present to soften him up and maybe make him like me before I told him Jennie and I were getting married. I got Brian a 1961 Roger Maris baseball card—the year Roger hit 61 home runs. I told Jennie my plan to give her dad the card and tell him we were getting married. She thought it was a great idea and invited me over Sunday for dinner and board games with her family.

Sunday night, I drove to the Sadusky house and circled the block three times. "I'm going to marry your daughter," I kept saying out loud. I thought I shouldn't ask him for permission because I had already asked Jennie and she said yes, so we were doing it no matter what he said. So tell him, "I'm going to marry your daughter." He had already given me the key to his house. Might as well have been the key to the chastity belt—he knew we weren't just watching Disney+ in his daughter's room on the nights I slept over. Right?

I walked in the house and was greeted by one barking dog this time— Ruby. The other dog, Bella, had died earlier that week of old age. Max told Ruby, "Be quiet, it's just Dustin." Max high-fived me and I walked to give Jennie a kiss, who was sitting at the dining room table.

"Where's your dad?"

"Watching TV. Are you going to do it now?"

I just smiled and walked through the kitchen and toward her dad, who was sitting on the couch with his head locked on the TV. I pulled out the card that was in a hard plastic clear case from my shirt pocket and put it in front of Brian's face. I startled him, but he took what I was holding and examined it.

"Is this real?"

"Yes. 1961," I said.

"This is the year he hit 61," Brian said, looking at me.

"I think Mantle would have got him if he didn't get hurt."

"Or if he didn't drink so much."

Brian went back to looking at the baseball card, so I said without thinking, "I'm going to marry Jennie."

Brian didn't move or say anything, and I stood there quietly waiting for his response. Then I looked at the TV and the closed captioning was on. I looked at the coffee table—and his hearing aids were on it. Brian was a little hard of hearing. He didn't hear me tell him I was going to marry Jennie. I thought, *I had to ask your daughter to marry me twice. Now I have to tell you twice?*

Brian started to hand me the card back. Instead of telling him what I came to tell him *again*, I said, "Oh no, that's for you."

"Are you sure?"

"Yes." And I shook his hand firmly. I said what I came to say. He shook my hand and took the card—so Jennie is mine. A deal's a deal.

I walked back to the dining room and sat next to Jennie at the table.

"You told him?"

"I told him."

"Did you ask or tell him?"

"I told him I'm going to marry Jennie."

"What did he say?"

"Nothing."

"Nothing?! And you gave him the card?" Jennie looked surprised.

"He loved the card."

"But he said nothing about us getting married?"

"I don't think he heard me. He was looking at the card and his hearing aids were out."

"What?! I can't believe you did that!"

"I told him!"

"No—that you gave him a Roger Maris card. I'm worth at least a Mantle."

"No, you're worth a Ruth. That's why I call you Babe, babe."

Jennie smiled at me and her eyes got big. Then her dad walked in to show her the card, and Jennie said, "Oh, it's not mint?"

"It's Maris," Brian said.

"Yeah, it's a Maris," I said.

Brian left the room with his card, and I told Jennie, "You're not mint."

Jennie lightly started jabbing me in the arm, and I hugged her like a boxer breaking up the punches. She hugged me back. Then we heard her mom call from the kitchen, "Dinner is ready."

We walked into the kitchen. There was a pot boiling with lobster tails, a second pot with corn on the cob, and a bowl of salad. We filled our plates and walked back to the dining room. The kids walked in and sat after us. Their plates looked much different than ours—chicken nuggets shaped like dinosaurs for the boys and noodles with butter for Sophie.

"You guys don't like lobster?" I asked.

"Gross," all three said.

"They are the worst eaters," Jennie said.

"You're eating lobster butts," Max said.

I looked at my plate. I was eating lobster butt. I had never thought about it like that. I silently prayed and thanked God for my lobster butt, and Jennie held my hand while I did.

After dinner, we all cleared the table and Linda brought out a board game. She explained the rules, and I nodded like I understood but really had no idea. I figured I would just wing it. We rolled dice and moved our pieces, then had to look at pictures on cards and guess whose card it was without letting anyone know who you guessed for. I was confused. It was just the kids, Linda, Jennie, and me. Brian had gone back to watch TV. I figured I could at least beat Max. No—I came in last.

We played a couple more different games before the kids had to go to bed. They had school in the morning. Jennie tucked all the kids in, and then we went to her room. I shut the door. Then Jennie said, "Make sure you lock it." And I thought to myself, *Key to the chastity belt,* and I locked the door.

Chapter 10

Midnight Rain

Monday night, Jennie came over to my house to enjoy a fire in my backyard after she put the kids to bed. Her parents were home to watch the kids, and she'd leave my house around 5 a.m. to get home before the kids woke up. I had a bottle of white wine waiting for Jennie, and I was drinking a six-pack of IPA beer that night.

She arrived at my house a little after 9 p.m. and let herself in with her key. I popped the bottle of wine and poured Jennie a glass. Then she took it from my hand and went to the freezer to get two ice cubes to put in her glass.

"Classy," I said.

"Oh, it's ok for you to put an ice cube in your bourbon but I can't put some in my wine?"

Jennie had a good point, but I said, "I remember my first glass of wine."

"No, my first wine was Boone's Farm," she said, then we both started laughing.

"That stuff was so bad!" I told her.

"The strawberry kiwi wasn't that bad."

"Ok, I admit I drank the pina colada one in high school."

"And that's how you got into hairdressing?"

Jennie was quick with a burn. I gave her a high-five as we walked into the backyard where I had already started the fire. There were two old sun-worn plastic chairs around the fire, and we sat in them. Jennie played music from her phone. She chose Willie Nelson to start the playlist, then we looked to the stars. It was a clear night for now, but rain clouds were blowing in from the east.

"Do you still have your telescope?" Jennie smiled mischievously as she asked me.

I knew what the smile was for. In high school, my dad got my brother a telescope for Christmas from Costco. My brother didn't want it—my dad just thought it was cool and a good deal. The telescope sat in the den of our one-story house collecting dust. My junior year of high school, I started smoking weed and listening to '70s rock, mostly Pink Floyd. One night, I got stoned and took the telescope out to the front yard to look at the moon. Jennie saw me from her room on the second floor of her house across the street from mine and yelled at me from her open window, "Stop trying to watch me change!" I was embarrassed and high and yelled back, "I'm looking for the dark side of the moon." Jennie came downstairs and walked across the street to my house, where I was standing with the telescope set up in my driveway, and she told me, "You can't see the dark side of the moon because it's dark. What you see is the sun's reflection off the moon." She was right.

"Take that smirk off your face. I remember the night you're thinking of, and I wasn't spying on you!"

"Well, you did see me change once."

Jennie was right again. I had seen her change once by accident. I was bringing out the trash cans to the street and happened to look up to her window and saw her topless. She found out about it at school because I told all my friends, and it had gotten back to her. I was sixteen.

"Now I see them all the time," I said.

We started talking about everything that night by the fire and eventually got to the topic of God.

"I trust God with everything because He is God, and I'm just me."

"Doesn't the Bible say you're not supposed to have sex until you're married?"

"I haven't gotten to that part yet."

"Don't you teach Sunday school?"

"I lead a group of sixth-grade boys. It's mostly Noah's Ark and Adam and Eve stuff."

"What about adultery?" she asked.

"Well, that's like sleeping with a married person. It does say not to covet thy neighbor's wife. Good thing it doesn't say not to covet thy neighbor's daughter."

"I have to tell you something, and please don't get mad?"

"You can't ask me that."

"Just don't get mad?"

"What?"

"I got a D.U.I."

We were both silent, and I took a long drink of my beer. "When?"

"Back in January."

"Oh, way before we were dating. What happened?"

Jennie explained to me that her ex-husband was giving her a lot of trouble, and she was dating Jeffrey, who wasn't very good to her. That morning, she had dropped the kids off at school, then got a bottle of wine from the gas station and drank it by the lake. Someone saw her drinking alone at 8 a.m. and called the cops. The cops pulled her over just out front of her parents' house.

"It was the morning, and I had already just given up for the day. I wasn't happy with my life," she said.

"And now are you happy?"

"Very happy." She said it, but her eyes looked sad as she was waiting for what I would say next.

"If you're happy now, that's all that matters, babe. We will get through this. I got a D.U.I."

"When?"

"When I was 25. I got pulled over leaving the bar. I was only a mile away from the house. The cop followed me for a mile and pulled me over when I pulled into the Jack in the Box to get him off my tail. He said he pulled me over for not coming to a complete stop leaving the bar. That was bullshit. I was stopped and saw him waiting at the light a quarter mile away. He asked me to say the alphabet backwards. So I turned my back to him and said a-b-c-d-e-f-g-h-i-j-k-l..."

"No, you didn't?"

"He didn't think it was funny."

"You're not mad?"

"No, but when we get married, you're staying on your own insurance." I laughed.

She gave me a big hug and said, "I'm sorry."

"Don't be sorry for things you did before there was us, ok?"

Jennie nodded, with one lonely tear going down her cheek. I noticed her glass was almost empty and the fire was burning out, so I said, "Let's go inside and get a refill. You're not driving tonight, right?" Jennie shook her head no, and we walked inside and turned the TV on but didn't watch it. We just kept talking. She finished her wine, and I finished the last of my beers.

It was 12 a.m., so we started to go to the bedroom and stopped because we heard thunder.

"It's raining!" Jennie said very excitedly, with childlike innocence in her eyes. She grabbed my hand and led me outside, but I walked back in to grab another bottle of wine.

"Sorry, I only have red wine left."

"That's perfect. Sit with me."

I took a seat next to her on a wicker bench I had sitting on my covered patio and poured us two glasses. We sat in silence, taking in the smell of fresh rain and the sound of thunder and lightning from the clouds. We started kissing and kissing and kissing some more before she stopped me.

"Should we wait till we get married?" she said sarcastically.

Without thinking, I took Jennie by the hand and pulled her into the rain onto my rocky backyard.

"You're crazy—we're getting wet."

"Do you love me?"

"Yes. Why?"

"Then marry me?"

"I am going to."

"No, right now, right here. Marry me?"

"You're serious?"

"Adam and Eve didn't need a piece of paper from the state of Arizona to be married. They just needed God. He is all that matters." The rain was coming down harder as I held both of her hands.

"Before God, I take you, Jennie, to be my wife. Do you take me to be your husband?"

"YES!"

"Then kiss your husband." And we kissed and held each other until thunder broke us up. The two of us were completely soaked from the rain.

Jennie's wet hair had gone onto her face, and I brushed it away. "Let's go to the bedroom and take off these wet clothes. We're not sinning anymore."

"I love you so much, Dustin."

"I love you so much, babe. And we will have a wedding. This was just for us and God. So you pick a day."

Chapter 11
Jennies 40th Birthday

Tuesday was the day before Jennie's 40th birthday. I had work until 9 that night. I hadn't planned anything for her birthday. Everything had been going so fast. I did get her a present, but I thought she would have plans with her best friends for the big 4-0. She didn't. Jennie was going to meet with them on the weekend to get their nails done and go to dinner.

Wednesday, October 6th, Jennie's birthday, I had work until 9 p.m., and I had clients booked all day. Tuesday, she came over when I was off work, and we walked to the lake with my backpack packed with the Batman blanket and a bottle of wine.

We sat at the lake talking and laughing while a pontoon boat slowly trolled the lake until around 11:50, then we walked back to my house. I kept looking at the time on my phone.

"Are you expecting a booty call?" Jennie asked.

"No, checking the time. I have to get you home before curfew or your dad will kick my ass."

Jennie smiled and I opened the door to let her in. The time was now 12 a.m., and I kissed Jennie and said, "Happy birthday!" Then I left her alone and ran to my office to get her present.

"You're going to leave me on my birthday? Jerk!"

I came back into the room holding a snowboard in a snowboard bag and said, "Happy birthday, babe. Open it."

"For real?"

"Happy birthday!" I said again, and Jennie hugged and kissed me, then grabbed the bag and opened it. She pulled out a dark blue and gray Burton snowboard with the picture of a woman's head in the middle of the board and her hair blowing in the wind. Then I handed her a small box wrapped in birthday paper. She opened the box and put on her Blenders goggles that were teal and pink.

"I love it, baby, thank you." And she kissed me with the goggles on.

"I've only been snowboarding once and had to be taken down the mountain by the snow patrol. I know you go all the time, but I suck," she said.

"Third present—free snowboarding lessons by me."

"What if I'm not good?"

"You won't be, but I know you, and you don't like to give up. So you will, eventually."

"I want to go snowboarding with you right now!"

"Well, it's October 6th, so we have a few months. Besides, I still need to get your pants, boots, and jacket."

"More presents?" Jennie asked.

"Yes, more presents, babe. You need to try them on to make sure they fit."

"And you're teaching me?"

"Yes."

"I'm going to bang my snowboarding instructor."

I laughed. "Well, you already are, and you're 40 now. Do you still say 'bang'?"

"Oh, make love? No, I'm going to bang you, babe, until we are old and gray." Then Jennie rubbed my gray beard. "You're already gray," she said and smiled.

"But not old," I said.

"No, not old. You're like a grown man who thinks he's still a kid. Let's never get old, baby."

"Never," I said, and we kissed.

"Babe, I have to go home. The kids and my parents will be up early for my birthday."

I grabbed my keys and said, "Let's go."

Jennie grabbed her snowboard and said, "The kids are going to be so jealous."

"I have a feeling I'm going to be buying a lot of snowboards."

"But teach me first so I can help teach them?"

"You got it, babe." I locked the door to my house and drove the two of us home to Anchor Dr.

We walked into her parents' house quietly and into her bedroom, then went to sleep. The kids were up before the sun was up. "Happy birthday, Mom!" they shouted. All three kids were in the room with cards they drew for her. Jennie's dad left, and he made an excuse that he had to go to ASU for work. Jennie told me he was going to get her rainbow cake from Chompies in Tempe. The kids left for school, and so did her mother, who worked as a teacher nearby at Patterson Elementary School.

"We are all alone?" I said.

"Birthday sex before my dad gets home!" she said.

I love this woman so much. After that, we laid in bed until we heard the garage opening, and then we got dressed quickly so as not to be caught by her dad. Brian called out, "Jennie," and we walked downstairs, where he had Jennie's favorite—the rainbow cake from Chompies. Jennie gave her dad a kiss and a hug and said, "I thought you forgot," even though she knew he didn't. I had a slice, and it was amazing. It tasted as good as it looked. So colorful. It was like you could taste the colors.

"Do you like it?" Jennie asked.

"It's like if you can taste a Jack Johnson song, babe!"

"Is it always better when we're together?"

"Always." I reached for another slice, and Jennie stopped me.

"Save some for the kids, Dustin."

"Ok," I said, and then hung around for an hour until I had to leave to get ready for work.

"I wish you didn't have to work today."

"Me too, but I have nine clients, and I need to make money for three more snowboards. I'm sorry I didn't take it off."

"It's ok. I'll see you after work?"

"Of course." I kissed Jennie again and said, "Happy birthday, babe."

"I love you."

"I love you more."

"You can't say you love me more!"

"Thought I couldn't say 'I love you too'?" Jennie looked frustrated, so I said, "I love you, and happy birthday."

"Thank you."

I went home and got ready for work. It was a long day in the salon, but it went by fast with no breaks. Every day went by fast at work since Jennie came into my life. It was like I just got through work to see her.

I got off work after 9 and called Jennie. She was home. She had cake and ice cream with the kids and put them to bed.

"You're not going out with your friends tonight?"

"I'm a mom. My friends are moms too. Besides, who goes out after 9 on a Wednesday?"

"I do. Why don't you change, and I'll take you out to downtown Gilbert?"

"Why don't you just come over here and go to sleep with me?"

"I will, but…"

"It's the top of the 6th and the Dodgers are down?" Jennie replied.

"Do you want to watch the game?"

"OK, pick me up, but I'm not changing or getting ready."

"Let's go to Fat Cats, then." Fat Cats is a family fun center one mile from the house. They had a bar and the game on.

"Hurry up!" she said.

I went home, changed my clothes, and picked Jennie up. We were at the bar by the top of the 7th inning. We saw some friends we went to high school with who knew it was Jennie's birthday and bought us a round of shots.

"Babe, we can go anywhere you want," I said.

"I just want to be with you, and I know how much you love your Dodgers."

"You just didn't want to get ready," I said.

Then Jennie ordered another shot of Patrón. "It's my birthday!"

"It's your birthday! Cheers."

We soon forgot about the baseball game, and I got us a $50 game card and we started playing arcade games and winning tickets. We played Skee-Ball and a basketball game, as well as slot-machine-like games to win tickets. We tossed rings onto bottles and played air hockey until our card was rejected for lack of funds. We went to the ticket redemption counter to get our prizes. I got an army man with a parachute. Jennie got a princess crown and handcuffs.

"Handcuffs?" I asked.

"They're for you. Let's go home."

I am the luckiest man in the world.

Chapter 12

The Great Outdoors

Sunday came and it was time to take the kids camping for a night at Woods Canyon Lake. The kids were on October break, so we all had Monday off. I packed my car the night before and went to church at 9 a.m., then drove home to pick up Chichi, and then to pick up Jennie and the kids. I didn't go to Sunday school that day and had someone cover for me. I was at the Sadusky's around 10:30 in the morning, and Jennie's dad Brian was waiting and offering camping supplies. I let him know I had everything. Camping was something I had done my whole life. I grew up thinking camping was vacation. When I was in elementary school and heard other kids talking about going to Hawaii for vacation, I always wondered how they brought their tents on a plane.

We loaded their bags in my packed Scion XB, and the three kids got in the back seat, Jennie up front with Chichi in her lap. Jennie's parents smiled and waved as we drove away. Then we had to make a stop at the QT for snacks for the drive. Jennie got Slim Jim's and coffee for the two of us.

Sophie was the only one who knew we were getting married. Jennie told her first. Jennie told me Sophie said, "I want you to be happy, and you are happy, and Dustin makes you happy, and we like him."

I let the kids get whatever they wanted in the store because I was on a stepdad audition: Doritos, Kit Kats, donuts, Ring Pops, and Takis. The only thing they didn't get were napkins.

We drove the two hours up north to Payson with very little fighting from the kids, and Jennie in control of the music in the car. Then the snacks ran out, and the fighting began.

All three kids said, "Are we there yet?"

We had just turned off the highway and were only ten minutes away from the campground.

"Not even close," I said.

"We are there when we are there," Jennie said.

Then Jennie whispered to me with her empty coffee in hand, "We are almost there?"

"Yes, babe, we are here."

I pulled into the dense Ponderosa pine woods with Douglas firs driving on the paved road, and we drove back to the Spillway Campground at Woods Canyon Lake. We pulled up to our campsite.

"Get out," I yelled.

"Yay!" they all screamed in excitement, and I started unloading the car by myself as the kids explored and Jennie stayed near me watching. I went to set up our tent, then went back to the car and got the kids' tent out.

"Hey guys, you need to set up your tent." Then I walked back to set up ours. I finished pretty fast with Jennie helping me. We were missing one pole for the entry. I had let my ex-girlfriend Rachel's daughter borrow my tent when we were dating, and she returned it missing a pole.

I looked at the kids. They were just standing around the unopened tent, so I walked over to them.

"What's up, guys?" I asked.

"We don't know how," Noah said.

I had assumed they did, since I did at their age. So I took the tent out and handed the kids the poles.

"Connect these," I told them, then started to unfold the tent. The kids did, and then they asked for more things to do. So we put the poles through the tent holes and we all lifted it up together to connect the poles to the pins in the bottom of the tent. Their tent was up, and the kids celebrated like they had just built a house.

"Go get your sleeping bags from the car," I told them.

They went, then Jennie handed me a can of beer.

"Good job, Dad," she said.

Max came up behind us and asked, "Can we go fishing now, Dustin?"

"Get the fishing poles. I'll set them up for us," I said, and all three kids ran to the car to get the fishing poles and started arguing over who got what color.

I had brought four fishing poles for the five of us. Jennie didn't want to fish, so it was just me and the kids. I had a green, red, orange, and brown pole. I took the brown pole.

"This one is mine; it was my dad's."

I set the kids' fishing rods up in the campground for trout fishing with sinkers and swivels and left a 12-inch lead from the sinkers to the hook. I let the kids carry their fishing poles to the lake, and the five of us walked the 100 yards to Woods Canyon Lake from our campsite. I carried the tackle box and my fishing rod. Jennie carried the small cooler and walked Chichi on a leash. I also had my backpack on with the Batman blanket and a bottle of white wine inside.

We found a spot near the dam and unpacked. I put the blanket on some dirt and grass for Jennie and Chichi to sit on, then opened the bottle of wine for Jennie.

I put green Powerbait on Noah's hook to show him how, then I cast it for him since he had never been fishing. I handed him his rod and told him, "Let me know if you get a bite."

"How will I know?" Noah asked.

"You just will. Trust me, buddy."

I started to bait Max's hook and Noah yelled, "I think I have one!"

So I turned around and his fishing pole was bent in a U-shape.

"Pull up and set the hook, then reel down!" I shouted.

"What?" Noah screamed, scared and confused.

So I handed Max his fishing pole and ran over to help Noah.

"You got him, you just have to reel it in slowly."

"I don't want to. You do it, Dustin!"

"No, Noah, it's your fish. You got this."

"It's too hard, Dustin."

"You're on your own, buddy. I'm here with you. Get that fish!"

Noah reeled with all his strength and the pole continued to bend. Then I saw the trout. It looked big.

"Get the net!" I shouted.

"Dustin, take it!"

"I can't, buddy. It's yours."

Noah continued to struggle, but the fish got close enough for me to get it in the net. It was huge! I had been fishing this lake for 25 years and had never caught one as big as this. I was jealous and proud at the same time.

I took the fish out of the net with my hand and showed Noah, but he squirmed. I laughed and everyone clapped.

"Good job, Noah!" shouted Sophie, Jennie, and Max.

I was getting the hook out of the trout's mouth with some pliers and Max walked up to me.

"My turn."

So I put the fish on the stringer and cast Max's pole out, then handed it to him.

"You know what to do?"

"Pull up, then reel down after the fish bites."

It was his first time fishing, but he heard what I told Noah. Max was a very smart kid. They all were. I walked over to bait Sophie's pole and cast it out for her.

"Dustin, I have one!" Max shouted.

I looked over and saw his rod bent in a U-shape.

"Okay, Max, you know what to do?"

"Yeah, I got it," said the tiny little man.

Max pulled up and reeled down. He struggled but never asked for help. I saw the fish in the clear lake water and yelled, "Get the net!"

Sophie brought it to me and I got the fish in the net. This one was just as big as the last one. The two boys had pulled in bigger trout than I ever had, and they did it back to back. Jealousy set in very fast. I wanted those fish to be mine. I did everything! Then I heard their laughter and saw their smiles, and I was overcome with joy for them. I took the fish out of the net and showed Max, then put it on the stringer. I took Noah's fishing pole and baited it, then cast it. Then I had to tie a new hook on Max's line since his fish swallowed the hook. All of the kids were now fishing in the lake at the same time, so I walked over to Chichi and Jennie.

"Wow," I said.

"You're a good teacher, babe."

"I'm just lucky."

"No, I'm a lucky girl." Jennie kissed me, but it was broken up by Noah screaming, "I have another one!"

"Not again, I don't have one yet," Sophie said.

I rushed from the blanket to help Noah, but he was only snagged on the rocks. I broke the line, then tied him to a new setup.

"Got one!" Max shouted.

"Seriously!!" said Sophie.

I went to help Max, and he too was snagged on rocks. I broke the line and made him a new setup, then cast the pole for him.

"This is boring," Sophie mumbled.

So I walked over to her and had her reel in her fishing pole.

"You cast it this time. Find your spot," I told her. I showed her how to hold the line with two fingers against the pole, then flip the bail and cast. She did it, and it was a perfect cast about 30 yards off shore.

"Patience, dude."

"Ok, Dustin," Sophie said.

I walked back to set up my fishing pole. I picked it up and put the two rods together, then unconnected them and put them back on the ground near Jennie.

"Babe, don't you want to fish?" Jennie said.

I looked at the kids and the clear water, with reflections of the Ponderosa pine trees mirrored off the surface.

"I am fishing, babe."

I took a can of light beer from the cooler and walked over to the kids, leaving Jennie peacefully relaxed on the blanket, sipping her white wine and holding Chichi.

"Got one, Dustin!" shouted Sophie.

Her pole wasn't bent like the boys', so I walked over thinking she was snagged. Then I saw the fish in the clear water, and the rainbow coloring shined off the sun's glare.

"I got the net, Sophie!" Max yelled as he dropped his fishing pole and rushed to his big sister's aid.

I let Max net the fish. I took the fish out of the net and took the hook out with my fingers—it was hooked right on the lip. This fish was much smaller than the boys'. Sophie looked disappointed.

"Hey, you're the only one that cast your own pole and caught a fish."

"Yeah," Sophie said and smiled.

I put her fish on the stringer, then handed her the pole to bait and recast. The kids continued to get snagged, and I continued to tie more hooks. I felt like a deckhand. I eventually ran out of hooks, but we had three trout. We packed up and walked back to our campsite with me holding the fish on the stringer.

"You got a couple of good ones there," said a stranger as we walked through the campground with our catch.

"The kids caught them. Not me."

"He said a couple good ones? That's two. Mine sucks," said Sophie.

I put my arm around Sophie and said, "Next time is your time." She smiled, and the kids ran back to camp with Chichi, leaving me and Jennie alone.

"This place is so relaxing," Jennie said.

"It's one of my favorite places."

"I love your favorite places, baby."

"I'll show them all to you. This last summer I came here alone twice, just me and Chichi."

"Is it better with us?"

"It's more work, but yes, it's better. Let's go get ice cream?" I said.

"We haven't had dinner yet, Dustin."

"The campground store closes at five, and we need to get wood. It's 4 o'clock and a ten-minute walk."

"Well, the kids will love it," Jennie said.

"And you?"

"I want a drumstick."

We dropped off the fish at the campsite, and I cleaned them quickly with Max watching.

"You ripped out the guts!" Max said.

We went on the short hike to the campground store. The kids took turns holding Chichi on the leash, and we walked the windy dirt trail that went by the lake and led to the store. I tied Chichi to a bench, and she lay down in the shade under the bench. We all walked into the store, and the kids scattered, looking down every aisle of the small store.

"Get stuff for s'mores," I said.

Jennie and I went to the two large freezers of ice cream.

"They have so many choices," Jennie said.

"Ice cream is always the best camping treat."

The kids came up to us with marshmallows, Hershey bars, and graham crackers, then picked out their ice cream. I chose a Big Stick. It was always my Pappy Earl's favorite, and he always bought me one when we went camping. Sometimes we would get one before dinner, and he'd tell me, "Don't tell your grandma."

Jennie paid for our things, then the five of us sat on the bench outside and enjoyed our treats with Chichi watching Max. She knew he couldn't finish his ice cream sandwich.

"I'm full," said Max.

"Chichi!" Jennie said. Then Chichi finished Max's ice cream.

We walked back, and I carried the wood to camp. The wood was damp from a recent rain, so when we got back to camp, I had to chop it with my hand axe to get to the dry center.

"What are we doing next?" Noah asked.

"Let's go shoot my BB gun," I said.

The kids all looked excited, and Jennie said, "You brought a BB gun?"

"Well, I have to protect you."

"With a BB gun?"

I lifted my shirt and showed Jennie my concealed 9mm Glock. "I'll protect you with this, but let's have fun with the BB gun."

"Okay, Rambo."

I took the BB gun, and we all walked into the woods until I found a spot for us to shoot. I placed three empty beer cans as targets on a fallen old tree trunk about 20 feet from us. I shot first and hit all three cans. The cans rattled as the BB swirled around the can. I loaded the Daisy Red Ryder for Jennie and handed it to her. She hit one out of three. The kids all went next, each getting three shots that I loaded for them. They all missed. Jennie laughed. We went several more rounds, Sophie being the only one strong enough to load the BB gun herself. In the last round, Sophie went 3 for 3.

We picked up the beer cans with holes in them and walked back to camp to start a fire and cook. The fire would not light. The wood was still too wet. To top things off, Noah forgot to bring a sweatshirt, and it was getting cold, so I gave him my hoodie. I chopped the wood more and added the cardboard from the beer box. Then the fire started to take off. The kids clapped like I was a hero. It was better camping with them than alone. I had a team. If the fire didn't start and I was alone, I'd just go to bed. But I needed this for them.

We boiled water and cooked the kids ramen noodles. Picky eaters. I had brought a steak for me and Jennie to share. I slowly cooked it in my cast iron skillet for her with butter and garlic. Max was still hungry, so the two of them shared the steak, and I ate the trout that I put in the cast iron skillet after their steak was done. After dinner, I pulled out my metal marshmallow sticks and handed them to the kids. They burned more than they ate, but we had fun. We had plenty of marshmallows but ran out of chocolate because the Hershey bars were within arm's reach of Max. For a small kid, he had a big appetite. He just couldn't finish ice cream. The fire died down and the kids went to their tent, so I put the fire out. Jennie and I were walking to our tent, and we heard fighting from the kids' tent. Max was annoying his brother and sister, so we took Max to sleep with us. Max wasn't mad. The kid smiled like he got what he wanted.

It was very cold without the fire and without my hoodie, so the three of us got close in the tent on my queen air mattress. I held Jennie, and Jennie held Max, and Max held Chichi, and we fell asleep—until I woke up alone in the middle of the night.

I looked around the tent and found Max and Chichi in the corner of the air mattress. I left the tent to find Jennie. I found her lying down in the dirt. I rushed to her and tried to pick her up, but she lay like dead wood, saying, "Where are the kids?"

"They are sleeping, babe."

"Do my parents know they are here?"

"Yes, they watched us drive away."

"Are the kids OK?"

Jennie looked confused and not herself. I struggled to get her out of the dirt and back to the tent. I lifted her over Max and onto the air mattress. I wrapped her in the sleeping bag and extra blankets. She kept mumbling like she didn't know where she was. I held her tighter and told her we would go home as soon as the sun came up. She started to act normal and apologized. I held her, and she held Max, and they went to sleep—but I didn't.

In the morning, I lit a fire for the kids because it was cold, and I started to pack the car. I took Jennie to the front seat and turned on the car to get the heater going. The kids all got in the car to be warm as well, and I packed everything up quickly. I threw my tent away in the campground garbage to pack faster, and drove us home to Gilbert after putting the fire out with water and ice from the cooler. I stopped for coffee at a Circle K in Payson for Jennie. The kids went into the store to get something to eat. I gave them some money and stayed to talk to Jennie.

"I'm OK, baby," she said.

"Babe, I'm so scared. We need to go to a hospital!"

"I'm OK."

"No, you're not."

"I had a stroke a couple of years ago. I didn't ever tell anyone."

"Is that what you had last night?"

"Please don't tell my mom."

"If you're sick, we need to get help, babe."

"I'm OK, I promise. We are getting married, baby."

"No, we are married, babe."

"I know, honey. I'll get better. I think it was the high altitude and the wine."

I was upset, but I believed her because I wanted to.

The kids came back to the car, and Sophie handed me the change. Then I went inside to get Jennie and me a coffee, and we drove home to Gilbert. Jennie texted her ex-boyfriend Jeffrey about getting her things he had stored for her at his work. He was upset that she was dating me. He soon stopped texting back. Jennie had first reached out to me trying to get him help because he had mentioned to her that he went to church randomly one day a few years ago, and on that day I was getting baptized. Jennie was the second of his girlfriends to tell me the same story. I told Jennie the same thing I told the other girl: "Church is at 9 and 10:30. I'll meet him there." He never showed up. When he found out Jennie and I were dating, he told her he was happy for her because he couldn't make her happy and that I could. Then he told her I was a homosexual and that I did hair for a living and was gay because only gays do hair. I found it funny because I've been called gay for over twenty years for being a male hairdresser. I also found it funny he thought the guy having sex with his ex-girlfriend every night was gay.

I dropped Jennie and the kids off, then went home to unpack and shower. Jennie called me, saying she got the storage unit down the street for her things and asked if we could take some of her stuff from her parents' garage over there. I told her yes and drove over. We loaded my Scion XB up with boxes and drove half a mile to the storage unit and unloaded it.

"We'll get the rest of the stuff this week from Jeffrey," I said.

"He won't text me back."

"Tell him I'll come get your stuff and not to worry—I won't try to blow him."

"Dustin!"

"He thinks I'm gay! He probably thinks I'm going to show up singing show tunes and try to redecorate his house."

Chapter 13
Lets Go To The Fair

I had taken off a Wednesday to take Jennie and the kids to the Arizona State Fair. I was waiting for the kids to get out of school when my dad stopped by my house. He had sold his house and was moving to Montana. He wanted to drop a few things off that were mine. We had small talk.

"So, you're getting married, I hear?" my dad said.

"Yeah, I was going to tell you, just haven't had a chance."

"Marriage is great. I'm happy for you."

"Thanks, Dad. I'm pretty happy. So, you guys are leaving today?"

"No, tomorrow."

"I'm taking the family to the fair today. I'll stop by tomorrow."

"Sounds good."

My dad gave me a solid handshake and a hug, then drove away. Something felt off. I went back inside and got ready for the fair, then drove to pick up Jennie and the kids.

We drove with the three kids in the back and Jennie in the front. I joked to them about which kid was going to throw up on a ride first or who would chicken out on a ride. The drive only took thirty minutes, and we were there in the beautiful hood of downtown Phoenix—decorated in graffiti, homelessness, and street vendors selling the cheap toys and stuffed animals from the fair, only without having to pay for admission.

I paid to park in the fairgrounds parking lot. We all got out of the car, and the sun was still up as we walked to the entrance. Jennie got the tickets, and I handed the kids each a twenty-dollar bill for a souvenir.

"If you don't buy anything, you get to keep the twenty," I told them.

"Dustin, they are going to keep the twenty and not get anything," Jennie said.

"I'm planning on it. You can't get anything at the fair for twenty bucks. You think I spent sixty dollars, but I think I saved a hundred."

I put a hundred dollars on a game card, and we walked into the food area of the fair. We all wanted different things, so we split up. Jennie went for the giant turkey leg, Sophie and Noah went for fresh powdered donuts, Max a giant slice of cheese pizza, and I went for the giant corn dog that was well over 12 inches. We all got lemonades to drink and walked and played the carnival games. The games don't take cash anymore like they did when I was a kid. Now they take a prepaid card, and the carnies scan it. Before I knew it, the card was empty, so I put another hundred on it, and we walked to the rides.

Jennie and the kids all waited in line for the bumper cars, and I waited by myself, holding everyone's drinks and food while trying to take pictures of Jennie and the kids. Jennie was such a bad driver, even when it came to bumper cars. Max was riding with her, and they ran into every wall and were targeted by other drivers as the weak ones, so they took a fun beating. When the ride was over, they came over to me.

"Why does my turkey leg look smaller?" Jennie said to me.

"Holding fee," I said.

Then we all walked over to some roller coasters and let just the kids ride a few of them. They were all getting along and having fun with no fighting! I thought to myself, *Being a stepdad is going to be easy.*

After the rides, we went to the petting zoo. It was my favorite for many reasons, but today it was my favorite because it was one of the only free things to do at the fair. The kids went to pet a dairy cow, and I noticed Jennie eating her turkey leg in front of a giant caged turkey. So I took a picture.

"You savage, Jennie! Showing that caged bird his future."

"See you next month, Mr. Turkey. Gobble gobble."

Max wandered away to pet a llama. I saw him and told him, "Watch out, they spit."

"Animals don't spit, Dustin," Max said.

Just then, a little girl screamed. The llama had spit on her.

"Told you, bro."

Max laughed and said, "OK, I trust you."

We walked over to the pigs, who loved being petted like big dogs, and they oinked in joy. There was a donkey, who the kids all named Eeyore, and some quarter horses. Then we came to the goats, and we bought some pellets to feed them. Max got too close, and the goats found a bag of Skittles Max had in his pocket, and they took them.

"Those are mine, goats!" he said as he tried getting them back.

I stopped him and said I'd get him some more. Then we walked to ride the giant Ferris wheel. I put another hundred on the card because this ride was fifteen dollars per person—so seventy-five dollars to take the family on a few spins. It was dark now, so the fair was lit up with lights like the Las Vegas Strip, and I knew the view would be beautiful from the top.

We got on the ride, and Jennie sat with Noah on one side, and I sat with the other two kids on the other side. When we got to the top, Jennie told Sophie and Max to switch spots with her. Then she sat on my lap and pulled out her phone to take a selfie of the two of us. It was our first selfie. I tried to look cool, but I was scared. We were so high, and the kids were shaking our pod. I'm not a big fan of heights, and my stomach felt tight. But the view from the top was beautiful. Every color light you could think of decorated the rides and food stands, and we could see the downtown Phoenix skyline with its tall buildings and lights. It was so pretty, you forgot you were in a bad neighborhood.

After several spins around the Ferris wheel, our ride came to a stop and we got off. The kids wanted to ride a water log ride, so we gave them the card and told them to go. Jennie and I went and grabbed a funnel cake with powdered sugar. The kids yelled at us from the line that the card was declined! So Jennie rushed over to get it and put more money on it.

"What are we at, four hundred now?" I said.

"Five if you count food and parking."

"Our trip to Jerome cost this much." I laughed.

"And that was twenty-four hours. We've been here three."

"I forgot to tell you I have a room booked in Bisbee at a haunted hotel for the Saturday before Halloween. Can your parents watch the kids?"

"Another haunted hotel!"

"You knew what you were getting into marrying me."

"Yes, and I love it! I've never been to Bisbee."

"You'll love it. Rusty and his girlfriend are coming."

"Rusty who threw up in your kitchen sink last week?"

The week before, my friend Rusty asked me to meet up for a beer after work. I hadn't seen much of my friends lately, so I agreed. I told Jennie I was going to stop by Native, the sports bar by the house, to have a beer with Rusty. She told me to take my time and that she was already at my house. Rusty had already been drinking when I showed up. One beer always turns into two with friends, and with my friends, it turns into four with shots. My house was only two blocks away, so I talked him into sleeping at my house in the guest bedroom since he didn't look like he should be driving. He agreed.

We got to my house, and he walked in right past Jennie and into the guest room and passed out. I sat on the couch with Jennie, and within an hour, Rusty came out of the room, walked past my guest bathroom, past Jennie and me on the couch, past my kitchen trash can, and to the kitchen sink—where he threw up.

Before I could get mad, Jennie was up and running the sink and splashing water on his face. He stumbled back to the room and said, "Goodnight, Dustin."

And I replied, "I hate you."

The kids came back from the ride and we shared our funnel cake with them, then walked over to a building that was more of an indoor swap meet.

118

The kids looked at some of the anime things they had. Max used his twenty to buy a Pikachu figure, but the other two kids decided to save their money, and I got a giant pickle from a jar for Jennie.

From there, we walked over to the Great American High Dive show at the fair. This was free. The kids had fun watching as the divers put on a good show with comedy and death-defying dives. The kids were also getting tired. So after the show, we went for one more ride—the giant swings. Sophie and Noah could go on it, but Max was too short, and he cried. Jennie tried to console him in a loving motherly manner, with her hands on his shoulders as she tried to hug him. But he pulled away.

"Max, they won't let you on," Jennie said.

"It's not fair! I'm always too small! You told me if I eat all my food, I'll get big and strong! But I'm not, and I eat everything, and Sophie and Noah don't eat anything and they're bigger!"

Jennie looked at me and said, "Feel free to step in, stepdad."

This was a chance to say something powerful and motivational to Max—a real dad moment. Something like *David was small but he defeated Goliath,* or *Big things come in small packages.* Instead, I said, "Did you try walking on your tippy toes?"

Max took my hand and got on his tippy toes and said to me, "Come on, Dustin."

"No, guys!" Jennie said and stopped us.

"Max, how about instead of a ride, we go play some games?"

"OK, but Sophie and Noah can't play!"

"Deal."

I walked Max to play some games and Jennie watched the kids on the giant swing. After their ride, they came over to us and wanted to play the game.

"No, you're too big," Max said.

I laughed, but then the three kids started fighting, and I looked at Jennie.

"Time to go home," Jennie said.

The kids tried some "But—!" and a few "Sorries!"

"No, we are going home. You have school tomorrow."

Jennie was so stern the way she said it that I thought I had school tomorrow too and started walking to the car.

"Dustin!" Jennie said with her hand out.

I looked back at her, then walked back to hold her hand as we walked to the parking lot.

All that money spent and the good time we all had ended with the kids fighting. And I remembered my mom and dad breaking up the fights between my brother and me at the fair growing up. I thought, *I can't wait to tell my dad about this tomorrow.*

But the next day he left for Montana and didn't tell me bye. He never was good at goodbyes.

Chapter 14

A Bisbee Hallowen

The next few weeks went by with Jennie and me spending every night together. I found myself spending a lot of nights at her house. I'd come over after work, and she would have a plate of leftovers that she cooked waiting for me in her room. We would sneak out to the park across the street from her house to have a smoke and some beers—the same park we would sneak out to in high school to have a smoke and some beers. We'd sit on the grassy mound and talk.

"Would it be weird if we moved back into this house one day?" Jennie asked.

"With your parents?"

"No, us and the kids. The house is paid off, and it's my inheritance. My brother gets the Pinetop house."

"I would love to grow old with you on Anchor Dr.," I told her.

"It will be perfect. When the kids move out, I will use my room as my writing room and write books."

"Me and you back on Anchor Dr. sounds like a fairy tale love story."

"Love stories happen in real life, Dustin."

"Let's save up and buy a house, then one day when we move into this house, we can rent it out."

"Perfect, baby. I am going to write a book, you know."

121

"I know you will, only I'm nervous."

"Of me writing a book?"

"You watch a lot of murder shows, babe. I don't want to be part of the plot."

"Don't be dumb. I want to write a love story. What do you want?"

"I want to be in your love story."

"You will, but what do you want in life?"

"I have everything I ever wanted in life right now, so I'll take a Pepsi."

"Diet Pepsi, maybe." And she pushed on my stomach.

"It's a dad bod, babe!"

On Saturday, October 30th, I picked up Jennie and we drove down south to Bisbee for a Halloween block party to stay at The Bisbee Grand Hotel. My friend Rusty had canceled last minute, but I wasn't mad because we were sharing a two-bedroom suite. So now Jennie and I had it to ourselves. We'd be back the next day in time to take the kids trick-or-treating, but tonight was adult Halloween—a time for the parents to have fun.

We drove south through Tucson, then headed east to Bisbee, passing through the small towns of Benson, St. David, and Tombstone. It was all beautiful desert views until we passed Tombstone and started to drive up in elevation, and the landscape slowly turned from desert bushes to ponderosa pines. We were on a two-lane road when we approached a tunnel.

"Hold your breath, babe," I said, and we both did because you always hold your breath going through a tunnel for luck.

When we came out of the tunnel, it was a different world—pine trees and a view looking down on an old mining town that was covered in old houses that whirlpooled down to the town center.

"Is this real?" Jennie said.

"I knew you'd like it."

We drove down into Old Bisbee, a town famous for copper mines and being part of the Old West. The movie *3:10 to Yuma* starts out there. We drove through the small town that seemed like a movie set at Universal Studios—two-story old brick buildings with side roads that went to dead ends. Staircases seemed to pop up out of nowhere throughout the town, and it reminded me of the drawing *Relativity* by M.C. Escher. We had perfect timing because there was a parking spot outside our room on the street, so I parked.

"We're here," I said.

"This is a bar, not a hotel, babe."

"Get out."

Our room was the door next to the bar. It was originally a store with the hotel on the second floor, but they turned it into a room. The room had two storefront windows and a door.

"Doesn't look like a hotel, Dustin."

I got out of the car and opened Jennie's car door, then walked to the bar and opened that door.

"Come in."

Jennie walked hesitantly, like I was playing a trick on her. We both walked to the bar and were greeted by a female bartender.

"Hi, we'll take two shots of Jameson and two pints of the Bisbee draft. Also, I'm checking in. Dustin Elkin for the Captain's Suite."

The bartender came back with our drinks and the key to the room. I paid cash for our drinks. The room was already paid for because I had to pay when I booked it almost a year ago.

"Do I need to show you the room?" she asked.

"No, I've been here before." I took the key and handed Jennie her shot.

"Of course you've been here before," Jennie said, rolling her eyes.

"It's usually a guy's trip," I said.

"Will you take me somewhere you've never taken a girl someday?"

"For real?"

"Yes."

"Well, if you want, we can go to Apache Junction."

"I hate you."

"I love Arizona! You've lived here your whole life, and I'm showing you new things. Just let me be your tour guide."

"Show me the room, Sherpa."

"Sherpa?"

"Yes, go get my things and carry them to the room."

We laughed and took our shots, then drank our beers. I got Jennie's bags and walked her to our room.

I opened the door to what looked like an antique shop. Once inside the room, it opened to a living room with a couch on the left and a TV on the right that was hidden in an armoire. By the TV was a table that had enough room for six people to eat. Straight ahead from the entrance were French doors that opened, and a hallway to the right of them. We walked through the French doors to the room with a queen bed.

"I love it," Jennie said.

"This isn't our room." I took her by the hand and led her through a second door in the room that went to a long hallway. Jennie stared at the ceiling as it was high, and I led her to our room next door with a California king bed and threw her bags on the floor.

"It's amazing, Dustin."

"I'm not finished." Then I led Jennie down the long hallway to the bathroom and showed her the soaking bathtub sitting alone to the left side of the room, the sink center, the shower to the right with a big mirror next to it, and the toilet hidden in the corner.

"Can we take a bath?" Jennie asked.

"After we eat."

"I am hungry."

I went and got the rest of our bags from my car parked outside our room, and Jennie walked the hotel room in awe.

"When did you book this room?" she asked.

"February. Why?"

"Like the tickets to Guns N' Roses, huh?"

"Yeah, I just wing it."

"I like that."

"The last time I was in this room was with Dave and Rusty. Rusty put his bags on the bed, and when he walked back into the room, they were thrown on the ground."

"Another haunted hotel with Dustin Elkin," Jennie said with a smirk.

We left the room and walked to a Mexican restaurant just a few blocks north of our hotel and stopped in a couple of antique stores to browse, but we didn't buy anything.

At the restaurant, the waiters were dressed for Halloween. We sat on the patio, and our waiter was dressed as a pirate. You could tell he wasn't happy having to work dressed in a Halloween costume, but he gave us a fake smile and chips and salsa. We ordered and enjoyed our food on the patio with the pleasant Bisbee breeze. Jennie held my hand from across the table as we sipped margaritas. I paid for our check, and we walked back to the room.

As soon as we walked in, Jennie said, "Bath time."

I looked for the kids, then realized she meant me. I handed Jennie some bath salts I had brought, and she went to prepare the bath. I opened a bottle of wine for her and then opened a beer for me. I kicked off my shoes and sat at the table and drank my beer.

"Baby, the bath is ready," Jennie said.

I walked down the hallway with my beer and into the bathroom, where Jennie was already in the bath with music playing from her phone.

"You didn't bring me a drink?" she said.

I ran back to the table, grabbed her wine and a glass, then finished my

125

beer, got a new beer, and ran back to the bath. I poured her a glass, then took my clothes off and climbed into the bathtub. We lay in the bathwater listening to music and drinking our drinks. We were there so long the water went from hot to cool, and my beer was finished, so I was drinking wine from the bottle. I poured Jennie the last of the wine into her glass.

"We need to get ready for the party," I said.

"Let's just stay here, baby."

"Are you serious?"

"No, I'll get ready."

We got out of the bathtub and went to change into our Halloween costumes. I dressed as Adam Sandler's *The Waterboy*, with football shoulder pads, his jersey, and a helmet. Jennie dressed as a football referee. We stepped outside our room and I heard a voice:

"Dustin?"

It was my friend J Low, who happened to be there for the party. I introduced him to Jennie and said we'd meet him at the block party later. There was a speakeasy bar twenty feet from our room, so we went there first. We walked into a room full of people dressed in Halloween costumes. People recognized my costume.

"Gatorade is better! Water sucks!" a stranger shouted.

"Are you stu-stu-pid?" another stranger yelled.

They were all having fun, and the last guy bought us our first drinks. After that, we went to the Bisbee Grand and had a beer, then walked one block south through a dark alleyway to the Copper Queen Hotel for the block party. We had to pay a cover because we weren't staying at the hotel. Once inside the gate, I saw my friend Tyer, who was dressed as Bob Ross with a painting palette, and his pregnant girlfriend, who wasn't drinking but came out to have fun anyway. J Low showed up with no costume. I met these two guys years ago—they were bartenders at Crabby Don's. We all just happened to be in Bisbee.

I walked Jennie inside the hotel and up the stairs to show her the balcony that overlooked the party.

"I came here two years ago dressed as Batman," I said to Jennie.

"I remember seeing the pictures of you on Facebook."

"I met this girl, and she was dressed as Harley Quinn."

"I don't want to hear a story about you picking up some girl and living your Batman fantasy."

"It's a good story, babe, trust me. So I leave my friends at the block party and walk Harley Quinn inside the hotel to the bar to get us some drinks. The whole time I'm talking in this deep Christian Bale Batman voice."

"Nerd," Jennie interrupted.

"Anyway, this fight breaks out behind us—two girls, one dressed as Snow White and the other dressed as Cinderella. Total catfight. Then Snow White's boyfriend comes and starts helping her beat up Cinderella."

"What's he dressed as?"

"Kylo Ren. So there are these three Disney princes fighting. Then Cinderella's boyfriend comes into the fight, and he is dressed as the Red Power Ranger. The four of them are just going at it. Harley asked me if I was going to do something about it. I said, 'I'm not really Batman,' in my normal voice. Then out of nowhere comes this steroided-out, buff cop wearing sunglasses and shorts, and he just beats the shit out of the four of them in like a couple seconds, then he takes off."

"Cops can't do that," Jennie said.

"That's what Kylo Ren said. He was pissed that his lightsaber broke in the fight, then said he was going to sue the Bisbee police for assault. Turns out the cop wasn't a real cop—just some guy dressed as a *Reno 911* cop. The drunk *Reno 911* cop saw a fight and decided to throw down. After the fight, no one saw him again."

"What happened to Harley Quinn?" Jennie asked.

"I don't know. I think she left with some Joker."

Jennie laughed, and the two of us went back downstairs to the party.

We all drank for a while at the party, but Jennie and I left because I had to show her more of Bisbee. So we went to another bar—that really is what you go to Bisbee for, to bar hop. We walked the half block to St. Elmo's, one of the oldest bars in Arizona. We ordered vodka Red Bulls because we needed the Red Bull. We talked to everyone we didn't know, then got separated. Neither of us had our phones.

Drunk and panicked, I went to find Jennie at another bar. But she wasn't there. I got worried and had another shot to calm my nerves. I walked out into the street yelling, "Jennie!"

And people yelled back, "H2O!"

"Jennie!" I shouted continuously, walking alone through the streets until I heard:

"Babe!"

It was Jennie. She had walked back to our room when we got separated.

"I thought I lost you. I've been looking for you," Jennie said.

Someone yelled at me, "Mama said!"

I replied to Jennie, "Mama said you're the devil, and ma mama..."

"Come back to the room and I'll show you my boobs, Bobby."

So we went back to our room.

In the morning, we woke up and showered instead of taking a bath. The room included a free breakfast at the bar, but I wanted to go to Bisbee Breakfast Club.

"It's free. We will eat here," Jennie said.

"I'll pay."

"You already did for this breakfast. You are married to a Jewish woman, so you will not win this, Dustin."

"We still need to pick a day and a spot, my Hebrew queen."

"Breakfast first, Dustin. Then we will wing it."

"I like your style."

We didn't pack our things. It was 9 a.m. and checkout was 11. We walked next door and into the bar for breakfast. Our server gave us our menus, then said, "We have a build-your-own Bloody Mary bar."

"We're good," Jennie said.

"We have octopus hot dogs to put in your drinks," the waitress added.

"Come on, Dustin," Jennie said as she pulled me from my seat and toward the Bloody Mary bar.

We ate our breakfast, and it was good—but the Bloody Marys were better. Then we packed and drove home but stopped in Tombstone because Jennie had never been there. We walked to the gunfight site of the O.K. Corral but didn't see the gunfight reenactment because we had to get back to the kids in time for Halloween. Instead, we walked to the old courthouse and paid admission. The building was now a museum of the town's historic past.

"You know they do weddings here," I said.

"You want to get married in Tombstone?"

"Just saying."

An employee heard us and said, "Yes, only $60."

We kept walking through the building and out to the gallows where they used to hang people.

"We can get married here!" I told her.

"No, not here, babe. But in the courtroom where they tried Doc Holliday and Wyatt Earp for murder at the O.K. Corral."

"Are you serious?"

"I'm your huckleberry."

And we kissed. This woman knew me more than I knew myself. This was the perfect spot.

"Let's get married now?" I said.

"Okay."

We held hands and walked to the check-in.

"Hello, we'd like to get married," I said.

"Fantastic. This is a brochure," she said, handing us each one. I handed mine back.

"No need for that. We want to get married now."

"Well then, do you have your marriage license?"

"No, we'll take one of those too."

"I'm sorry, this is a museum, not a real courthouse anymore. The closest courthouse is in Bisbee."

"We were just there."

"It's okay, baby. Just not meant to be today," Jennie said.

"But it's Halloween! How cool would it be to have our anniversary every year on Halloween?"

Jennie took the brochure and led me by the hand out of the courthouse like a kid who didn't get what they wanted at Target.

"You promise we'll get married here?" I asked.

"Only if you're good."

We got in the car and drove home. Jennie started pulling up western-themed weddings on her phone. She tried showing me things while I was driving. I agreed to everything.

"Why don't we just come back in a few months with a wedding license and get married—just the two of us? Then we can save up and have a party later on our one-year anniversary," I said.

"In August?"

"Yes. August 21st—the night you came over to my house for the first time and we made tacos."

"Then we can make tacos for everyone at the wedding party!"

"I like it."

"Just the two of us?" Jennie said, sitting quietly in thought. Then she said, "Let's get married in February."

"Okay."

"February 2nd."

"Okay."

"February 2nd, 2022. Just the two of us. 2/2/22."

"That's perfect! You just came up with that?"

Jennie smiled and sipped her water. Then we shook hands and both said, "Deal."

We got back to her parents' house around three. The kids weren't home yet from school. I dropped her off, then went home to unpack and set up for Halloween.

Around 5 p.m., I came back over to Jennie's house to pick them up. Sophie was already gone—she went to a friend's house to get ready to go trick-or-treating. Max came down in a DJ Marshmello outfit, and Noah and Jennie were arguing.

"Put it on!" Jennie yelled from upstairs, so I walked up.

"What's the problem?" I asked.

"Noah doesn't want to wear his costume," Jennie said.

"Put it on," I said to Noah.

"I don't want to wear it," Noah said.

"You picked it out, right?"

"Yes."

"Your mom paid for it?"

"Yes."

"Then put it on or pay her back."

"Ughhhhh," Noah groaned and went to get dressed.

"Thank you, Dustin," Jennie said.

Jennie and I weren't dressed in our costumes yet. Jennie grabbed hers from her unpacked bag, and we went downstairs. Noah came down shortly after, wearing a pink wig.

"What are you supposed to be?" I asked.

"An anime character," Noah said.

"I can see why you didn't want to wear it."

"Mom!!"

"Dustin, stop! Noah, you look cute."

"Let's go, Marshmello and Pretty in Pink."

"Mom!"

"Dustin, stop," Jennie said.

"Yeah, come on, Pretty in Pink," Max added, walking out the door holding his orange plastic pumpkin basket.

We said bye to her parents, and I drove us back to my house, where Jennie and I got dressed and the kids shot pool in the garage.

Several of our friends came to the house. I gave the adults drinks and their kids full-sized candy bars. A lot of my friends always come to my house on Halloween to park, then walk to the neighborhood between Jennie's and my neighborhood. The subdivision was called Spinnaker Bay, and it was featured on the news every year as one of the best spots in Phoenix to trick-or-treat.

"We almost got married today, but apparently you need a license! I have a driver's license, fishing license—and now I need a marriage license!" I told my friends.

Jennie walked into the room wearing her referee costume. I was wearing my Waterboy costume and grabbed Jennie, then said, "Mama said she's the devil. But I like Jennie, and Jennie likes me, and she showed me her boobs. And I like them too!"

I served up some shots of vodka, pineapple juice, and Sprite that I had made in a punch bowl. The kids were getting restless, so the adults grabbed some beers for the road and we made our way to Spinnaker Bay. We walked down the greenbelt by the power lines. A random kid ran by us and tripped over his own feet, spilling all of his candy onto the grass. Noah rushed to help him pick it up.

"Noah?" said Spiderman.

Spiderman recognized Noah from school, and he got embarrassed in his pink wig and walked off. I ran and caught up to him.

"You okay, bro?"

"I don't want to wear this!"

"Don't wear it, buddy—own it!"

"Huh?""You have character, dude. Show it."

"What's character?"

"What people think of you is their perception of you—good or bad. Who you really are is your character. Who you really are is a good guy who wants to smile and have fun! So smile and have fun, buddy. It's Halloween. Let's get some candy—and don't forget to skip while you walk."

So I started skipping.

"If you stop skipping, I promise I'll have fun tonight," Noah said.

"Deal! And if you don't have fun, I'm going to walk you to school tomorrow wearing your pink wig and skipping."

Noah put a forced smile on his face.

"Keep it going, you pink-haired anime king."

And he walked back to the group. Jennie was close by, listening.

"You're kind of good with kids, even though you tease them."

"Kids tease each other all the time—I'm just speaking their language."

"Max, stop!" Noah shouted.

Max was skipping now as he walked.

Jennie gently slapped my shoulder. "See what you started."

"Max, stop. We can skip tomorrow to school if Noah doesn't have fun tonight."

"I'm having so much fun, Dustin," Noah said with another forced smile from his cheeks. But his eyes smiled. He was having fun.

We walked through the park and past the basketball court to Spinnaker Bay. Every house was decorated and lit with purple and orange lights. Pumpkins, cobwebs, skeletons, and scarecrows decorated the lawns. Families sat in their driveways and handed out candy to hundreds of children—some with plastic pumpkin buckets and others with pillowcases. We walked house to house saying, "Trick or treat." A few houses handed out shots of alcohol to the adults walking their kids. Multiple Halloween songs played at the same time, and the air was filled with smoke from the fog machines.

It took us about an hour to get through the neighborhood, then we started to walk back home, stopping in two other neighborhoods on the way. We got through these streets much faster, as most of the houses were dark with their lights turned off and not participating in Halloween. We got back to my house—just Jennie, the kids, and I. It was close to 9. The kids played some games in the garage. Jennie and I had a drink, then we all walked back to their house, eating candy from the kids' Halloween buckets.

When we got home, Jennie let the boys lay in her bed with us, eating candy as we watched *Hocus Pocus*. Max fell asleep first, and Noah was fighting to stay awake.

"Time for bed," Jennie said.

Noah got up and walked right to bed without any arguing, and I picked Max up and carried him to his bed on the top bunk in the room next door. I came back into Jennie's room and locked the door.

"Are you ready to be bad?" Jennie said.

"Oh yeah."

Then Jennie lifted Max's orange plastic pumpkin filled with candy.

"We can't eat it all, babe," she said.

"All the candy is half off tomorrow. I'll replace it all—and double it!"

We lay in bed, eating candy out of an orange plastic pumpkin, and watched *A Nightmare on Elm Street*.

Happy Halloween.

Chapter 15

Church and the Swap Meet

Jennie and the kids had started going to church with me on Sundays. After church, we would go to the Mesa outdoor swap meet to walk around and let the kids get a couple of things. The Sunday after Halloween, I picked them up at 10 a.m. and drove us to church. I helped out with Sunday school at 10:30, so Jennie had to sit alone at church this week. The junior high has one service at 10:30, and we wanted Sophie to go to that.

The five of us were driving to church on a happy Sunday.

"Why do we have to go to church?" Noah asked from the back seat.

"Yeah, I don't want to go," Max said.

"I like it. I see a lot of kids from school there," Sophie said.

"Why do we have to go?" Noah asked again.

"Max and Noah, we have to go because you two are bad. If you act good, then we don't have to go anymore," I said.

"Really?" asked Noah.

"Yes. If you guys don't fight all week, don't lie, do your chores without being asked to, and do what your mom says—then we don't have to go to church."

"That's impossible, Dustin!" Max said.

"Exactly. That's why we need Jesus. He did it all for us, so we come to say thanks."

"Jesus did our chores?" Noah asked.

"In a way, yes. But hey guys, don't you want to go to the swap meet?"

"Yes!" they all said.

"No church, no swap meet, okay?"

We pulled into the church parking lot and parked, then checked the kids into their classes. I walked Jennie to the main church, then I left to go to my Sunday school class.

I walked into the room and was greeted by my sixth-grade boys.

"Dusty McAwesome!" they all said.

We walked outside to play gaga ball before church service started and made fun of each other's football teams.

"Cardinals are trash, Dusty McAwesome," said one of the boys wearing a Dallas Cowboys jersey.

"We are at church. Can we be nice?" I said.

The kid wearing the Dallas Cowboys jersey also had a candy Ring Pop in his hand.

"Enjoy that Ring Pop. It's the only ring you guys are getting this season."

"Burn!" shouted the kids.

"I thought you said we were supposed to be nice at church?" the Cowboys fan said.

"I said enjoy it," I replied.

They called for us to come in—service was about to start. We gathered in the building and sat on the carpet. My friend Paul, who was in charge, took the stage to play a game with all the kids called The Impossible Shot. One kid from each group went up on stage to throw a water bottle across the room into a trash can. The winner got candy. No one made it. That's why it's called The Impossible Shot.

A couple of kids came on stage to sing some worship songs with the words on a screen. The kids sang along, but my job was to keep the boys calm. They didn't sing—they yelled the words to get attention. I let them go for a while until I got looks from other leaders, then tapped the boys on the shoulder to calm down. They laughed.

After worship, we sat back down on the carpet and watched a video of two guys acting goofy and then explaining the story of Nehemiah returning to Jerusalem with the blessing of the Persian King Artaxerxes to rebuild the walls of Jerusalem. When it was done, my group took a corner of the room to talk about what we just watched.

"So why did Nehemiah return to Jerusalem to build a wall?" I asked the group.

The kid in the Cowboys jersey raised his hand, and I picked him.

"To keep the Mexicans out?"

"No, bro. There was no Mexico," I said.

"Why not?" they asked.

"It didn't exist yet," I said.

"Why not?"

"The New World hadn't been discovered."

"Why?"

"The Old Testament takes place in Israel," I said.

"My friend is Mexican and his name is Ezra. Isn't that Jewish?"

"Yes, it is."

"So the Jews were Mexican?"

"No. Guys, Nehemiah came back to rebuild the wall to protect Jerusalem after praying and fasting for four months. You guys want to play gaga ball?"

"Yes!" they all said.

"Okay, let's pray first. Anyone want to lead the prayer?"

"I do," said one of the boys.

He said, "Dear Lord, please bless us and forgive us our sins, and we love you and thank you for loving us. Amen."

"Amen," we all said.

"Why do we say amen after we pray?" one of the boys asked me.

"You know when you play football and you get in a huddle to tell everyone the play? After you say the play, you say break! That's what amen is. Break. Now let's go run the play."

"If you don't say amen, does that mean God is still listening?" another kid asked.

"God is always listening," I said.

"Like the government?" another boy asked.

"Only if you have an iPhone."

I led the boys outside to play gaga ball until their parents came to get them, and I left to meet Jennie and get the kids.

Jennie asked me, "How was Sunday school, babe?"

"So hard I want a beer."

"Babe!"

"Kidding! But I do want pizza."

We picked up the kids from their classrooms and went to Barro's to have pizza and sodas. I watched some of the Arizona Cardinals football game on the TV while we ate, then we went to the Mesa outdoor swap meet.

It was a short ten-minute drive, and we parked and walked to the tents that covered the asphalt mall. I gave the kids ten dollars each to get something. As soon as we walked in, we saw a beef jerky stand, so Jennie and I walked over to get a bag for later. The lady who sold the beef jerky was well into her 50s and had several hickeys on her neck.

"Looks like she had a good time last night," Jennie said.

I laughed and held Jennie's hand, then walked to where the kids were looking at cacti. Jennie walked Sophie and Noah to another stand, but I stayed with Max. He was intrigued by the cactus.

"Are these real, Dustin?"

"Yes, Max."

"Can I get one?"

"If you have enough money."

They were small cacti in small pots for six dollars.

"I have enough."

"Then pick one."

Max grabbed one—but not by the pot, by the cactus itself.

"Dustin, it's stuck to my hand."

I looked at him, and it was dangling and stuck in his little hand. I pulled it off him quickly, but a couple of needles were stuck in him.

"Ouch!" Max said.

"Follow me."

I put the cactus back and led Max down the aisle until we found someone selling random tools. They had hammers, dental tools, train spikes, used nails—then I found tweezers. I took the tweezers and pulled out the needles. Then the stand owner came up to us.

"Can I help you?" he asked.

"How much for the tweezers?"

"Three dollars."

"Sold."

I handed him three one-dollar bills, then handed Max the tweezers.

"What's this?" Max asked.

"Your souvenir."

"I don't want this. I want the cactus."

"You don't get the cactus. You picked it up by the needles!"

"You didn't tell me I couldn't do that."

"Well, don't do that."

We walked and caught up to Jennie and the kids, who were looking at crystals.

"Hey guys, how are you?" Jennie asked.

"I got tweezers because I grabbed a cactus and we had to get the needles out," Max said.

Jennie looked at me, confused, so I kissed her. And kept kissing her until we were interrupted by an old man tapping me on the shoulder.

"You mind not doing that, son? My wife is going to want me to start kissing her too," the old man said.

We laughed, and I said, "I'm sorry, sir," then shook his hand. He was wearing a Vietnam veterans' hat. He was joking with us, of course, then he walked back to his wife, kissed her with tight lips, took her hand, and led her away.

The five of us walked three more aisles, and the kids spent their ten dollars on things they would lose interest in by the end of the day.

Chapter 16
Thanksgiving

On Wednesday, Jennie came to the salon to get her hair done. I only cut hair, so my friend Mike Z colored Jennie's hair, then I cut it. I got Jennie a coffee from Black Rock Coffee next to the shop while her hair was processing from the color. I shampooed and conditioned Jennie's hair, then walked her over to my station where I combed her out, then cut her hair. Afterward, I blow-dried Jennie's hair and finished by curling it to give her beach waves. When her hair was done, I went to walk her out.

"Don't I have to pay?" she asked.

"No, babe. Mike did me a favor, and I cut your hair. Oh—take these."

I handed Jennie a couple of dry shampoo cans from the retail shelf.

"Ring this up for me," I told the receptionist. I got a 40% discount on products.

"I get free haircuts, color, coffee, and hair products?"

"Yes."

"The perks to banging your hairdresser, huh?"

"I'll call you when I get off, babe."

"I'll see you at home, baby."

We kissed, and I went back to work. We continued spending every night at each other's houses. At my house, we watched the fire burn in the backyard, and at her house, we watched movies in her bed and did other things.

One morning I woke up in Jennie's bed, and the boys were up and trying to get in the room.

"Why is the door locked?" they said.

So I got dressed and let them in, then went back to lying on the bed. Jennie went and sat at her desk, and the boys got on the bed and started jumping. They didn't bother me because I could still see the TV, so I didn't say anything.

"Don't jump on the bed! How many times do I have to tell you boys not to jump on my bed? It's old and it will break!" Jennie yelled.

The boys stopped jumping.

"That's not fair. We heard you guys jumping on the bed all night and you didn't break it," Noah said.

"And you guys are bigger than us," Max added.

The room was quiet and still. I looked at Jennie.

"Yeah, Jennie, it's not fair we get to jump on the bed and they don't."

Jennie looked embarrassed and said, "Fine. Everyone jump on the bed."

And the boys did.

I got up to use the bathroom and whispered in Jennie's ear, "When you move in with me, our room isn't next to the kids' room. We can jump on the bed all the time."

Thanksgiving was coming up, and Jennie, the kids, and her parents were going to their house in Pinetop to spend the holiday. Her brother Matt was living there with his son Cameron, who was a senior in high school. I couldn't go because I only had the Thursday for Thanksgiving off and had to work Friday at 3 p.m. Jennie was sad we wouldn't spend Thanksgiving together, but she understood—it was a 5-hour drive. Jennie and her family left for northern Arizona on Wednesday, and I went to work. That night, I got off work and went to have a beer at Fat Cats by myself.

"Any plans for Thanksgiving?" Sean, the bartender, asked.

"Jennie and the kids went with her family to Pinetop for Thanksgiving, so I'll just go to a friend's house, I guess."

"Why didn't you go?"

"I'm out of vacation time, and I work Friday at 3."

"Really? I've seen you make that trip lots of times for one day to go snowboarding, Dustin."

He was right! I wanted to spend Thanksgiving with Jennie. I could do it.

"Thanks, Sean. Close my tab—I have to get some sleep."

I texted Jennie: "See you tomorrow, babe."

"Really?!"

"Yes. I'm going to leave around nine in the morning. Can I bring Chichi?"

"YESSSSS! I love you sooo much!" she texted.

I paid my tab and thanked the bartender, Sean, for the words of wisdom, then went home to sleep. I woke up at nine in the morning, threw some clothes and things in my backpack, showered, got dressed, and walked to my car. I opened the passenger door for Chichi. She jumped in, and we headed north for Pinetop.

I stopped in Show Low for a bottle of wine and a six-pack of beer. I was at the Pinetop house by three. Jennie came out to greet me.

"You really came, babe! I love you so much!"

"I really came?"

"You didn't have to, but you did."

"Thanks for inviting me. Since my parents got divorced, I've been spending Thanksgiving at a friend's house every year."

"And now you have a family, baby."

We kissed and walked inside with Chichi. I had forgotten that Brian brought his dog, Ruby, and Matt also had a pitbull named Vegas. They were both old dogs, but they got the scent of Chichi, and the chase began. The boys helped separate them, but after ten minutes, the dogs were all calm and somewhat friends.

The house had a living room with a kitchen, one bathroom downstairs, and two bedrooms. Then upstairs had another bedroom, bathroom, and a loft. The master bedroom was downstairs and had a back door that opened up to a wood deck patio and a view of the woods. Matt was living in the master bedroom, and his son was in the other room downstairs. Brian and Linda took Cameron's room. The kids all slept in the loft, and Jennie and I took the upstairs bedroom.

Matt was cooking all of Thanksgiving dinner by himself. He wanted to. He treated us like guests. Jennie took me and Chichi for a walk around the neighborhood, with Max coming with us and walking Chichi.

"Max has been telling us about his dream all day," Jennie said.

"What was it about?"

"Oh, he'll tell you."

Max started explaining his dream, and I couldn't keep up. It was an amazing story of nothing and everything awesome, with no real beginning or ending. I just laughed and agreed with him. We made our way back to the house in the cold Pinetop air. Being from Phoenix, the cold was pleasant, and I embraced it.

"Thank you for coming, baby."

"Thank you, babe. I'd seen you post on Facebook about this place. It's prettier in real life."

"Everything is prettier in real life, baby," Jennie said.

"Like pictures of you."

"What?"

"You look beautiful in pictures, but right now is the prettiest I've ever seen you."

"Why?"

"Because I'm trying to get laid."

"You had me for a second, jerk."

"Because you look happy, babe. You're prettiest when you're happy," I told her.

"Then keep making me happy, baby." And we kissed.

"You guys are kissing again!" Max said, holding Chichi on the leash.

"I bet you a dollar you and Chichi can't beat us back to the house," I said.

"Oh yeah we can. Come on, Chichi." And they ran away. Then Jennie and I kissed a while longer.

Jennie and I walked back into the house, and I gave Max his dollar. Thanksgiving dinner was ready, so I opened the wine. Jennie didn't like to drink around her parents, so Brian and I drank the wine. The food was amazing. Jennie's brother Matt was a great cook, and for the first time on Thanksgiving, I had collard greens. The kids, of course, had dinosaur-shaped chicken nuggets.

Brian led a short prayer, then we ate. The collard greens were my favorite, and without finishing my plate, I went back for more. We all ate and talked, and I handed Chichi turkey under the table. After dinner, we all went to sit on the couches. There were three couches. Jennie and I sat on the loveseat. I drank a beer while Brian finished the wine, and we started to watch Christmas movies. I suggested *Die Hard* but was outvoted, so we watched *Christmas Vacation* and kept watching Christmas movies until, one by one, they all went to sleep—leaving just Jennie and me on the couch.

Jennie played the Ryan Reynolds movie *Just Friends*—the story of a guy who was in love with his best friend in high school but was in the friend zone. Then he comes back to his hometown years later for Christmas and decides to get the girl he couldn't get in high school, who is now living at her parents' house trying to finish school to be a teacher. It sounded familiar to me.

"This is us, babe," I said, and Jennie laughed.

"You never tried, Dustin."

I never did try. I was always intimidated by her and afraid of her rejecting me. Just knowing Jennie was good enough for me—but I always wanted more. Now, for the first time in my life, I had more.

"Let's go to bed, Dustin."

The house was quiet, with the exception of the TV. Everyone was sleeping, so we walked upstairs to our room to go to sleep. I held Jennie, and we cuddled in bed. Then she kissed me.

"*Just Friends*? OK, boy across the street who's on vacation with his crush and her family. You are left all alone in a bedroom with the girl you always wanted. What do you do?"

I did it, and it was amazing. Childhood fantasies do come true.

Chapter 17

Happy Hanukkah

Jennie had taken a job at a CVS pharmacy as a manager because her ex-husband was trying to get custody of the kids, and she needed a job that showed she worked. The irony was that he had never paid Jennie any child support and owed her sixty thousand dollars. He was trying to get the kids so he wouldn't have to pay her. He was married to the woman he cheated on Jennie with, and they had a three-year-old son. The woman also had three other kids from a previous marriage.

To add to this, Jennie's ex-boyfriend Jeffrey had never returned her text. His dad owned the company he worked for and had sold the company. No one told Jennie, and all of her things—and the kids' things—were thrown away.

Things were hard for Jennie, but she smiled and invited me to celebrate Hanukkah with her family, which started on Sunday, November 28th.

"I'd love to, but all I know about Hanukkah is the Adam Sandler song," I said.

"It starts at sunset, baby."

"Should I bring a joint or a blunt?"

"No! Why would you?"

"Drink some gin and tonica and smoke some marijuanica?"

"No, Dustin. That's not what we do."

"What do we do?"

"We light candles and say a prayer."

"OK, can I bring my own candles?"

"You have Hanukkah candles?"

"I have candles."

I showed up to the Sadusky house with Roman candle fireworks. The kids were excited, but Jennie took them from me and hid them. We all gathered around the kitchen table to light the menorah. Jennie grew up taking Hebrew classes, and she said the prayer in Hebrew—and it was the most beautiful language I had ever heard. Afterward, she said the prayer in English for the kids to understand:

"Blessed are You, our God, Ruler of the Universe, who makes us holy through Your commandments and commands us to light the Hanukkah lights."

Then the kids all lit a candle on their menorahs. Afterward, they were each given a present from Linda.

Hanukkah kicked off the Christmas season for me. The next weekend, I went to pick up Jennie and the kids to look at Christmas lights a block from the house at the Gilbert Riparian Preserve. Max had fallen asleep, so we left him with his grandparents, and the five of us—Chichi included—went.

Sophie wore some jeans that had so many holes in them that shorts would have covered her legs more.

"It might get cold out. Do you want to change?" I asked.

"I'm wearing jeans," Sophie said.

"OK," I said.

We drove and parked, then walked up to a pop-up coffee stand and ordered holiday drinks. Jennie and I got peppermint café mochas, and Sophie got hot chocolate. Noah didn't know what he wanted.

"What do you want, Noah?" Jennie asked.

"I don't know," he said.

"You don't have to get anything," I said.

"No, I want something," Noah said.

"So pick something," Sophie said.

This went on for a couple minutes before I just ordered him a hot chocolate. Then we walked to the gate, and a man scanned our tickets. We started our walk around the Gilbert Riparian Preserve, which was lit up in lights and filled with Christmas airblown figures. We walked around the man-made lake and into the desert landscaping. It didn't take long before Sophie complained she was cold. Those jeans.

It was a short walk—only fifteen minutes—then Jennie, Chichi, and I had a picture taken near the lights. The kids took the picture of us while fighting over who got to take it. So they each took turns. I didn't mind the fighting. I was holding Jennie and Chichi as Jennie and I kissed for the picture. It felt like we were in a Christmas snow globe, and this moment was locked in time.

On December 21st, I woke up next to Jennie in her bedroom and she told me, "Happy four-month anniversary!"

"What?" I said as I was still waking up.

"You forgot?" Jennie said jokingly.

"No, I didn't. I got you a present."

"You did not! I was kidding," she said.

"It's in my car—hang on."

I ran outside to my car. I had gotten Jennie a Bible because hers was thrown away with all of her things in storage. It wasn't meant to be an anniversary gift, but I went with it. I wrote in it, "Happy anniversary," and put the date 12/21/21. Then I ran it up to Jennie in her room and handed it to her.

"A Bible?" she said.

"You said you wanted one for church."

"It's huge!" she said as she examined it.

"That's what she said."

"Dork. But thank you."

"I know you like to write, so the big one has more room for you to write. You're the first girl I've ever given a Bible to."

"I love it. Thank you."

Chapter 18
Christmas Time

C hristmas Eve, I went to church with Jennie's brother Matt. He was in town for Christmas and Jennie had to work at CVS. We lit candles at church to celebrate the light of the world that was given to us. Then I went back to the Sadusky house and waited for Jennie to come home from work.

Jennie came home after 9 p.m. and was tired, but the two of us opened a bottle of wine and started wrapping the kids' Christmas presents. I got each of the kids a present from Jennie and me: Max got a piano keyboard, Noah a drawing table, and Sophie some black Doc Martens.

Jennie has a system and a saying to get the kids their presents: "Something you need, something you want, and something to read." We wrapped the presents from Santa, then went to sleep. I woke up early around 5 a.m., kissed Jennie, and said, "Merry Christmas!"

We made love, then Jennie made coffee, and we lay in her bed enjoying the silence until we heard little feet run down the stairs—then back up to our unlocked room. The door opened, and it was Max.

"Santa came! Come see!"

The two of us got out of bed and walked with Max down the stairs to the Christmas tree where Sophie and Noah were waiting. The tree was lit, and presents were all around it.

"You have to wait for Nana and Papa," Jennie told the kids. So Max went back upstairs to wake them up. Matt was sleeping on the couch downstairs, and his son Cameron came down from the boys' bedroom where he was sleeping. Linda came down with Max and went straight for the coffee.

I went to the fridge and took out a bottle of champagne I had brought over and poured it with some Donald Duck orange juice to make mimosas for the adults. Jennie had to work later, so she didn't have one. After enough suspense, we let the kids start opening their presents. Max opened his keyboard and was excited. Noah opened his drawing table and was confused. Sophie opened her black Doc Martens and screamed in excitement.

Then I handed Jennie her present from me. She opened it and smiled at me.

"Brown Doc Marten boots?" Jennie said.

"I always remember you having brown Docs growing up."

"I love them!"

Then Jennie handed me her present. I opened it.

"You got me a real TurboMan!"

Jingle All The Way was my favorite Christmas movie. We watched it at the Pinetop house. The kids kept opening presents and I kept refilling everyone's mimosas. Then I handed Jennie her second present, and she opened it.

"Birkenstocks!" Jennie said.

"Well, when I got you the Docs, it made me think of you wearing these in high school. You always wore these two shoes, and now we're so old that they're back in style."

"You remember what shoes I wore in high school?"

"I remember you eating cold pizza and drinking a Diet Coke at the bus stop in the morning."

"I love you, Dustin. Open this."

Jennie handed me another present. I opened the gift and it was a chef's cutting knife. I loved it.

"To cut our steaks. I love when you cook for me," Jennie said.

"And I love to cook for you."

We kissed and embraced each other as we watched the kids open more presents. After the presents were done, Jennie ran upstairs and came down with the Roman candles from Hanukkah.

"Let's go outside," Jennie said.

The kids jumped up and rushed to Jennie to take a firework from her hand. Then we walked to the park across the street from the house to light them. There was a fog hovering over the grass and we shot the Roman candles into it.

I looked back at Jennie's house, then to the house I grew up in, and then back at Jennie smiling with the kids. I was a 41-year-old man living the dream of a 15-year-old boy.

The kids' dad soon came to get them and drive them back to Utah for a week. I went inside. I didn't want to see him. I didn't like him, but I didn't want the kids to know that. I didn't think it was right for them to spend Christmas in a car for 8 hours.

After they were gone, Jennie and I went to my brother's house for Christmas where my mom was. Jennie drove because I was drunk. We ate and exchanged presents, then Jennie dropped me off at my house on her way to work at CVS.

"I'll be back when I get off, babe."

"I'll pack my car for our trip tomorrow."

"I can't wait to go snowboarding!" Jennie said.

After she left, I walked inside, opened another beer, then passed out on the couch. Mimosas always knock me out. I woke up alone a few hours later and started to pack my car for our snowboarding trip in the morning. Jennie came over after work and we went to sleep.

In the morning, we woke up, showered and changed, then headed north to Flagstaff to spend the night and go snowboarding at Snowbowl early Monday morning.

We had a cheap hotel off Route 66 in downtown Flagstaff called the Rodeway Inn. It was a basic, plain small room with a queen bed that took up most of the space. It was also next to the train tracks.

"Jerome Grand, Bisbee Grand, now the Rodeway Inn, babe?" Jennie said, not very impressed compared to where I had taken her before.

"It's Christmas break. We're lucky to get this room. Everyone from Phoenix is here. Next time we'll stay at the Monte Vista Hotel. That's my favorite hotel in Flagstaff," I said.

"Must be haunted."

"It is." I laughed, and she did too.

We unpacked and changed into warmer clothes, then left the room to explore downtown Flagstaff. It was a cheap hotel, but it was also in the heart of downtown, so we could walk everywhere. The sun was still up, and we walked down a wet alley with old snow pushed to the side that was melting.

"It's so cold, baby," Jennie said.

"Didn't you go to college here?"

"One semester, then I switched to ASU where it's warm!"

I put my arm around her and tried to warm her up. We walked into a shop and I got her some gloves for her cold hands. Then we went back to walking around the town, going in and out of several stores before we found a bar— The McMillan. I remembered going to this bar in my early twenties when I visited my friends who went to NAU.

"They have great wings. Let's eat," I told her. We walked in and sat at a booth, then I walked to the bar and came back with two Jägerbombers and set them on the table.

"Oh no, baby, not those!" Jennie said.

"Come on, I used to drink these all the time here."

"You were twenty-one. Now you're forty-one."

"You said, 'Let's not get old.'"

"I hate you," she said, then we drank them.

Our waitress came and we ordered two dozen wings and two tall drafts.

Then two more Jägerbombers. We continued this for two hours. When the wings were gone, we decided to go back to our room to go to bed. The waitress brought our check and Jennie grabbed it.

"Let me get it," I said.

"You got the room; I can get this." Jennie handed the waitress her debit card.

"How much was it?"

"$180!"

"Wow, the room was only $66!"

"I hate you!" Jennie laughed and threw a napkin at me.

"Next time we'll get a $180 room and a $66 bar tab," I said.

"I forgot Jägerbombers are fun!" Jennie said, laughing.

We stumbled back to our room to go to sleep.

I woke up at 6 a.m. to the loud sound of the train passing by and the freezing cold. I looked around the room and saw the window was open. Jennie wasn't cold at all.

"Babe, the window is open!"

"I know. When I opened it, I was so hot."

"It's snowing outside!"

"Oops."

We both moaned and Jennie said, "I hate Jägerbombers!"

We put on our snowboarding gear, packed our things, and went to have breakfast at The Place. It was the best breakfast in town. I always ate there when I was in Flagstaff. We ordered coffee, then biscuits and gravy, eggs over easy, bacon, hash browns, and sourdough toast—and split it.

When the check came, Jennie said, "Oh, you can get this one." So I did.

"How much was it?" she asked.

"$25."

"For all that food? How did I get the Jägerbomber tab?"

"I tried to get it."

We left the restaurant and drove north through the town, then made a left at a sign that said Grand Canyon and Snowbowl. It was only a thirty-minute drive, passing the snow-covered pine trees and up the mountain. We parked and got out of the car and put our snowboard boots on. I helped Jennie with hers. Then we carried our snowboards to the lodge to get our lift tickets. Jennie's lift ticket included a free lesson, so I walked her over to drop her off at ski school.

"I thought you were going to teach me?" she asked.

"I am, but you take this class first, and I'll get some rides in. When you're done, I'll take you up the lift."

"OK," Jennie said but didn't smile.

"You know what? Let's go to the bunny hill—me and you."

"No, you go, baby."

"I said I will teach you. Come on."

We walked to the bunny hill and I helped Jennie into her bindings.

"So how do I stop?" she asked.

"Don't worry about that."

"What do you mean, don't worry about that?"

"You will fall before you have to stop."

"Baby!"

"Get up. Today we learn heel side. Just lean back, facing down the mountain, and sway your hips. You want to lean back on your heels. Transfer your weight to the left to go left, and right to go right."

I got up and went twenty feet down the hill to show her, then stopped.

"Now you go."

Jennie got up and made it two feet, then fell forward.

"Try to fall back, not forward," I said.

Jennie rolled around in the snow like a wounded beach seal trying to flip over.

"Dustin, come get me!"

"I can't go up the hill—you have to come to me."

She did. She got up and pointed her right foot straight down. And down the mountain she went, screaming! I went after her, but she stopped after catching a front edge and flipping.

"Don't you even say I need to fall backwards, Dustin."

Jennie made it to the bottom, and we took the snow escalator back up the bunny slope and went down again with the same result—only she yelled at me for showing off because I kept spinning in circles the whole way down.

Jennie looked beat after two runs, so I asked if she wanted a break. She did, and I walked her to the lodge so she could get coffee. I left her to do some solo runs. I only did one run, then put my board in the snowboard rack and went to get Jennie.

I found her sitting at a table with a family, a glass of white wine in one hand and beef jerky in the other.

"Thought you were getting coffee?"

"Oops?"

"Where did you get the jerky?"

"These nice people made it at home and offered me some. I'm not going to say no to free jerky."

I had left her alone for 45 minutes, and she had made new friends. That is just Jennie.

"Come on, let's go snowboarding."

We walked and got her snowboard—but not mine.

"What about yours?" she asked.

159

"I don't need it. Come on."

We walked back to the bunny hill, and I strapped Jennie into her bindings as she sat down in the snow. Then I helped her up.

"We're doing toe side now," I said.

"You said heel side first?"

"I changed my mind. Hold my hand and lean toward the mountain, facing me. I won't let go."

"Promise?"

"I promise, babe. Now swing to the right, then swing to the left."

Jennie did, and I glided her down the bunny slope.

"I didn't fall!"

"You did good. Now let's do it again."

And we did it again, with me holding her hands and gliding her down the bunny slope. By the third time, I was letting go, but when she got scared, I'd grab her hands and let her know, "It's okay to fall."

"But I don't want to fall," she said.

"Everybody falls. It's important to get back up."

The fourth run down, she made it without me holding her hands.

"I did it!"

"You did it, babe! I'm so proud of you!"

Jennie hugged and kissed me while strapped to her snowboard.

"This is the best birthday present ever. But you barely got to snowboard, Dustin."

"It's okay. I had fun with you."

"You took us fishing and didn't get to fish either?"

"Snowboarding and fishing are just an excuse to get up north. It just feels good here. I like it better with you, but it's definitely easier by myself."

"I love you," she told me, then slipped and fell on the slushy snow.

"Are you ready to go home?" I asked.

"Yes!"

We walked back to grab my snowboard, then back to my car, and we drove back to Phoenix. We had to make one stop—Rock Springs for a pie. This time, blueberry crumb.

Chapter 19

Happy New Year

The kids were back from their dad's in Utah and in time to spend New Year's Eve with Jennie and me. Sophie went to stay at a friend's house for a sleepover, and Jennie had to work until eight that night. I picked up the boys at six from their grandparents. Brian and Linda didn't plan on staying up until midnight, so I brought Brian a six-pack of Heineken and Linda a six-pack of White Claw so they could at least have a drink on New Year's Eve. Then I drove the boys and me back to my house.

The boys were excited because I had fireworks for us to light. It was lightly raining, but I promised them we could still light the fireworks.

"Water puts fire out, Dustin. How can we light them in the rain?" Max asked as we walked into the house.

"They're waterproof, buddy," I told him.

The boys walked into the house and saw the mountain of fireworks that filled the kitchen table. I had gotten the biggest box of fireworks from Costco. Max stood next to the box of fireworks, and it was bigger than him. His eyes got wide as he continued to look at the table that had mortars, Roman candles, bottle rockets, sparklers, and one giant box that had a clown jester printed on it. Max was especially interested in the big box.

"That's the grand finale, Max," I said.

"Can I light it?" Max asked.

"Not this year, buddy. But one day, when you are older," I said.

It was just the three of us, and the rain had stopped, so I took some of the smaller fireworks out front for the boys to light. We started with snakes that I let them light with a multipurpose lighter from the kitchen junk drawer. They enjoyed watching the small black pellets catch fire and grow from the cement. They also lit some smaller cone fireworks, each of the boys taking a turn with the one lighter.

Some of my friends had shown up, as well as my brother and his new girlfriend, and my mom with her boyfriend. I opened the garage so everyone could play pool and enjoy the arcade while the kids lit fireworks. I started a fire in the backyard and put a metal cover over the firepit to keep the rain from putting it out.

To keep the boys from lighting all the fireworks before midnight, I gave them some plastic slingshots that shot LED-lit arrows into the sky. I gave the two boys three arrows each. Ten minutes later, the arrows were all on top of the roof of the house. To keep their attention, I set up medium- and large-sized fireworks on barstools in the entryway of the house and made a shooting gallery where the boys took turns shooting the fireworks with a Nerf gun. Every firework they hit with a Nerf dart, they got to light.

Jennie walked in from the garage a little after eight with a bag of clothes to change into from her work clothes. She saw the Nerf shooting gallery and asked,

"What are you boys up to?"

"Winning fireworks! I'll get you a big one, Mom," Noah said.

Jennie smiled and went to the bedroom to change. When she came out, we all went outside to light the fireworks the boys had won. When we came back into the house, I taped one-dollar bills to a life-size cardboard cutout of Chuck Liddell. Same rules applied—if you hit the dollar with the Nerf dart, you win the dollar. I made Jennie and me some vodka Red Bulls, and we went out back to the fire.

"How was work?" I asked.

"Blahhhh," Jennie replied.

"I'm sorry."

"I think I want to go back to teaching," she said.

"That sounds great!"

"I thought it would be good since I would be at work at the same time the kids were gone to school and be home on the weekends with them."

"That sounds perfect! And you could have Sunday off and we can go to church."

"I know you love the Sunday school class, but could you miss some so I don't have to sit alone?"

"I didn't tell you—Jeff is helping me in class now. So I can miss every other week and sit with you."

"Davidson?" she asked. Jeff had been my best friend since high school, and he grew up on the same street as Jennie and me.

"Yes."

"Does the church know how bad you boys were in high school?"

"That's why we volunteer—to try and keep them from making our mistakes. Try to be the cool adults they can talk to when they can't talk to their parents."

"Dustin and Jeff, Sunday school teachers. Who would have thought?" Jennie said.

"Dustin and Jennie getting married. Who would have thought?" I said.

"One month away! We need to get our marriage license, baby."

"We will next week, okay? Get a Monday off, and I'll take you to breakfast, then the courthouse."

"Can I light some fireworks now?" Jennie asked.

"I thought you'd never ask. I have some special ones for you."

We walked inside and I grabbed a mortar cannon and some shells, then loaded it as we walked to the street to light it. I placed it on the wet street and handed Jennie the lighter. She lit it and walked away as a loud shot left the cannon and into the lightly rainy sky. Then came a loud boom, and the sky was covered in green sparkles that drizzled down to earth until fading away. The people in my garage cheered, and Jennie said, "Again!" So I loaded her another round, and I let her light it. Afterward, I hid the cannon on the side of the yard and put the kids in the front with sparklers.

"Why did you do that?" Jennie asked.

"When the cops come by, we just wave and look like we just have snakes and sparklers."

"Are you serious?"

Minutes later, a cop car rolled by and slowed down to look at us.

"Happy New Year," I said as I lit more sparklers.

The cop drove away.

"You're a genius," Jennie said.

"Let's get another drink."

The boys wanted to play in the garage, so I took the lighter with me, and Jennie and I walked to the fire in the backyard to put some more wood on it. We continued to go back and forth from the backyard to the front yard to light fireworks for the next three hours until it got close to midnight. Then I opened a box that had twenty-four cans of silly string and passed them out—two apiece—to everyone at the party. I took the large grand finale jester firework to the street with Jennie, and the party started the countdown...

10... 9... 8... 7... 6... 5... 4... 3...

At 3, I lit the firework.

2... 1... "HAPPY NEW YEAR!" everyone shouted as an arsenal of mortars shot out of the box, lighting up the night sky in every color of the rainbow along with the sounds of loud booms that shook the ground.

Chichi was locked away in the closet of my room with the TV on loud and every dog treat she could dream of.

I kissed Jennie.

"Happy New Year, babe."

"Happy New Year, baby."

This special moment was broken up by Noah and Max shooting Jennie and me with silly string. We fired back and made our way onto the driveway where everyone was chasing each other with cans of silly string until the cans were empty and my driveway was no longer gray, but colored much like the sky when the fireworks had lit it up. The water from the rain had added to the mess, and the silly string was sticking to the ground.

"Baby, the mess?" Jennie said.

"I got it. Noah and Max, you want to make twenty bucks?"

"Yes!" they both said.

"Grab the brooms from the garage and sweep up all the silly string, and I'll pay you."

"No, Dustin. You got all these fireworks and all the silly string—they will clean because they are thankful."

The boys got the brooms and started sweeping the driveway. I walked inside with Jennie and sat her on the couch, then went out to check on the boys, who were moving very slowly.

"Guys, this job sucks, I know, but I appreciate you doing it. And I'll still pay you."

They started moving much faster, and while they were occupied cleaning the driveway, I got to sit alone with Jennie on the couch. Well worth twenty bucks.

Chapter 20
Max and Me

On Sunday, we all went to church, and I sat with Jennie at the 10 a.m. service. We held hands and only let go when Jennie wanted to write in her new Bible. After church, I dropped Jennie and the kids off at their house. I went home to watch the football game with some friends. Jennie called me saying her best friends Margo and Ashley were in town and they wanted to get lunch with her and Marry. The high school cool girl Mount Rushmore. But she couldn't go because she had the kids.

"I'll watch them," I said.

"You have your friends over."

"They don't care if I'm here."

"Stop."

"Seriously, my friends live here. Yours are in town for a day."

"The kids don't want to go to your house because you don't have the internet."

"I have an arcade!"

"They like Wi-Fi more."

"Okay, I'll take them to do something."

"Really?"

"Yes."

"Since we are moving in soon, I'll just have the internet set up this week at your house, and I'll pay for it."

I didn't have Wi-Fi because I watched TV on my 60-inch flat-screen with antenna bunny ears. The only football game I cared to watch was the Cardinals, and they were always televised. I got the basic channels, and when I wanted to watch a movie, I picked from one of my hundreds of DVDs.

"Sounds good, babe. I'll head over now," I said. I told my friends I was leaving and to lock up if I wasn't back. They had beer, pizza, and a football game. They were fine. It was like leaving kids with soda, pizza, and Wi-Fi.

I went to the Sandusky house and kissed Jennie on her way out.

"Thank you so much, Dustin."

"We're getting married soon, babe. I'm supposed to do this."

"We are married, baby."

"I know. Go see your sisters—tell them I said hi."

Jennie drove away, and I tried to rally the kids. Noah was drawing in his room. Sophie was in her room on her phone. Linda and Brian were doing their own thing. I didn't know why they needed me.

Then Max came running down the stairs.

"What are we doing?" he asked.

"Let's go—laser tag?" I said.

"Sophie, Noah, let's go!" Max said.

"I don't want to go anywhere," they both said.

"Take Max, please," Linda insisted.

I knew then that it wasn't the kids that needed watching—it was Max. He craved fun and was an absolute lunatic when he was bored. Much like myself. It was Brian and Linda's day off, and they wanted to relax. So I took Max to laser tag.

I drove the two of us two miles down Greenfield Road to Main Event—another family fun center, much like Fat Cats, only this one had laser tag. We walked inside, past all the games, and to the main counter.

"Two for laser tag," I said.

The teenager working gave me our tickets after I paid, and we walked over to the laser tag arena. I strapped Max into his harness, then I put mine on. Each harness had a number associated with a name. I chose Batman, and Max chose Captain America. After we were strapped in and ready, a group of five thirteen-year-old boys came in and chose their laser tag harnesses. It was just the seven of us now.

Just before they let us in the room to play, Max looked nervous.

"What's wrong, bro?" I asked.

"I've never done this before, Dustin."

"That's okay."

"It's a laser, and lasers hurt, Dustin. I don't want to get hit."

Max thought we were really getting shot. So I told him,

"Stay behind me and I will block you."

"Okay, let's go!" Max said.

Then we ran through the two-story black light maze seeking cover before the fight started. It was me and Max vs. five 13-year-olds. We took the high ground on the second floor. Then the fight started.

Max and I sniped the kids from the second floor, but they made their way up, so we made our way down, blasting with Max behind me. My harness was hit, and I was out of play, but I protected Max from the thirteen-year-olds.

"Not fair—you're blocking!" they yelled.

Then my harness turned back on, and I shot the two that were in front of us.

"Life's not fair, kid," I said, and Max and I ran for cover to hide.

"Let's get them, Batman," Max said.

"You ready, Captain?"

"Yes," Max said, with determination in his eyes.

We ran through the course, blasting away like The Mandalorian protecting Baby Yoda.

One of the 13-year-olds yelled at me, "It's not fair! I can't shoot the little kid because you're blocking him—and you're fat!"

"You're mom's fat," I said.

"You don't know my mom!" he said.

My harness lit back up and I was in play again, so I shot the kid.

"Everyone knows your mom."

I was talking trash to 13-year-olds. But this was war.

A siren went off and the game was over, so we all walked over to the base to see our scores. The kids laughed. Batman finished last. On the scoreboard, you could see who shot you the most. I was shot the most by Captain America—9 times.

"Max!" I said.

"You were in my way," Max said.

The 13-year-old boys laughed.

"You want to go again?" I asked.

"No blocking," one of them said.

"If you beat me, I'll buy you all ice cream."

"Deal!" one of them said.

So we stood in the black light room and waited to be released back into the war zone.

"I don't think we can beat them," Max said.

"No, we can't. But I can."

"What?" Max said as they let us into the war zone to hide.

"You're on your own, kid," I said as I disappeared into the maze.

I kept a close eye on Max while playing. All of the 13-year-olds had Max as a target. For the first time in my life, I realized why Batman had Robin. It was to take the eyes off of Batman! I crept through the darkness, taking them out one by one, as Max took the shots for me. He was a good Robin.

The siren sounded, and the game was done. We walked back to the base to see the scores. Batman was second. Captain America   last.

"You owe us ice cream!" they all shouted.

I helped Max out of his harness, then took mine off.

"Yaya, meet you at the ice cream counter," I said.

The 13-year-old boys ran to the ice cream counter.

"Max, let's go!"

"But the ice cream?"

"We don't buy the enemy ice cream."

The two of us walked fast to my car and drove away. I didn't feel bad. These weren't underprivileged kids. They all had brand-new Air Jordans on their feet and perms in their hair. Plus, they called me fat. If I had won, I would have bought them all ice cream, because I'm not a sore loser—but a great winner.

We were driving home, and Max said,

"I thought we were getting ice cream?"

So I drove to Cold Stone.

"We are, bro."

We went to Cold Stone on Val Vista. I used to work there in high school. I was fired for making out with another female employee named Britni. I was cute, she liked it, loved it, and had to have it.

I ordered a "Love It" half sweet cream and chocolate with brownies and cookie dough. Max ordered vanilla.

"Just vanilla?" I asked.

"Yes."

"Add something, please."

"Okay… sprinkles."

The two of us sat on a curb and ate our ice cream.

"I'm full," Max said. The kid never finished ice cream.

There was no Chichi, so I let him throw it away.

"Thanks, Dustin. This was fun."

"You had a good time?"

"Oh yeah. Those kids are probably still waiting for their ice cream. We got them good."

Chapter 21

Going to the Courthouse

On Friday, January 7th, Jennie and I went to get breakfast at The Farmhouse in downtown Gilbert before we went to get our marriage license. The Farmhouse was my favorite breakfast spot in town. I had been going there since my family moved to Gilbert in 1994. They had the best biscuits and gravy in the world.

I wrote my name on a handwritten list, and we had to wait outside on a bench for my name to be called. Two elderly women were walking down the street in the bike lane and went to step up on the sidewalk, but one of the women fell and hit her head. She was being helped up by her friend, and I thought I should go help, but they both looked embarrassed. Jennie didn't think—she just rushed to their aid and helped them both.

"You're really just going to stand there, Dustin?" Jennie said.

I walked inside and asked a waitress for some ice in a bag and napkins for the woman. I walked back outside and handed them to Jennie, who gave the women our seats on the bench, placed the ice bag on the woman's head, and wiped a small cut on her head with the napkins. Another waitress called my name, and Jennie gave our place in line to the two old women, then put my name back at the bottom of the list. We took our seats back on the bench.

"Always be kind, Dustin."

"I like it. I'm glad I'm marrying you."

It was a beautiful day out—sitting with Jennie on the bench in the 70-degree weather with a slight breeze, and Jennie in her oversized black sunglasses, was perfect.

Eventually, we were seated at a table. I ordered a full order of the biscuits and gravy for Jennie and me to share, along with eggs over easy, bacon, hash browns, and sourdough toast for myself. Jennie ordered a country omelet. We drank our coffee and waited for our food.

After breakfast, we were going to get our marriage license at the Gilbert courthouse. I felt nervous, like for some reason they weren't going to give it to us.

"So we just walk in and they give us our marriage license?" I asked Jennie.

"Pretty much."

"We don't have to take a test?"

"No."

"Because I failed my driver's license test three times before I got it."

"Babe, are you nervous?"

"No. It's just... I've never gotten anything good out of that courthouse."

"You are nervous."

"Okay, yes I am. What if I mess up being a husband?"

"You will mess up—and that's okay, because I won't give up on you. So you'll be fine."

Jennie smiled and looked confident in what she just said. Suddenly, I wasn't nervous anymore. Looking at Jennie, with her two hands on her coffee cup, I knew I'd be a good husband.

Our food came, and the waitress put the biscuits and gravy between the two of us and our plates in front of us. She refilled our coffee, and Jennie and I held hands for a quick prayer, then dove into our food.

"These are the best biscuits and gravy in the world!" Jennie said.

"I can't believe you never come here."

"The best things were always right in front of me, and I never knew it.

Now you're showing them all to me," Jennie said, as she stole a piece of bacon from my plate.

"Babe! You can't steal my bacon!"

"What's yours is mine now, baby."

I could only laugh. Jennie was right.

"Besides, you always eat my leftovers! I go to sleep thinking I have lunch for tomorrow and find an empty styrofoam container in the morning. Why do you put it back if it's empty, Dustin?"

"So I don't feel like I ate it all?"

Jennie rolled her eyes and dropped her head. Then I handed her my last slice of bacon. She took it and said,

"Thank you. That's sweet."

The waitress came by to check on us.

"How is everything?" she asked.

"Perfect. Can I get another order of bacon?" I said.

"Dustin!" Jennie said.

"Two orders?" I asked.

"No, we're fine," Jennie told the waitress.

We finished our food, and I paid our tab. Then we drove a mile south on Gilbert Road to the Gilbert courthouse. They were open. The building was almost empty except for the security guard who made us go through a metal detector, and the three women working at the counter. We walked up to the counter holding hands.

"Is this where we can get a marriage license?" I asked.

"Yes," a middle-aged woman working the counter replied.

"Okay, how much is the fine?" I asked.

Jennie jabbed me in the ribs gently.

"It's not a fine, Dustin. It's a fee," Jennie said.

"Sorry. I've only paid fines in this building. This is my first fee," I said.

"It's a marriage license, not a marriage ticket, sir," the clerk said.

"License to bone," I said.

"Baby, please walk away and let me talk. I love you," Jennie said.

So I walked away and sat down, getting on my phone. Jennie came back to get me a few minutes later.

"It's $83," Jennie said, and I pulled out my debit card.

"They only take cashier's checks or money orders."

So we drove across the street to a liquor store to get a money order, but they didn't do it there. At the liquor store, I ran into a friend of mine, Adam, that I used to cut hair with in Scottsdale.

"What are you doing, bro?" he asked.

"I'm getting married!"

"No way!" Adam said.

Then I introduced him to Jennie and explained what we were doing. After that, Jennie and I drove across the street to the QT gas station. We got a cashier's check but had to pay cash for it, so Jennie and I emptied our wallets and came up with enough after I bought some gum and took twenty dollars cash back.

We walked outside, and I saw a cop standing out front.

"Hey, asshole," I said.

"Dustin!" Jennie said to me.

"Dustin!" the cop said, then gave me a hug.

He was a guy I was friends with in high school named Jacob. I told him what we were doing, and he joked and said,

"Hey, do you need my handcuffs?"

"We already have some," Jennie said.

Jennie and I drove back to the courthouse and got our marriage license, then back to my house. Jennie was very tired, so we took a nap. I let her sleep longer, and I went alone to her parents' house to get the kids when they got home from school.

Chapter 22
Nothing Is By Accident

I was driving to work Thursday morning. I had to start work at eight, but I left earlier than usual to stop and get a coffee from Starbucks, because I had a gift card from Christmas, and that morning Starbucks sounded good. I remember thinking my manager was going to freak out because I was early instead of late. I pulled up to a red light in the third lane just south of Elliot Road on Val Vista, next to the Gilbert Post Office. There was a Starbucks to my left and one to my right inside the Safeway grocery store, but I was going to stop at one closer to my work.

The light turned green, and I accelerated through the intersection. An early 2000s Cavalier sped past me in the middle lane. A car in the first lane turned its left blinker on to get into the middle lane and started to move over. The speeding Cavalier was in their blind spot. I knew they were going to hit. But they didn't. The Cavalier swerved left to avoid hitting the car and instead clipped the front of my Scion XB, sending me over the curb and into the median. I was airborne, and everything was moving in slow motion. I had no control of anything, and all I could think was, This is how I die, and that I'd never see Jennie again. A loud bang stopped the slow-motion experience.

I woke up to a woman tapping on my window.

"Are you okay?" the woman asked.

I felt my face and then my body, then nodded. I was okay. I wasn't dead. The airbag had deployed as my car ran into a tree. The tree stopped me from hitting oncoming traffic. I pushed my car door open, undid my seatbelt, and exited the car. Traffic was stopped on both sides of the road. The Cavalier was flipped upside down a few hundred feet from me.

"Are they okay?" I asked a stranger.

"Yes, they got him out and he is walking," they said.

The police were there almost immediately. They asked if I was okay and then asked me what happened. Several people had stopped who saw the accident, and they all said it was the Cavalier's fault.

I texted Jennie, "I just got in a car accident. I'm okay but can you come pick me up at the post office on Val Vista."

"Okay baby," she replied.

I then sent a picture of my car to my manager and said I was in an accident and wouldn't be in today. He was happy I was okay and blocked my books for the next couple of days.

I gathered my things from the car, and the police officer handed me some paperwork. Then I stared at my totaled Scion XB. It was the first brand-new car I had ever purchased. It had been paid off since 2018. I thought about all the trips around Arizona we had been on together and that we would never do it again. I got sentimental about the car. I loved that car. My friends called it the "toaster." That car saved my life. It was a toaster. The Brave Little Toaster. I stared at my car until I heard Jennie's voice.

"Baby!"

I walked over to her with my things, and she gave me a hug.

"Ow," I said.

"Are you okay?"

"I'm fine, just really sore."

"Do we need to go to the hospital?"

"No, can we just go home?"

"Of course, baby."

I got in on the passenger side, and Jennie drove us a mile back to my house. We walked inside.

"You can't die! We are getting married in a week!"

"I didn't die!"

"We need to go to the hospital. You might be hurt and don't even know it."

"I'm fine."

"What if you're not?"

"Okay, let's go to the bedroom and see if I'm okay?"

"You almost died, and you want to have sex?"

"If I can have sex, then I'm fine."

"If we have sex, then you are going to the hospital to get checked."

"Sex first, then the hospital?"

"Deal," Jennie said and led me to the bedroom.

"But be gentle, babe. I was just in a car accident."

"Then we can tell the doctor that's how you broke your back."

After, Jennie went home to get some things and asked her mom if she could watch the kids after school because she was taking me to get checked out at urgent care. Jennie also called in to work at CVS. It was her last week before she started substitute teaching.

While I was alone, I called my insurance company to make a claim. Jennie was back home before I was off the phone. I finished the phone call.

"How do you feel?" Jennie asked.

"Really tight and sore."

We went to urgent care, and I was looked at. Everything was okay except for the bruises from my seatbelt and my swollen face from the airbag. Then we went home.

"I'm not leaving you today, Dustin! I almost lost you! Even if I annoy you, I'm staying with you all day."

"I'd like that. Let's take a nap on the couch."

"They set the internet up at your house this week! We can watch Beverly Hills 90210."

"Sounds perfect."

Around 4 p.m., Jennie went home to say hi to the kids and let them know what happened today.

"Can I take you to dinner for sushi tonight?" Jennie asked as she was leaving.

"Yes, but why sushi?"

"I almost lost you, and we've never had sushi together."

Jennie went home to her parents and was back within 30 minutes and told me the kids were glad I was okay. We laid on the couch for a few more hours, then Jennie drove us to the sushi restaurant, Ra. I was doing Dry January and hadn't had a drink since New Year's Eve. The waitress came to take our drink order.

I said, "I'll have a sake bomber, Kirin Light."

"Really, Dustin?"

"It's been 20 days. I'm good."

"Make that two," Jennie said.

I was quiet. Jennie kept asking me questions, but I gave short answers. The car accident kept playing over and over in my head. I had never seen life in slow motion before.

"What's wrong, Dustin?"

"I'm okay."

"No, you are not."

"I'm fine."

"Please tell me. This isn't like you!"

I started crying. I tried to hide it and wiped my face with my shoulder, but the tears wouldn't stop. Jennie didn't say anything. She just looked at me and held my hands.

"When my car hit the curb and I was going into the tree, I thought I was going to die. And all I could think was I'm never going to see you again— and that hurt so much more than dying."

"But I'm here, baby."

"I know. I've just never been scared like that in my life. I wasn't afraid of dying. I was afraid of not seeing you again."

Jennie started to cry, and the waitress came back to take our sushi order.

"Another round of sake bombers. We're Ubering home," Jennie said.

"Oh yeah?"

"Life's too short. Let's live every moment, baby."

"Cheers to every moment with you."

"Cheers. We are getting married in a week!"

"Cheers to Mr. and Mrs. Elkin."

We kissed and ordered several rolls of sushi and even had dessert. It was a great ending to a day that started out so bad.

Chapter 23

I'm Your Huckleberry

February 2, 2022, we were getting married. I got off work the night before and told Jennie I was going to sleep alone at my house because I thought you're not supposed to see the bride the night before the wedding day.

My friend Derrick called me on my way home. He was an old friend who was always in rock bands. He looked like Johnny Depp if you ordered him off of WISH. He was with his wife and wanted to get a drink. I said I couldn't because I was getting married in the morning. He insisted I meet him for a drink, so I did. We met at Native Sports Bar, where he bought me a few rounds.

"Lame bachelor party, dude," Derrick said.

"My life has been a bachelor party. I'm okay."

"No invite, bro?"

"We're having a party in August. You're invited. It was just supposed to be me and Jennie, but her mom wanted to come. Then her dad. Then the kids. Then her brother and nephew."

"Who's going to the wedding for you?"

"No one."

"I would have gone to Tombstone!"

"I know, bro. We're just keeping it small."

"Well, cheers to you, Dustin!"

We drank our shots of Jameson and I went home and to bed.

I woke up at 8 a.m. Jennie was calling me.

"Don't forget the rings," Jennie said.

"I won't, they're already packed in my bag."

"Max is riding with my parents and Noah and Sophia with us."

"Okay, I'll be over in an hour."

I showered and put on some basketball shorts and flip-flops with an oversized shirt for the drive, then I laid on the couch and enjoyed my quiet three-bedroom house that I had all to myself with Chichi. After today, I'd have a wife and three kids moving in. Everything would change.

I fed Chichi and kissed her goodbye. My friend was coming by to feed and check on her. We'd be back the next afternoon. I grabbed my Adidas soccer bag full of my things and walked out the door, ready for the rest of my new life to begin.

I showed up to Jennie's and was greeted with,

"You're late, Dustin!"

"Well, let's go."

"I'm not ready."

"But I'm late?"

I grabbed Jennie's and the kids' bags and packed them in Jennie's Jeep. I had a new used car from the accident, but I was returning it and couldn't put miles on it.

It was getting close to 10 a.m., and we had a three-hour drive to Tombstone. We were getting married at 3 p.m., so Jennie would have close to two hours to get ready. The courthouse was just two blocks from where we were staying.

I finally got everyone in the car and we drove to the Quick Trip for snacks. No road trip is complete without snacks. Once everyone was back in the car, we drove south to Tombstone, Arizona.

I picked up $2 scratchers at the QT and gave them to the kids in the back seat if they answered an Arizona trivia question right.

"What's Tombstone famous for?" I asked.

"Pizza?" Noah said.

"Gunfight at the OK Corral," Sophie said.

"Right, and who was in the gunfight?" I asked.

"Doc Holliday, Wyatt Earp, and his brothers," Sophie said.

"Not fair, Sophia is looking at her phone," Noah said.

"That's okay. You both win this round because you learned something," I said and handed them two scratchers each.

"Teaching them to gamble, Dustin?" Jennie said.

"I'm going to teach them so much! Wait until we do family poker night!" I said.

"Yay, poker!" Noah said.

"You don't even know what that is," Sophie said.

"Sounds fun," Noah said.

It started to rain just as we drove past Tucson.

"It's raining on our wedding day, Dustin!" Jennie said.

"I think it's good luck," I told her.

"Really?"

"Yes, just like the first time I married you in the backyard when it was raining."

Jennie smiled and grabbed my hand to hold.

We pulled into Tombstone just before 1 p.m. I stopped at the gas station to get beer, wine, and cheap champagne. I saw some Hostess cupcakes and got them since we didn't have a wedding cake.

After the gas station, we drove two blocks to our cabin called Katie's Cozy Cabins. There were four wooden cabins lined up in a row, and our cabin was the first one. We walked up the porch that had a porch swing, and I opened the door and the kids rushed in first.

The cabin had a loft, and the main floor had a small kitchen with a two-burner stove, a refrigerator, a small table with two chairs, a futon couch, a bathroom with a shower, and a room that had bunk beds. The queen bed was up in the loft and you had to climb a ladder to get to it.

The kids ran up the ladder immediately and treated the cabin like a clubhouse.

"Can we stay here tonight?" Noah asked.

"Not tonight, buddy, but we'll come back and we can all stay here another time," I said.

"Can you get my things so I can get ready, Dustin?" Jennie asked.

I went outside and brought in her bags, and Jennie started doing her makeup at the small table. Linda had shown up to take the kids so we could get ready. It was 1:30, and I decided I'd take a shower and get ready.

I pulled my clothes out of my bag and put the wedding rings on the table.

"Is that the wedding ring? Can I see it?" Noah asked.

I gave it to him to look at. I realized I didn't have my brother there.

"Do you want to be my best man?" I asked.

"Are you serious?" Noah shouted.

"Yes."

"What do I have to do?"

"You're in charge of the ring. Can you handle it?"

"Yes."

"Do not lose it, Noah! It's your one job."

"I won't. Thanks, Dustin," Noah said, smiling.

I went into the shower. When I came out, it was just Jennie doing her makeup. Linda had taken the kids back to their hotel. The rings were sitting on the table. I decided I was going to play a trick on Noah and I put the ring in the pocket of my jean jacket.

"2 o'clock, babe," I said.

"I know, baby."

I grabbed a beer from the fridge and walked outside to sit on the porch swing. The weather was gray and windy. It was beautiful. I swung on the porch swing until I finished my beer, then I walked back into the cabin to grab another beer.

"Will you curl my hair while I finish, baby?"

"I'm not working today, it's my wedding day."

"Dustin!" Jennie yelled at me as I shut the door and sat back on the bench with my beer.

"It's 2:30, Jennie," I yelled.

"I know, jerk."

"You can't call me a jerk on our wedding day," I shouted so she could hear me.

"I love you, jerk."

"That's better."

I finished my beer and walked inside the cabin.

"It's 10 minutes to three, babe. We have to go."

"Let's drive there."

"Parking sucks in Tombstone. Trust me—it's faster if we walk. And I want to walk with my bride down the streets of Tombstone on this gray and windy day."

"Is it windy?"

"Barely. Come on!" I said and grabbed her by the hand to lead her outside.

Jennie stopped me and asked, "How do I look?"

"Like the most beautiful woman in the world."

Jennie had her blond hair curled, a white short dress with brown cowboy boots on, and a flower tiara my nephew Kaden's mom, Dana, had made for Jennie. Dana had her own flower business, The Floral Theory. Jennie's only request for the wedding was flowers from Dana. Since Dana was family, she did it for free and made Jennie a bouquet as well.

"Let's do this, Dustin," Jennie said.

"I've been waiting for this since 8th grade, Jennie."

The two of us held hands and walked east on Allen Street on that gray and windy day—February 2, 2022—feeling like Doc Holliday and Wyatt Earp, two best friends ready to take on the world.

When we got to the OK Corral, we made a right to the courthouse. As we walked up the steps to the courthouse, a gush of wind came and blew the flower tiara off Jennie's head and whipped her curls in front of her face. I picked up the tiara from the ground.

"Fix it, Dustin!" Jennie screamed.

I smoothed out Jennie's hair with my hands and put the curls back, circling the locks in my fingers, then placed the flower tiara back on her head.

"Perfect," I said, and held the courthouse door open for Jennie to walk in.

Inside, Jennie's parents were standing with the kids, her brother Matt, and his son Cameron. Jennie walked to her mother, and I walked to the counter to check in.

"Hi, we're getting married at three. Elkin?"

"Okay, that'll be $60."

I gave the woman my debit card, but because of the storm, it wasn't processing.

"This happens a lot with storms here," the woman told me.

Eventually, my card went through, and we all walked up the stairs to the courtroom where Doc Holliday and Wyatt Earp were tried for the gunfight at the OK Corral. When we got to the room, we met Pastor Joey for the first time—the officiant for the ceremony. Jennie had booked him. He was a nice guy dressed in old western attire, though his cowboy outfit looked too small. He looked like a grown man wearing a kid's Halloween cowboy costume.

"Dustin and Jennie?" he asked.

"Yes," I said.

"Okay, let's go up here to the front," Pastor Joey said.

Jennie and I followed him, and before I could take my hat off—

"Dear family and friends, we have gathered here today..." Pastor Joey began.

I threw my hat off. We had started. He continued with, "Do you, Dustin, take Jennie to be your wife, through sickness and health, till death do you part?"

"Yes," I said.

"You're supposed to say 'I do,' Dustin," Jennie whispered.

"It's my first time."

"And do you, Jennie, take Dustin to be your husband, through sickness and health, till death do you part?"

"I do."

"Do you have the rings?" Pastor Joey asked.

"Noah, the ring?" I said.

"What?" Noah replied, looking scared from the courtroom pews.

"The ring I gave you to hold—to be my best man?"

"No, you didn't," Noah said.

"Yes, he did. I was standing right there," Sophie chimed in.

"Noah, the ring," his grandma said sternly.

The poor guy looked so scared I figured he had enough, so I pulled the ring out of my pocket.

"Here it is," I said, and placed it on Jennie's finger.

Then Jennie took my ring and placed it on my finger.

"By the state of Arizona, I now pronounce you husband and wife. You may now kiss the bride."

Jennie had a mischievous smile on her face as she stood in the same spot Doc Holliday stood when he was acquitted of murder for the gunfight at the OK Corral. I thought Doc probably had the same smile that day back in 1881.

We kissed, and I held Jennie, and we kissed some more with our eyes closed. When I finally opened my eyes, I saw my wife glowing—beautiful and smiling with those big blue eyes. I did it. I had married Jennie Sadusky from across the street, just like I always wanted to.

Jennie hugged her mom, and I shook Brian's hand. Then I went to the kids and said, "Now I get to ground you guys too!"

Pastor Joey came up to me and asked about payment. I assumed Jennie had already paid since she booked him, but I pulled out my debit card.

Pastor Joey said, "Oh no, this is Tombstone. We do cash here."

"Jennie?" I said.

"I have the cash in an envelope in my purse," she said.

I looked in her purse. There was no envelope.

"Babe, there's no envelope."

"I switched purses at the cabin. I forgot!"

"It's okay. How much is it, Pastor Joey?"

"$75," he said.

I pulled out two twenties from my wallet.

"Does anyone have any cash?" I asked.

Brian had a twenty, Linda had a ten, and Max had two dollars.

"That'll do," Pastor Joey said. Then we signed the marriage certificate, and he took the $72 and left like he had a bookie to pay.

"So we're married?" I said to Jennie.

"Yes! Forever and ever, baby!"

We started walking out, but everyone began looking at the exhibits in the building. It was, after all, a museum. I found myself alone, looking at a picture of the great Native American chief Geronimo, who had surrendered in this part of Arizona.

I thought to myself how I wished I had some friends and family here for this moment. I was so happy, I wished they were here—but it was my fault. I didn't invite anyone. It was just supposed to be Jennie and me. I was happy Jennie's family came.

Then a small tear ran down my face as I realized Jennie was my wife. I turned around to see Jennie standing behind me.

"Are you already regretting this, Dustin?" Jennie asked, rubbing the tear off my face with her thumb.

"No. I always cry at weddings, babe."

We kissed and walked outside with everyone.

"Let's go eat!" Brian said.

"Big Nose Kate's. We're going to walk—we'll meet you there," I said.

Brian got in his car with everyone except Jennie, Max, Linda, and me. They drove off, and I laughed because the restaurant was so close.

Then it started to hail—small ice pellets raining from the sky.

"Make it stop, Dustin!" Jennie said.

I grabbed Max and Jennie by the hand.

"Run!" I yelled. And we ran for cover at the OK Corral.

We made it inside the OK Corral to escape the hail. A woman working the counter let us know the final gunfight reenactment had been canceled due to weather.

The four of us browsed the souvenirs. I got Max a marshal badge and a silver metal cap gun with a brown plastic belt and holster.

Jennie and Linda walked to the restaurant with Max to meet everyone, and I ducked into a wine store to get Jennie and me a bottle of wine to save and drink on our one-year anniversary. The brand was Passion Cellars—one of the bottles we had in Jerome. The clerk let me know the winery was in Camp Verde, but the grapes were grown not too far from Tombstone, near Patagonia. I paid $60 for the bottle and went to meet everyone across the street at Big Nose Kate's.

Big Nose Kate's was named after Doc Holliday's girlfriend, Kate, who had a knack for getting her nose into everyone's business—thus the nickname "Big Nose Kate." Kate never owned the bar; it was just named after her. The bar was originally called the Grand Hotel and opened in 1880. The Grand was one of the finest hotels in the state. Doc and Wyatt frequented the hotel. The Grand caught fire and burned down in 1882, and the long bar was the only thing to survive.

I walked up to the long bar where Wyatt and Doc once stood and ordered a shot of Bulleit bourbon. I had heard once that it's called a "shot" because in the Old West, bullets were the same as currency and you could pay for a whiskey with a bullet from your belt. I took my shot and paid cash.

At the table, Max was getting his gun out of the packaging. Noah, Cameron, and Sophie were on their phones, and all the adults studied the menu. I didn't need a menu—I knew I was getting the Reuben.

Linda ordered champagne for everyone, and we toasted. Brian and I got some tall draft beers. After we ordered, I took Max outside so he could shoot his cap gun.

Max started blasting his cap gun on Allen Street as soon as we walked onto the wood deck boardwalk. Smoke left his silver-colored revolver, and the smell of firework gunpowder was pleasant—it reminded me of the cap gun fights I had in the streets with my friends as a child.

"Max, don't shoot the window," I said.

"It's not a real gun, Dustin," Max replied, then fired near a man walking down the middle of the street dressed as a cowboy with a red sash.

The man fell to the ground.

"Dang it, son, will ya watch where you shoot that dang thing?" the cowboy said.

Max just stared at his gun, mouth wide open, smoke leaving the chamber. The cowboy got up and brushed himself off.

"Max, say you're sorry," I said.

"I'm sorry," Max said.

The cowboy tipped his hat and walked along. The people of Tombstone are great fun. Max reloaded his cap gun with another red ring and just shot at the birds this time.

"I keep missing," Max said.

"Just keep trying, and stay away from the windows."

"Okay."

After a couple more reloads, we went inside to eat. The food was waiting for us at the table when we got there. Brian and I had another tall draft after dinner, then Brian paid the tab.

After Big Nose Kate's, we walked down Allen Street to the Birdcage Theater, which is now a museum but was once the center of town for shows, food, hookers, drinking, and gambling. It was all of Las Vegas under one roof. We took the tour of the building, and Max walked with his cap gun drawn to shoot ghosts.

After the tour, Brian and Linda took everyone back to their hotel, and Jennie and I walked to our cabin and swung on the porch swing, enjoying the sunset with glasses of cheap wine.

The sun was gone and it got cold, so Jennie went inside to change and I followed her. The movie Tombstone was playing on the TV.

"That movie was playing at Big Nose Kate's," Jennie said.

"It's playing everywhere in town. Let's go to another bar?" I said.

"I'm your huckleberry," Jennie replied.

"Wait, we have to consummate the marriage first."

"You're a daisy if you do."

"Babe, is that a yes or no? I believe that's a death threat?" I asked.

Then Jennie led me into the room near the futon couch.

"Bunk beds, babe?" I asked.

Then Jennie pushed me onto the bed.

"I'm on top!" she shouted.

We made our marriage official by making love in bunk beds, then made our way back down Allen Street to Virgil's Bar. Everything in Tombstone is named after someone associated with the gunfight at the OK Corral.

We were playing a game as we walked down Allen Street, telling each other what one celebrity we were allowed to sleep with. Jennie's was very boring—Brad Pitt. Mine was Jodi Arias.

"Isn't that the girl who stabbed her boyfriend to death in Mesa?" Jennie asked.

"Yeah, but she's hot."

"How would you murder me?" Jennie asked as we walked into the old western-themed bar and sat at the bar.

Immediately I said, "I'd strangle you with a Slim Jim—your favorite snack—and talk like The Macho Man the whole time."

Just then, a female bartender came up to us. She was a big woman, missing a few teeth, dressed like a hooker from the 1880s. She was really nice though.

"What'll you have?" she asked.

"Old fashioned for me—Bulleit bourbon—and a Tito's vodka cran for my wife."

The bartender started making my drink by pouring crushed ice into a plastic cup. I hated it already. Before I could say anything, she asked, "What brings you to Tombstone on a Wednesday evening?"

"We just got married today at the courthouse," Jennie said.

"Congratulations," said an older couple at the end of the bar. "Put those on our tab," they added.

We told the couple thank you. Then I noticed the bartender pouring heavily into my drink—bitters and simple syrup. She didn't know what she was doing. But at least I didn't have to pay for it. The bartender dropped off our drinks.

"Congratulations. I've been married five times. Hell, killed one of them," the bartender said as she walked away.

A man at the end of the bar, sitting alone, said, "I remember that."

"Welcome to Tombstone," I whispered in Jennie's ear.

Jennie was very interested in what the bartender had said.

"What happened?" Jennie asked the bartender.

"Me and my husband were doing the nasty before my shift, and he started moving all crazy, so I finished up and told him to do the dishes on my way out the door. When I got home, the dishes weren't done and his lazy ass was still in bed. I started to yell at him, then I realized he was dead. Poor son of a bitch was having a heart attack while we had sex."

The bartender walked off to get the man at the end of the bar another beer.

"That! That is how I kill you, Dustin," Jennie said.

The line from the movie Tombstone that Doc Holliday said to Big Nose Kate popped into my head: "It's true, you are a good woman. You may also be the Antichrist."

My drink sat in front of me untouched. The couple that bought our drinks raised their cups for a toast, so I raised mine, but I didn't drink it.

"Drink your drink," Jennie said.

"I don't want it."

"Don't be rude. Those people bought them for us."

"No. I don't want it."

"All the Jägerbombers you made me drink in Flagstaff?"

"It's okay. You don't have to drink it. I don't mind if my husband is a little bitch."

I raised my cup to Jennie and chugged the whole drink, then spit some ice back into the plastic cup. The bartender saw my empty cup.

"Make you another?"

"No, I'll take a bottle of Coors Light, please."

I grabbed my phone, pretending I was getting a call, and walked outside.

"Where are you going?" Jennie asked.

"My mom is calling."

"Tell her I said hi."

I walked out of the bar and into the dark dirt street of Tombstone. No one was around, and I vomited bitters and simple syrup onto the historic Allen Street. I was sure Doc Holliday had vomited a few times on these streets as well.

I wiped my face and went back into the bar and sat with Jennie and drank my beer. The beer was cold and smooth, and I finished it in two drinks, then ordered another.

"Are you thirsty?" Jennie asked.

"I just threw up."

Jennie laughed at me. "You didn't have to drink it if it was that bad, Dustin."

"Now I'm hungry. Let's go to Doc's. They still serve food."

Jennie paid for my beers and we left the bar, walking east on Allen Street.

We walked into the bar where there was one man singing karaoke and another couple at the end of the bar. I pulled a $100 bill out of the ATM. We sat down at the cash-only bar and I ordered two Jägerbombers.

"No, baby," Jennie said.

"Okay, just one. I don't mind if my wife is a little bitch."

Jennie glared at me. "How about two shots of Patrón Silver?"

"Deal," I said.

"Salt and lime?" the bartender asked.

"Not for me, but training wheels for my husband."

"We'll also take two vodka Red Bulls and a Tombstone supreme pizza."

The bartender walked away to get our shots.

"They really make Tombstone pizzas here?"

"Yes. After the silver mines ran dry in the 1950s, the town started making frozen pizzas. It's the number one export of Tombstone. Tourism and pizza are what keep this town alive."

"I've been eating Tombstone pizza my whole life. I had no idea they made them here—or how they got their name."

I couldn't keep a straight face and started laughing as the bartender dropped off our shots.

"You're lying, aren't you?" Jennie asked.

"No, I'm teasing."

"I believed you!"

"Cheers, Mrs. Elkin."

"It's not nice to tease your wife."

We took our shots of Patron and I laughed.

"Do you want to go back to the cabin and have sex right now?" Jennie said.

I started pulling money out of my wallet to leave for the bartender.

"What are you doing, Dustin?"

"Paying the tab."

"We haven't even got our drinks or pizza—oh, the sex? Yeah, I was teasing."

"When I tease it's funny. When you tease, it's just mean."

The bartender brought our drinks and then our pizza. We enjoyed the lonely karaoke singer serenading us with Billy Joel's The Piano Man. We had more shots of Patron and drinks until the pizza was gone, then I paid cash and we walked outside to the empty, dark dirt street. There were no streetlights, and the only building that had lights on was another bar—The Crystal Palace.

We walked down the middle of the dirt road, arms locked, and passed the bar, then past the OK Corral and back to our cabin. Once inside, I opened the bottle of champagne.

"I'm going to put on something comfortable," Jennie said and slipped into the room with the bunk beds.

I was excited. It was our wedding night and I wondered what she was putting on for me. I looked for some glasses to pour the champagne into and found some in the cabinet by the sink. They weren't champagne glasses, but they would do. I filled the glasses with champagne, then turned to see Jennie. She was wearing Ugg boots with loose sweatpants, a loose t-shirt, and a white fluffy jacket that made her look like a sheep.

"Babe, I thought you were putting on some lingerie?" I said.

"Nope, it's cold. I have some in my bag you can wear."

I took pictures of her with my phone to remember the moment.

"Stop!" Jennie shouted.

I stopped taking pictures, then handed her a glass of champagne.

"We didn't have a first dance, Dustin."

I took out my phone and played Can't Help Falling In Love. It was Eddie Vedder covering the Elvis song. We put the drinks on the table and slowly danced around the small cabin.

"You dance like an 8th grader at the Christmas formal," Jennie said.

"Dancing is like NASCAR—I only go left."

The song finished, then Jennie looked on her phone to play another song. I saw the Hostess cupcakes on the table and went to get them. I opened them and walked over to Jennie, who was looking at her phone.

"Hey, babe!" I said, then smeared the cupcake on her face. We didn't have a wedding cake. Jennie laughed, then punched me in the stomach. I leaned over and she took the cake off her face and wiped it on mine. I took out the other cupcake.

"No, don't waste it, baby. I want to eat it," Jennie said.

I handed Jennie the single cupcake, then turned to get our drinks. I turned back around and Jennie smashed the cupcake in my face.

"Sucker!" Jennie said.

"I am a sucker. I married you."

"I really fucking love you, baby."

Jennie swearing while saying she loved me made it feel like more than just "I love you."

"I really fucking love you, babe," I said, then I kissed her with Hostess cake on my face.

We woke up in the morning and Jennie didn't feel well. Our sheets were wet from her sweating during the night. I packed up the room while Jennie lay on the futon. We were too drunk the night before to try and climb up the ladder to the queen bed, so we slept on the futon.

Brian and Linda took the kids for the night so that Jennie and I could be alone on our first night as man and wife in our house. Jennie was tired and slept most of the way home. When we got home, I unpacked, then Jennie and I watched TV in bed all day. She didn't know what was wrong. She said she just didn't feel well—like something was off.

Chapter 24
Valentine Day

Jennie and the kids moved in that weekend. I had emptied my office for the boys' room, and Sophie took over the guest room. Noah argued that he wanted his own room even though he shared a room with Max at their grandparents' house. Noah didn't think it was fair that Sophie got her own room.

I got another Scion XB. The car had saved my life, so I wanted the same car. Toyota had discontinued the model, so the only one I could find was used, on Carvana. I got a white one this time—a slightly newer 2015 model. I took the used car to my friends at AAMCO Mechanics to look it over. The alignment was off, and the paint had some problems. My friends told me the paint on the bumper didn't match the white on the rest of the car and that Carvana had probably replaced it. My friends at AAMCO found me another Scion XB on the Carvana website—this one black—so I asked to trade it in. Carvana has a 10-day return policy.

Carvana brought the black Scion to my house and took away the white one.

"I wish Carvana had married us," I said to Jennie.

"Why?"

"So I could trade you in for a black one too."

Jennie rolled her eyes, then got in the car with the kids and Chichi to go for a ride. We went to get donuts at Bosa Donuts, then stopped at the Circle K for sodas.

"Can I get water?" Noah asked.

"No, get a soda," I said.

Noah came back with a bottle of FIJI water.

"Sodas are a dollar. I'm not paying $5 for water. Put it back. We have bottled water at home."

Noah got a Polar Pop cup and filled it. When we got home, I found out he filled it with water from the soda fountain.

"Noah!" I said.

"I wanted water!"

"Then don't get anything!"

"You said fill up my cup!"

"No I didn't."

That day I had to set up the boys' bunk beds. I had no directions, just fifty pieces of wood and two hundred bolts and screws. Jennie was tired and lay in our bed watching TV. It took me about five hours to put the bunk beds together, and I even had extra pieces. Max climbed up the ladder and it fell off. I fixed it. The room was too small for the bunk beds. The ceiling fan hung slightly over Max's top bunk. I found this out when the fan hit Max on the head.

"Let's just not turn the fan on, guys," I said.

The next week was the Super Bowl, and Valentine's Day the next day on Monday. I was cleaning the house Sunday morning, getting ready for my Super Bowl party. I had the sink running when I heard Jennie.

"Come into the bedroom. I want to give you your Valentine's Day present early while the kids are gone with my mom."

"Babe, I'm cleaning."

"It will only take a minute," Jennie said.

I thought to myself, Valentine's Day present, kids are gone, only take a minute? Jennie wanted to have sex! I left the sink running and ran into the bedroom to find my beautiful wife on our bed with a book. It was a children's book by Shel Silverstein—The Missing Piece.

Jennie saw the disappointment on my face.

"You don't like it?" Jennie said.

"No, I love it. I just thought you meant sex "

"It's my favorite book. I wrote in the book for you."

"I'll read it after sex."

"Baby!"

"I'll read it now."

Jennie wrote: Dustin, Thank you for being the most amazing person. Thank you for making me smile. Thank you for always holding my hand. Thank you for all the kisses. Thank you for always holding me. Thank you for you! You are my piece. I love you, Jennie.

I went into our closet and brought out her present since we were doing Valentine's Day presents early. Jennie hated flowers as a gift, so I got her a flower vase with the bottom filled with one of her favorite things in the world—Carmex—and instead of long-stem roses, I put a dozen Slim Jims.

"I love it! Will you read the book to me?" Jennie asked.

"Now?" I asked.

"You don't like it?"

"No, I love it. I will read it now." And I read it to her, starting with, It was a missing piece and wasn't happy…

It was the story of a Pac-Man-shaped figure in search of its missing piece to be whole. Sometimes it thought it had found the right piece, but it wasn't perfect and rolled on until it found its missing piece and they were perfect together. They fit perfectly, and the two pieces had fun until one day the Pac-Man-looking figure had to let go.

"You are my missing piece. There are blank pages at the end. Will you fill them out for me and finish the story, Dustin?"

"Of course, babe." And we started kissing.

"What's that noise?" Jennie asked.

"I don't hear anything." I kept kissing Jennie.

"No really, it sounds like a waterfall," Jennie said.

I ran to the kitchen and the sink had been overflowing for a while, and water was coming out of the lower cabinets as well as overflowing the sink. The entire kitchen was soaked. But it did smell like Fabuloso.

There was a knock at the door. My friends were showing up for the Super Bowl party. Jennie let them in and they all laughed at me as I slipped on the floor and grabbed every towel in the house to soak the water up. Once the floor was dry, I started a fire in my Weber grill to cook the carne asada. More friends showed up and I made us all tacos as we played cornhole in the backyard and waited for the Super Bowl to start.

The Super Bowl party was just like the many Super Bowl parties I had thrown in the past. Everyone ate and drank and paid little attention to the game but looked forward to the Super Bowl halftime show. This year was one of the biggest halftime shows of my life: Eminem, Snoop Dogg, and Dr. Dre!

Jennie led me away from the group of people and toward our bedroom.

"Babe, we're going to miss the halftime show," I said.

"It's football season. Time to run the two-minute drill."

"I can do that."

We snuck into the room and locked the door and were back out into the party before anyone missed us. Linda had brought the kids back to our house and stayed for some tacos. The Rams ended up defeating the Bengals, then my friends all slowly made their way home.

I decided I would clean up the next day since it was Monday and my day off. It was also Valentine's Day, so I put out candy boxes we had gotten for the kids on the counter next to their lunch bags Jennie had made for them. Max was in our bed watching TV with Jennie, and we let him stay until he fell asleep. Then I carried him to his room and bed on the top bunk.

When I came back to the room, Jennie had Chichi in bed with her. Jennie had stolen my heart—and my dog. Chichi had to sleep wedged between Jennie and me in bed every night.

I woke up at 6 a.m. to the sound of Jennie blow-drying her hair and the boys yelling that Sophie had them locked out of their bathroom. The three kids shared the guest bathroom that was small, with a bathtub/shower, toilet, and one sink. I let the boys into our room to get ready since we had two sinks. I brought Jennie some coffee.

She had started working as a substitute teacher at Patterson Elementary with her mom. Jennie was working with special needs students. There was a shortage of teachers, so they hired her on for the rest of the year. Jennie left first for school, then Sophie for her bus stop. The boys were last to leave.

My house was closer to their school than their grandparents', so the bus didn't get them and they had to walk.

"Can't you just give us a ride?" Noah moaned.

"The school drop-off is a nightmare! It takes less time for you to walk than it does for me to drop you off."

"I like walking," Max said.

"Max likes it," I said.

"Max sings the whole walk to school!" Noah said.

"Good job, Max. You guys need to go. I'll see you after school. I love you," I said.

"Love you," they said, walking out the door.

The house was still a mess from the party. I chugged my now-cold coffee and started cleaning. I finished cleaning around ten, and Jennie texted me.

"What are we doing tonight for Valentine's? My mom said they would take the kids to dinner so we could do something."

"Taking you to a wine bar, then we can walk to the lake and share a bottle of wine and one of those adult Lunchables."

"A charcuterie board?"

"Yes. The one from Four Silos that you love."

"I'll be home at 3:30. I have bus duty today."

I decided to be productive and went to the gym. I sat in the parking lot of the gym on my phone for five minutes, then drove home. That was enough gym for the day.

On the way home, I stopped at an adult store on Gilbert Road called Groove. It was Valentine's Day and I was married, but I felt weird walking in. I had only been in an "adult" store twice in my life. Once when I was 18, and it was to get my brother a porno on VHS. I picked Debbie Does Dallas—a classic. The other time was with a girl I was dating. She thought she was funny and suggested this bong-shaped object. I asked if she wanted to smoke weed. She laughed and said no, it's a penis pump. So I yelled across the store to an employee,

"Do you have any vagina shrinkers? I'd like to make hers smaller." We broke up soon after that.

I was walking around the store and an attractive young lady came up to me and asked if I needed any help. I showed her my wedding ring like a cop flashing his badge so she knew I was legit.

"I'm looking for something for my wife."

"What does she like?"

"I don't know."

"What do you like?"

"I like naked. Do you have anything like the Emperor's new clothes?"

I wanted to get out of the store. I felt uncomfortable, surrounded by sexy hot mannequins wearing lingerie, staring and judging me. I asked the lady what she thought was fun, and she showed me. Then I took it up front and paid for it with cash so my bank didn't know I was a pervert.

I got home, showered, and changed to go get things for our date. I was wearing jeans, my Air Jordan 4s, a black trucker hat, loc sunglasses, and a Dixxon flannel that was checkered red and white. I took a picture in the mirror and sent it to Jennie since I thought I looked good. Jennie called me right away.

"You need to change. You look like a cholo picnic table," Jennie said and hung up.

I looked back in the mirror. I did look like a cholo picnic table. So I changed and went to the store for a bottle of wine and some chocolate, then to Four Silos for the charcuterie board. I had a beer while I waited for the staff to make the charcuterie board. I came home and enjoyed the silence of the house for an hour before the kids came home. I liked the silence, but I also liked the noise of bickering kids.

The kids came home and ate their Valentine's Day candy from school before Linda came to get them. Jennie showed up after Linda, then went to the room to change.

"We have two hours," Jennie said.

"I only need a minute."

"For our date, not sex, nerd."

"Let's get going," I said and slapped her on the ass.

I opened her car door for her, then we got in and I drove to the Divided Vine beer and wine bar. Jennie ordered a glass of white wine, and I ordered an IPA that was 11%. Jennie took some Tylenol from her purse to take with her wine.

"Are you okay?" I asked.

"Yes, I think I'm going through menopause."

"At forty?" I asked.

"I had my tubes tied after Max, remember? I read that can cause you to start menopause early. I think that's why I've been sweating at night in bed."

"You can still get pregnant though," I said.

"There's like a 1% chance," Jennie said.

"I'm 50% Mexican, babe. Trump can build a wall and your doctor can tie your tubes, but we're still getting in."

Jennie smiled and rubbed my head. "How does your brain come up with this stuff?"

"I was thinking if we did have a kid together, we could give him a good Jewish and Mexican name," I said.

"Like what?"

"Moses, Emmanuel, or Jesus."

Jennie laughed. "I wish I could give you a baby."

"You did. You gave me three, and I never had to change a diaper."

Jennie smiled and said, "I wish we waited to give each other our presents today."

"I have more presents," I said, and slid her my phone, which was opened to the Quay sunglasses website—her favorite sunglasses.

"Really?" Jennie asked excitedly.

"Yes, pick a pair."

Jennie handed me my phone back.

"You don't want a pair?"

"No, I do. I already knew which ones I wanted. Put in your credit card info, baby."

I paid for the sunglasses, then our drinks, and we drove back home to walk to the lake. I went inside to get the charcuterie board that was in a pizza box and my backpack with the Batman blanket inside and wine glasses. I also grabbed a beer from the fridge. I put the pizza box down out front and locked the door, then held Jennie's hand and we walked to the lake.

We got to the lake, and I took out the blanket and laid it on the grass for Jennie to sit on.

"I forgot the charcuterie board!" I said.

"Babe."

"I'll be right back. Pick some music on your phone for us to listen to."

I finished my beer and jogged home to get the pizza box that was sitting outside the door. I opened the door and grabbed another beer. Chichi saw me in the refrigerator, and I grabbed a piece of cheese from the refrigerator for her, then walked fast instead of jogging. I was tired.

I got back to the lake to find Jennie sitting on the blanket.

"I got it," I said.

"Did you get a wine opener?" Jennie asked, holding the unopened bottle.

"Seriously?"

"Give me your beer."

I handed Jennie my beer and turned around to jog home one more time. I went into the house, grabbed the wine opener from the drawer, another beer, and another piece of cheese for Chichi, and walked back to the lake.

"Got it," I showed Jennie the wine opener.

"Sit with me."

I sat with Jennie and opened the wine, then filled our glasses.

"Thank you, Dustin. This is perfect."

We sat on a grassy knoll with a view of the million-dollar homes on the lake. We could see the Superstition Mountains behind the houses, and there was an early moon rising with the sun still out.

I didn't say anything; I just rolled back to lay on the blanket. Jennie laughed.

"I signed up for Pat's Run in April. You should probably get in shape before my seventy-year-old dad beats you."

"Thanks, that's the motivation I needed. Don't lose to the seventy-year-old."

"My dad's in really good shape, so don't take it too hard when he does."

We lay on the blankets for a while until the sun started to go down and cast a shadow over the lake. One by one, the stars started to appear and the moon was now over the Superstition Mountains to the east.

"My mom just texted to say she is at our house with the kids, but to take our time—she will stay there with them."

"Give me your phone. It's my turn to pick a song."

I took her phone and played the Beach Boys' "God Only Knows What I'd Be Without You."

"I love this song," Jennie said.

We listened to the song while drinking our wine on the blanket in the grass. Then we listened to a few more songs and had another glass of wine.

"Can you believe we grew up here, and we ended up here together?" Jennie said.

"Sometimes it doesn't feel real. Like I'm going to wake up and everything was a dream."

"What would you do if you woke up and it was a dream, Dustin?"

"I'd message you on Facebook and ask if you'd like to come over to make tacos."

"Good answer," Jennie said and kissed me.

I looked up to the lake and stopped kissing Jennie and asked, "What house do you want, babe?" as I pointed to the houses on the lake.

"The big one straight across with the pool and the swim-up bar. What about you?"

"The one with the big windows in the living room. So even when we are inside, we can see the lake."

"We never see anyone that owns one of those houses sitting outside enjoying their backyard the way we enjoy looking at their backyards. It's a shame. We'd be out there every night. It's too bad we could never afford one of those houses on the lake, with me being a teacher and you a hairdresser. We'd have to win the lottery to ever have one of those houses. But still—it's nice to look at them."

"I stopped playing the lottery when I fell in love with you, Jennie."

"You're so cheesy, Dustin! Oh, why? Because I'm your lottery prize?"

"No, because if I ever won 300 million dollars, I'd leave you."

"Dustin!" Jennie yelled playfully and slapped my shoulder, then said, "You would not."

"Yes I would."

"And what would you spend your money on, babe?"

"Hookers and blow."

Jennie laughed and said, "You're a jerk."

"That's the problem with you women. All you heard was I'd leave you."

"That's what you said."

"What I said was I don't play the lottery because I'd rather have you than 300 million dollars."

Jennie's eyes tightened and she smiled as she sipped her wine and said, "What if you won the lottery and bought a house on the lake, then we gave the rest to charidi—didity—Love is what I got, it's within my reach and the Sublime style's still straight from Long Beach…"

I started to say, "It all comes back to you, you're bound to get what you deserve…"

Then the two of us finished with, "Try and test that, you're bound to get served. Love's what I got, don't start a riot. You'll feel it when the dance gets hot."

"Lovin' is what I got…"

"Come on, Dustin, let's go. My mom was being nice. I know she wants to go home and go to bed."

I packed up our things, and we walked back home and put the kids to bed. Then I got in bed with Jennie and gave her my present from Groove. She opened it.

"What is it, babe?" she asked.

"Cordless vibrating panties," I said.

"Are you trying to shock my hoo-ha?"

"Yeah, you'll look like Billy Idol in the video on top of the building

215

yelling mo, mo, mo, mo, mo, mo!"

"You're thinking of the video 'Dancing with Myself.' He says mo, mo, mo in 'Rebel Yell.' Anyway, how does this work?"

"I don't know. It has a remote. I thought you could wear them when we go miniature golfing. Please don't make me go back to the store and ask."

"I'll text Ashley. She will know."

"You have a dildo technician?"

"It's Valentine's Day, and I have another present for you."

Jennie started kissing me and turned the TV on loud. Then my leg cramped up from running and walking back and forth, and Jennie had to rub it.

"My dad is going to beat you."

"Can you not mention your dad when we are naked in bed?"

I went to kiss Jennie again, then my other leg cramped up too.

"Hookers and blow my ass. Give it up, loverboy. You're done," Jennie said.

Chapter 25

They say It's Your Birthday, It's my birthday too

Saturday, February 19th, I woke up in bed to the kids yelling, "Happy birthday!" in my face.

I looked at Jennie, confused.

"Sorry, Dustin, it was their idea. Happy birthday, baby." Jennie then handed me my morning coffee.

"What do you want to do?" Noah asked.

"Go back to bed," I said, placing my coffee down on the nightstand and laying back down in bed.

"No! Get up, get up, get up, it's your birthday," Max said while jumping on the bed.

"What time is it?" I asked.

"Seven," Noah said.

"Why are you up this early on a Saturday? I can't get you up this early for church on Sundays."

Noah joined Max in jumping on the bed and said, "Because church is boring."

I threw the blanket over them, then pulled them to the bed and trapped the two boys between my legs with a move I called the scissors. My dad used to use this move on my brother and me when we were kids.

"If you guys get out in 30 seconds, I'll get up," I said as the boys squirmed like flies caught in a spider's web. Jennie walked back into the room.

"Mom, help!" Max yelled.

"What's she going to do? Mom can't help you," I laughed.

Jennie walked up and grabbed my nipple, then twisted it. I immediately let the boys free and yelled, "Ouch!"

"Get up, I'm hungry," Jennie said.

Fearing another titty twister, I got out of bed and kicked the boys out of the room so I could take a shower and change. I wanted to go to breakfast at the Black Bear restaurant, but the kids outvoted Jennie and me, and we went to IHOP.

During breakfast, we planned our day. The kids wanted to do something fun for my birthday, so I suggested Golfland Family Fun Center. It was a place Jennie and I hung out at in high school. They had miniature golf, laser tag, bumper boats, and, most importantly, go-karts.

After breakfast, we went home to wait for Golfland to open. Jennie had to run to her parents' house to finish my birthday present. She left me with the kids and asked if I would cut Max's hair while she was gone. I put Max in the salon chair in the living room that I had moved from my office.

"Get in, Max," I said.

"Do I have to?"

"You heard the boss."

"Mom is your boss too?"

"I don't have a boss."

"Then why are you doing what Mom said?"

"Because she is the boss, OK?" I said.

"Can I cut Max's hair?" Sophie asked.

"I want to cut his hair too," Noah said.

"OK, we can all cut Max's hair," I said.

I took my clippers out and put a three guard on them to start Max's fade, and I showed Sophie and Noah how to start at the bottom with the clippers in their right hand and work their way up while using their left hand with a comb in it and pulling the comb down. They each took turns on Max's head.

"Your dad's mom and dad cut hair, and my mom cut hair too. So it's good you guys learn. You can cut your friends' hair in high school and make money."

"Is that what you did?" Noah asked.

"Yes. In high school, my friend's mom gave him $10 and told him to go get his haircut at Great Clips and leave the change for a tip. Neither of us had any money, so I told him I'd cut it for $5 and he could keep the other $5. Then we bought Mickeys with the money."

"What's a Mickey?" Max asked.

"It's like Prime. OK, give me the clippers. I'm going to finish—your mom will be home soon."

Jennie came into the room with a wrapped box. "Happy birthday, baby."

The kids ran to their rooms and came back with drawings of Marvel and DC comics and told me, "Happy birthday."

I opened Jennie's gift, and it was a shadow box frame with an old atlas map of Arizona, and she had placed a pin at every place I had taken her in Arizona.

"I love this, babe!"

"You really do?" Jennie asked.

"Yes, this is so cool. Let's fill the map with pins! Hey—Prescott?"

"I didn't put a pin there because we didn't go there."

"I know. I mean, I have never taken anyone to Prescott. I have never stayed the night in Prescott. Let's go there next."

"A place Dustin Elkin hasn't taken a girl? Must not be haunted," Jennie said.

"It's haunted. I'm just obsessed with Jerome."

"I'll go anywhere haunted with you, Dustin."

Looking at the map, I said, "I've never stayed in Tucson either."

"We can skip Tucson, baby."

"Let's go to Golfland first! Kids, let's go!"

And we all piled into the car and drove to Mesa for birthday fun in a fake castle.

We started with a round of outdoor miniature golf. Jennie won. Then we went inside the castle for laser tag. It was still pretty early on a Saturday, and we were the only ones in the laser tag arena. The five of us walked into the smoke-filled, glow-in-the-dark, blacklight medieval-themed battleground with knights and green dragons. We waited for the countdown to run and hide.

I was a little sour about Jennie winning in miniature golf, so I told the kids, "Whoever shoots Mom the most gets $20."

"You can't do that, Dustin!" Jennie said.

"There's no love in war, Jennie. See you on the flip side."

The game siren went off, and the five of us ran loose in the arena, seeking cover until the siren stopped and the game started. This was a chance to show the kids and my wife that I was the head of the household. That I was the alpha male. That I was the boss.

My harness lit up and I was hit.

"Got you, baby!" Jennie said from the first floor, looking up at me.

I yelled to the kids, "Mom's by the dragon—get her!"

Jennie screamed and ran away with her gun in the air.

I ran down the stairs and chased Jennie into a corner.

"Dustin, do you even know the first rule of being a parent?"

I had my laser gun drawn on Jennie. "Always say 'no' first when the kids ask for something," I said.

"That's rule #2. Rule #1 is it's me and you against the kids, always."

My harness lit up again and I was shot.

"Jennie!" I said.

"It wasn't me, it was Sophie," Jennie said.

"Let's get them."

Jennie and I rolled through the maze like a SWAT team, taking out Max and Sophie one at a time, but we couldn't find Noah.

"Has anyone seen Noah?" I shouted.

"Noah!" Everyone yelled. There was no response.

The game ended and the lights turned on, then Noah came out.

"Where were you?" Jennie asked.

"I was hiding. I didn't want to get hit. Lasers hurt."

The computer was down, so we couldn't see who won, and we moved back downstairs to get tickets for the go-karts.

Max was too short, so he would ride with me. Noah was questionable, so we measured him. He was a few inches too short, but he wouldn't believe me, so I took a picture with my phone to show him.

"It's because you took the picture with an Android! Why can't you get an iPhone like everyone else, Dustin!" Noah said.

"So my phone made you shorter?" I asked.

"Noah, you should eat your vegetables so you can get bigger," Max said, with his mother's grin on his face.

Max was getting payback for not being able to ride the giant swings at the fair.

"Just ride with your mom or Sophie."

"I want my own go-kart."

"Then you don't get to ride and you can sit and wait for us," Jennie said.

"Fine," Noah said and walked away.

I walked after him.

"Dustin, let him go. He has to learn he can't always get his way," Jennie said.

Noah took a seat in the bleachers, and the four of us stood in line. I looked at Max's hair and his bangs were cut in one spot really short. Jennie noticed too.

"Dustin, I thought you cut his hair?"

"I didn't do that."

"Dustin let Sophie and Noah cut my hair, but I didn't get to cut my hair, so I got Dustin's scissors and cut my hair too," Max said.

"Team building, Jennie. It will grow back," I said.

We climbed into our go-karts and put our seatbelts on, then waited for the green flag. Max and I against Sophie and Jennie. Max and I were off to a lead and lapped Jennie on the second lap.

"Hi, Mom," Max said as we passed her. Jennie had both hands on the steering wheel and screamed as we passed her. She was such a bad driver. Sophie stayed behind me, and I swerved left and right so she couldn't pass. Eventually, I let her pass on the inside, and she yelled at us as she passed. I saw Noah in the stands sitting alone. I could tell by the look on his face he wished he had ridden with us.

The emergency siren went off, and all of our go-karts stopped. Jennie had spun backwards on a turn, and they had to flip her around. Then we went for two more laps before pulling back into the parking bay.

"Noah, are you ready to have fun?" I asked.

"Yes, I'm sorry," he said.

"Ok, bumper boats!"

We walked back through the castle and past the mini golf course to the bumper boats. Noah was tall enough, but Max was not. Jennie sat with Max, and the other two kids and I each got in our own bumper boat.

"Do you guys want the water guns turned on?" the Golfland employee asked.

The whole group shouted, "Yes!" and the water fight was on.

Just like in laser tag, Noah took off to hide behind an island in the shallow pool.

"Sophie, let's get him!"

"Oh, yeah," Sophie said.

We cornered Noah and blasted him from both sides with our cannons, and he spun in circles trying to avoid the water.

"Stop! I'm getting wet," Noah said.

"Shoot back, Noah!" Sophia shouted.

Noah got away from us and went to the other end of the pool, but we chased him down.

"Dustin! Get Sophie too!" Noah shouted.

"Ok," I said, and I turned my water cannon on Sophie.

"Dustin! Not my hair!" she screamed.

Jennie and Max stood at the fence laughing.

"Get Sophie's hair, Dustin!" Max yelled.

"Max! Stop," Sophie said.

"I'm not even playing, Sophie," Max said.

Noah took this opportunity to escape, but I tracked him down and soaked him again. He was saved by his sister coming to his rescue for payback on me for getting her hair wet.

"Noah, use your cannon!" Sophie yelled. He did.

The two of them had their cannons on me, and I was getting soaked and ran for cover.

"Don't let Dustin get away," Noah said, and the two of them chased me across the pool in their bumper boats until I was cornered. I had my last stand and blasted them with water left to right as they blasted me back.

The siren sounded, and the water guns turned off. We were told over a loudspeaker to return back to the dock. We exited the gates, and Jennie took pictures of us. The kids were wet and miserable, and I was having the best birthday ever.

We went home to rest for a few hours. I usually spend my birthday snowboarding at Snowbowl in Flagstaff because they give you a free ski pass on your birthday. Then I'd spend the evening in downtown Gilbert drinking at the bars with my friends. For the first time in my life, I had a family of my own, so I wanted to spend it with them—but I also wanted to drink. Fat Cats was an easy compromise. Two family fun centers in one day. I like to party.

The sun was starting to go down, and the kids wanted to walk. It was just a mile away down the greenbelt. Jennie looked tired, but she agreed since the kids were excited to walk. I put on my favorite Air Jordan 1s and threw some firecrackers in the pocket of my jean jacket, then we started the 20-minute walk. We told Jennie's parents we were walking and to meet us there.

It was Jennie and the kids walking behind me with Sophie's friend, and I randomly threw firecrackers into the air.

"Firecrackers, Dustin? How old are you turning?" Jennie said.

"Age is just a number. I'll be doing this when I'm 80."

"I have a headache. Can you please stop?"

"I'm sorry."

"I'm sorry—usually I would be lighting them with you. I just feel off."

"It's ok. No more, I promise."

"You ran out, didn't you?" Jennie knew me so well.

We walked into the bright casino lights of Fat Cats and met Brian and Linda. My friend Brian Ahsoon was there too. Everyone just called him Ahsoon. Most of the guys I went to high school with all called each other by our last names.

Ahsoon was a 6'0", 350 lb Samoan and the nicest guy in the world, but you didn't want to get on his bad side. One time at the bar Crabby Don's, he knocked out three guys with two punches. When the guys woke up, Ahsoon was gone, and everyone in the bar acted like they didn't see anything.

My brother wasn't at Fat Cats. I hadn't talked to him since New Year's Eve. He woke up that night drunk by the fire with a light rain on him, then started yelling at me for posting too much stuff on Facebook and other things he had built up towards me. My mom's boyfriend drove him home to separate us. He still hadn't called to say congratulations on getting married. Two of my best friends, Jeff and Lethan, couldn't make it because something came up last minute with their families.

There are a few times when I get really drunk. The first is at any wedding with an open bar—or any party with an open bar, for that matter—and the other is on my birthday. My alter ego, Dusty McAwesome, comes out. That also happens to be what the kids at church call me.

Dusty McAwesome is a lot of fun but also a bit much to handle. Maybe it wasn't an accident Jeff and Lethan couldn't make it? Jennie has met Dusty McAwesome many times since we've partied with each other since high school.

"Please keep Dusty McAwesome away until my parents leave?"

"I can only give you an hour."

"It's Fat Cats!"

"I was kicked out of Peter Piper Pizza on my 21st birthday."

"Oh yeah, I remember that. Didn't you guys start wrestling in the ball pit?"

"You mean Thunderdome? Yes."

"Dustin!"

"One hour, babe."

And I walked to the full bar in the family fun center and had a shot of Jameson and a beer with Jennie's dad. I got each of the kids some game cards and myself one too, then Ahsoon and I went to play the Connect Four basketball game that had drink holders for our beers. It was like they wanted us to party.

We ordered the kids pizzas, pretzels, and chicken fingers. They were having so much fun, you would have thought it was their birthday too. Brian and Linda left after an hour, then Jennie smiled at me and said, "Thank you. Now go and get me a drink."

I got Jennie a shot of Patron Silver and a Stella beer. Ahsoon ordered the two of us something much different—the "beautiful," he called it.

The "beautiful" was a shot of Hennessy and a shot of Grand Marnier on the rocks.

It was like what Dr. Jekyll drank to let Mr. Hyde out—only instead of killing people, he turned into Stifler from the American Pie movies and just wanted to party. After two of those, the next thing I remembered was waking up back home in bed with Jennie staring at me.

"Morning, babe," I said.

"Don't you 'morning babe' me!" Jennie said.

"What did I do?"

"You didn't listen to anything I said last night!"

"I waited an hour?"

"Then I had to practically drag you out to the Uber!"

"We Ubered home?"

"Seriously, you don't remember the high school kid playing the basketball game on a date and you blocked his shot then said, 'No, no, no'?"

"I Dikembe Mutombo'd someone?"

"Oh, the Geico commercial? Ok, that's kind of funny."

"That's it?"

"Then you held Max over the goldfish bowl game so he could drop the balls in the cups."

"I remember that."

"Do you remember me saying to stop and then you charged the kids' cards again?"

"That I do not."

"I was tired and didn't feel good, and I wanted to go home, but you wouldn't listen and had the kids thinking I was the bad one."

"I really am sorry."

"I'm sorry. I wanted to have fun with you, but this stupid headache "

"Menopause?" I asked.

"I think so. Being a girl sucks!"

"Would you feel better if I had sex with you?"

"Dustin!"

"I'll take one for the team."

"You're too much."

"You're too hot. Blame yourself, not me. I'm going to take a shower and get ready for church."

"You're going to church? Aren't you hungover?"

"Extremely. But my pappy Earl always told me, when bad habits get in the way of your good habits, you need to back off on the bad ones. Church is a good habit, so I'm going. Bad habits aren't stopping me today."

"The kids are worn out and still sleeping."

"You guys go ahead and miss church today, and I think you need rest. So when I get back, I'll take the kids out to the park and to get lunch so you can have a quiet house for a few hours."

"I love you."

"Go back to sleep."

"I like the advice your pappy told you. Don't you need to go pick up his truck?"

"Yes, I just talked to my grandma this week. Maybe we can all fly out to L.A. and drive it home when the kids are on spring break next month?"

"That sounds good. You know what sounds better?"

"Sex?"

"No! A breakfast burrito from Filiberto's."

"Okay, I'll bring you one home after church."

Chapter 26
Stepdads Step up

Being a stepdad was nothing like I expected it to be. The hardest part was not eating the kids' Lunchables. You look in the fridge for a midnight snack and those little yellow boxes stand out like gold nuggets in a flowing river. They were like redneck charcuterie boards.

One evening at home, Jennie was laying in bed and I was making dinner when I heard Max scream from the bathroom, "Dustin!"

I ran from the kitchen to the bathroom to help Max, thinking he was in trouble or hurt. Max was standing by the toilet, smiling.

"Look what I did," Max said.

I looked around the room and saw nothing. Then I saw Max pointing at the toilet. My first thought was, Did you try to flush a loaf of bread down the toilet?

Then the smell hit my nostrils. I have a weak stomach, and Max had a problem pooping. He suffered from encopresis, which is basically a fear of pooping. When I started dating Jennie, she let me know that Max sometimes would soil himself because he refused to poop. I felt bad for the kid because I used to poop my pants when I was five. I don't know why—I just didn't want to use a restroom. My parents would find me hiding behind a tree. My favorite place to poop my pants.

I told Max I used to poop my pants when I was his age, but I had to stop because it's gross and if he ever pooped his pants at Fat Cats, they wouldn't let him back. He stopped pooping his pants shortly after. We also gave him a dollar every time he went to the toilet.

The smell of the bathroom was worse than the smell of a porta potty on day three of the Phoenix Waste Management Open. I felt like I was going to throw up. I covered my mouth and nose with my shirt and tried to flush the demon poop down the toilet, but it clogged.

I did the only thing I could think of. I ran out of the house and yelled, "Jennie!"

Jennie came out of our room and I heard, "Good job, Max."

Then Max came up to me outside and asked, "Where's my dollar?"

Another day I was home alone with the kids; Jennie was out tutoring. She still tutored a few kids after school.

Max and Noah were pestering their sister. Instead of putting a stop to it, I joined in.

"Not today, Dustin, I'm PMSing!" Sophie said.

I pulled the boys back and all three of us walked backwards out of the room and to the safety of my room.

"What's PMSing?" Noah asked.

"Do you guys remember COVID? It's kind of like that," I said.

"Is it contagious?" they asked.

"No, but we do need to practice social distance for three to five days. And if you have any chocolate, give it to her. Leave it outside her room like an offering to King Kong."

Another day, Noah came home from school and I happened to be home from work on a lunch break, sitting on the couch.

"Dustin, can you tell if a hundred-dollar bill is fake?" he asked.

"Yes, why?" I said, and Noah handed me a hundred-dollar bill. It was real.

"Did you find this?"

"No, my friend at school was handing them out."

"Handing out hundred-dollar bills?" I said.

Then Noah pulled more cash out of his pocket and said, "This too."

Noah had $160. I remembered when I was in elementary school, a kid was handing out money. Turns out he stole it from his mom. The next day at school, we all had to give it back. It was his mom's grocery money. Kids do really dumb things.

"Noah, we have to give it back."

"He gave it to me!"

"It wasn't his to give."

Jennie walked in the house from school and I explained what was going on. She found out which friend it was, and she happened to tutor the kid. So she called his parents, and they were missing close to $2,000. She let them know they might want to check their son's backpack, and that she would return what Noah had—if she could not say it was Noah who snitched.

Noah was disappointed, sitting on the couch. He had never had that much money in his hands at one time in his life.

"I shouldn't have said anything!" Noah said.

I took my wallet out and gave him a ten-dollar bill.

"That's it?" he said.

Then I pulled a one-dollar bill from my wallet and handed it to him.

"Thanks for pooping in the toilet."

Another day it was just the boys and me. Jennie wanted to go to the store, so I said I'd watch them. After an hour, the boys told me they were starving and wanted Happy Meals from McDonald's. The McDonald's was one block away and the boys were playing video games, so I left them alone for five minutes to get them food.

The Happy Meal only comes with four or six nuggets. McDonald's has a family pack that gives you four large fries and forty nuggets for only $17.99—the same price as two Happy Meals. The boys said they were starving, so I got the family meal. Twenty nuggets each for them.

I brought it home and Max came running to me at the door.

"That's not a Happy Meal!" Max said.

"It's better. You get twenty nuggets and two large fries instead of one small fry and only four nuggets."

Max started crying.

Noah came into the room, grabbed his food, and said, "Thanks, Dustin." Then he walked back to his room.

Max wouldn't stop crying. I tried to make him stop. Then Jennie walked in from the store with bags in her hands.

"What happened?" Jennie asked.

"I didn't get Max a Happy Meal."

"You always get Max a Happy Meal. Go get the rest of the bags from the car, please, Dustin."

I went to the car and got the rest of the bags in one trip, and when I walked in, everyone was smiling and laughing.

"What did you do?" I asked Jennie.

"Max doesn't always open the toy from the Happy Meal, so when he doesn't, I save it and put it in the junk drawer. I pulled one out and gave it to him."

"So when Max cries, we just give in?" I said.

"My dad is coming to take the boys for a couple of hours to the jump park. Then me and you can have sex. Will that make you stop crying?"

"You are my Happy Meal, babe."

"I wish you were a McDonald's," Jennie said.

"Why?"

"So I could supersize it."

"That's not funny."

Chapter 27
Going Back To Cali

I booked a plane ticket to LA for the second weekend of March so I could drive my pap's truck back home to Arizona. Jennie was going to get the kids and herself tickets to fly with me, but she waited a couple of days too long and the prices doubled, so she didn't get them. The kids were on spring break for that week. Max and Noah went with their grandparents to their house in Pinetop for the weekend, and Sophie stayed home with us because she wanted to hang out with her friends.

Jennie and I were laying around the house alone, waiting for me to go to the airport. I had to talk Jennie into giving me a ride to the airport.

"Why don't you just Uber?" Jennie said.

"Because I have a wife that has no plans for the day and is sitting next to me."

"I just hate the airport. I always get stuck and end up driving around two or three times before I get out."

"I'm not going to see you for three days, so I'd like to spend the car ride with you."

"One day. You're coming back on Monday. Today is Saturday, so you won't see me Sunday."

I went to kiss Jennie and she cut the kiss short.

"Honeymoon's over, huh?" I said.

"I really don't feel good. I haven't for a while, babe, I'm sorry."

"You need to see a doctor, babe. We haven't had sex in five days."

"That's not a reason to see a doctor, Dustin."

"It's like ever since we got married, our sex life has gone downhill. I thought this ring was like a Disney FastPass to sex with my wife. I thought I was going to be riding Mr. Toad's Wild Ride twice a day, but instead, it's like being in line for Space Mountain and it's always broken."

"First, Mr. Toad's Wild Ride sucks. Second, even if Space Mountain is broken, it's still the best ride and worth the wait!"

"Sex is just marital maintenance, babe," I said.

"And your check engine light is always on!"

"I can't help it. I'm a Chevy guy, but I'm built like a Ford."

"You do require a lot of maintenance. Want me to check your oil?"

"I'll pass. If I was a Ford, I'd be a Ford MustBANG."

"If I felt better, I'd sleep with you for that one."

"Rain check?"

Jennie kissed me and said, "Rain check."

"But you're taking me to the airport. Come on, I'll drive there."

Jennie still pouted.

"I'll stop and get you a Starbucks."

Jennie smiled and got off the couch and walked with me to the car. After Starbucks, it was a short fifteen-minute drive to Sky Harbor airport. I got out of the car, grabbed my one bag, and kissed my wife goodbye as she got into the driver's seat.

"Good luck getting out of here," I said.

"You have no idea how much I love you to drop you off at the airport!"

"Call your doctor, please."

"I will. I need to see my OB/GYN anyway."

"Yeah, I should see mine too," I said, and walked into the airport toward the self check-in kiosk and then to the security checkpoint, where they made me take off my shoes, chain wallet, and belt. After getting dressed, I went to the bar for overpriced draft beers and stingy-poured shots of whiskey. I was on my second beer when Jennie called.

"I just got home," Jennie said.

I looked at the time on my phone. "You dropped me off an hour and a half ago. Did you stop somewhere?"

"I got stuck in the airport loop and made three laps around before I could get out. Why is Sky Harbor shaped like a racetrack? I ended up on the 17 heading to Flagstaff."

"You really are the worst driver ever."

"I just called to say I'm sorry that I didn't want to take you to the airport. It's just this headache, and I'm tired all the time and cranky, and I threw up today."

"Are you pregnant? I saw two pregnancy tests in the bathroom."

"I can't get pregnant. Those were COVID tests, babe, and I don't have COVID, so we can rule that out. But I'm feeling better now."

"That's good. Hey, they just called my flight for early boarding. I need to chug my beer and go. I love you. I'll text you when I land."

"Airport drinking? Lucky. Have a safe flight. I love you."

I said, "I love you," then hung up my phone, finished my beer, and left cash for my drinks. Then I boarded my flight. I had two beers on the flight that I was supposed to pay for, but we hit some turbulence around Palm Springs and the flight attendants had to sit down and put their seat belts on. They never came back for my payment. Free beer is my favorite beer.

As soon as I landed, I texted Jennie and then my grandma. My grandma left with my uncle to pick me up after I sent the text. They were about thirty minutes away from the airport, and it'd take about that long for me to get to the airport pickup curb.

After I picked up my bag, I walked outside of the Ontario airport and only had to wait 10 minutes until I was picked up. It was great to see Grandma and Uncle Kevin. We got back to Baldwin Park and the first thing I did was take Pap's truck for a spin. The gray interior was perfect. My Pap took care of things. The engine sounded great. My grandma had the oil changed for me for my drive home.

When I came back from my joy ride around Baldwin Park, I did some chores around my grandma's house. My uncle walked with a cane from an accident, so I got on a ladder and changed out the ceiling lights and dusted the redwood beams of the ceiling in the living room. Then my grandma and I drove to pick up a pizza from the world's greatest pizza—Petrillo's. We made a pit stop at the AAA store; she wanted to get me AAA in case the truck broke down on my drive through the desert.

The next morning, I took Grandma to church at Calvary Chapel. Then after I took her home, I had to do something for my Pappy Earl. His favorite thing to do in the world was spend his days at the Santa Anita racetrack. The only places he drove the truck to the last ten years were the racetrack and Malibu to camp with our family in June. My uncle climbed into the truck with me and gave me directions to the track. It was the same route my Pappy took to the track every time he went. My uncle joked that if I took my hands off the steering wheel, the truck would know where to go on its own—like a horse to the stable.

We got to Santa Anita and parked, then walked to the entrance. My uncle Kevin paid my entry fee and bought me a beer and a racing program. Then he took a seat, and I went to walk the grounds and place some bets. I started where they saddle the horses. I was looking at these massive, muscular, beautiful animals and the tiny jockeys that mounted them. Once mounted, they trotted around a circle before going to the racetrack to take a lap before getting into the starting gates. I walked with the horses as they made their way to the track, then I walked inside to play a trifecta—my pap's favorite bet. The horns sounded, the gates opened, and away they go.

The horses rounded the first turn with the San Gabriel Mountains behind them as they hit the straightaway, and I made my way to the finish line. The horses ran past the finish line with the sound of a stampede. I checked my ticket. I lost. I wished Jennie was there with me. I had an idea. I took a picture of the racing program for the next race and sent it to her.

"Pick a horse and I'll play it for you," I texted her.

"Really? How fun! I'm so bored."

"Let's gamble, babe."

"Why is one of the horses you circled named 'Forgotten Vows'?"

"Because the jockey's name is Tyler Baze, and he is one of my favorites."

"Ok, then give me $5 to win on Funkenstein."

"Espinoza is riding that horse. Good pick, babe. But it's a long shot."

"You always go for the long shot, baby."

I walked to the ticket window and made Jennie's bet, then I walked back to the front to see the next group of horses getting saddled.

Santa Anita looked like Southern California. It was beautiful. Green grass and freshly planted flowers were everywhere. The building was classic and well preserved. The ground was littered with white losing tickets, looking like winter's first snow.

I walked with the horses to the track, then I placed my bet and waited for the gates to open. I lost again and added my tickets to the trash on the ground. Then I sent Jennie a picture of the next race and let her know we lost.

"$5 to win on Whiskey Vision," Jennie said.

"Another long shot. I like your style."

"Go make the bet—mama needs some new shoes."

"No, you don't."

Jennie had so many pairs of shoes, and half of them were still at her parents'. I went and made the bet. I did this for four more races, and we lost every one. But I had fun betting with Jennie and walking the grounds.

I found my uncle talking to some guys in front of the stable. He used to work there and knew a few people.

"You win, Dustin?"

"Not one."

"Don't feel bad—Pappy never won either."

"Then why did he come here so much, Kevin?"

"The thought of winning! Every time those gates opened, for fifty seconds, he didn't remember he was old. He just remembered the feeling of winning. Then he would lose and say 'shit.'"

"I forgot about Pap swearing at the racetrack. I think I learned to swear here."

We drove home from Santa Anita in Pap's green Chevy Silverado without a win, one last time.

That night we went to dinner at The Hat for pastrami sandwiches and chili cheese fries. I spent the night talking to my grandma about my wife and the kids. She couldn't wait to meet them.

The next morning, I woke up and had coffee with my grandma until around 11, then I had to go so I wouldn't get caught in traffic. I told them I would see them in a few months when the kids got out of school. I promised Jennie I would take her to Malibu. My uncle filled the truck with gas, then I drove Pap's truck to its new home in Arizona. On the highway outside Palm Springs, I got the truck up to 100 miles an hour. This old truck still had some life to live.

The truck had a cassette player and an AM/FM radio. Once past Palm Springs, I couldn't get a radio signal. I found a cassette in the glove box. It was the same cassette they gave you with the truck to test out the sound system. For three hours, I listened to Bob Seger sing "Like a Rock."

I pulled up to the house just after 5. The kids heard me and came running out to see the truck.

"Where's Mom?" I asked.

"In bed," Sophie said.

I walked to see Jennie and gave her a kiss to wake her up.

"Still tired?" I asked.

"Yes, but let's go see the truck."

We walked outside and the kids were all in the truck bed with Chichi.

"Can we go for a ride and ride in here?" Max asked.

"Heck ya!" I said, and shut the tailgate.

I opened the truck door for Jennie, then I closed it and got in the driver's side and started the truck up.

"Can you believe it, Jennie?"

"Believe what?"

"The two things I wanted the most in high school—I finally got."

"You wanted a tired wife and a truck that needs a paint job?"

"I wanted this girl and this truck. Don't worry—I'm going to fix you both up."

"I love you, Dustin."

"You can write your book on this. The boy across the street grew up to be the man I married. He got everything he ever wanted, and they lived happily ever after. The end."

"I do like love stories," Jennie said.

"Good—because we're living one."

Chapter 28
St. Paddy Day

It was the morning of March 17th, St. Paddy's Day, and I was getting the kids ready for school with Jennie. I was putting the corned beef and cabbage into the crockpot. This was the one day of the week I had to be at work at 8 a.m. Max walked by me not wearing green, so I pinched him.

"Mom! Dustin pinched me!" Max said.

"You're not wearing green, Max. I'll allow it," Jennie said.

I stuck my tongue out at Max and took him to his room to find a green shirt to wear.

"What's so special about St. Paddy's Day?" Max asked me.

"We wear green and eat corned beef and cabbage and drink Guinness and green beer."

"Sounds dumb."

"Dumb? It's one of the best holidays! Oh yeah, and you get to find the leprechaun's money."

"For real? He hides money?" Max asked excitedly.

"Oh yeah, the leprechaun hides his money in the bushes so he doesn't lose it when he goes out drinking at the bar for St. Paddy's. If you find it, it's yours."

"But doesn't the leprechaun need money to pay for his beers?"

"Leprechauns drink for free on St. Paddy's, so he doesn't need money."

"Ok, that makes sense, Dustin. I'm going to find all of his money and buy Pokémon cards."

Jennie left for school and Sophie left for the bus stop. Then I walked the boys halfway to school just because it was so nice out, then I walked home to go to work. I was off at 2 p.m. and had an hour before the kids got home. I had made $80 in tips that day and had the front desk at work break down $60 into two ten-dollar bills, four five-dollar bills, and twenty ones. Then I stopped at the dollar store and picked up a pack of paper black clovers. I taped the money, bill by bill, to the clovers and put a twenty-dollar bill on one. Then I hid them in the bushes in our front yard.

After, I left to get a pizza. I knew the kids wouldn't eat the corned beef, so I got them a pizza from Little Caesars.

I came back and walked into the house with the pizza. The kids had just gotten home.

"Pizza!" they all screamed.

"More corned beef for me and Mom. Where is she?" I asked.

"In your room. Yes, you got crazy bread," Sophie said.

"Why do you guys love crazy bread but don't eat the crust of your pizza?" I asked.

"It's not the same thing," she said.

I walked into our room, and Jennie was already in her sweatpants and lying in bed.

"I made dinner for us, babe."

"It smells great, Dustin. Sorry, I'm just tired."

"I got the kids pizza."

"You're the best."

"The leprechaun hid some money out front if you want to watch the kids find it?"

"The what?"

"Get up, babe."

I walked to the kitchen and found the kids eating pizza.

"I saw a leprechaun hiding money in the bushes today. You guys might want to jack him before he comes back for it," I said

"Ok, Dustin," Noah and Sophie said sarcastically and continued eating their pizza and looking at their phones.

Max dropped his pizza slice and ran out front. He returned a minute later with a five-dollar bill taped to a black clover.

"Guys! Dustin's not lying! Look what I found!" Max screamed.

Sophie and Noah dropped their pizza onto the table and ran barefoot out to the front yard. The hunt for the leprechaun's money started, and the kids searched through the bushes and yard for the cash. When the kids found a clover, they yelled. The noise was so great it got Jennie to come outside to watch.

"You're too much, Dustin," Jennie said as she smiled and kissed my cheek.

"There's that smile, babe," I said.

I put my arm around Jennie, and we watched the kids search for the leprechaun's money. Max, the only true believer in the leprechaun, had found the $20.

"I love St. Paddy's Day!" Max shouted.

Noah walked past him, disappointed and not wearing green, so Max pinched him.

"Hey!" Noah shouted.

"St. Paddy—you have to wear green. Right, Dustin?" Max asked.

"You got it, buddy," I said.

"I was wearing green, and I took it off after school," Noah said.

"Too bad, so sad," Max said as he walked inside counting his money.

I walked Jennie to the bedroom and helped her into bed, then went to the kitchen and made her a plate of corned beef and cabbage and brought it to her in the bedroom.

"Did you call the doctor yet?" I asked.

"I made an appointment for next Thursday. Will you take me, please?"

"Of course, babe," I said as I fed her some of the food.

"Ahsoon and Jeff are coming by to look at the truck," I said.

"And then?"

"Can I please go to the bar with them? It's St. Paddy!"

"You're wearing your Larry Bird jersey. I assumed you were going."

"Not if you say no. You don't feel good."

"The kids had the best St. Paddy's Day ever, and you made me dinner. Go have fun. But please—no Dusty McAwesome tonight?"

"Thank you! I'll just be down the street at the Irish pub, Molly Brannigans, if you need anything."

"Don't be out all night?"

"I won't."

My doorbell rang and I ran to answer it.

"She said I can go!" I screamed at my friends.

The three of us walked to look at my truck. I opened the hood to show my friends how clean it was, then Jeff took the truck for a drive. He came back.

"Bro! It rides so smoothly," Jeff said.

"Yeah, bruh, this is clean. Where's Jennie?" Ahsoon said.

"She doesn't feel good. She is in bed."

"And she's letting you go out with the three kids at home? I see why you married her, bruh," Ahsoon said.

"I have to go home," Jeff said.

"Seriously?" I asked.

"Yeah, man, I'm sorry. I told Amanda I was just coming to look at the truck."

"Then just me and Ahsoon? You ready, dude?" I said.

"Jump in my car. I'm driving," Ahsoon said.

Ahsoon had a white Dodge Hellcat. I loved his car. He went way too fast and scared the hell out of me, but I liked it. The two of us drove to the Irish bar, only it had a new owner now. The Irish bar had turned into an English pub called Union Jack's. There was no line to get in.

We walked from the car to the bar and were checked for our IDs.

I told the bouncer, "Kind of dead for St. Paddy's?"

"That's because this is an English pub, not an Irish pub," the bouncer told me.

"So what's the big day here? The Fourth of July?"

"Dude, you're going to get us kicked out before we get in," Ahsoon said.

They let us in, but it was so sad and dead that we decided to celebrate St. Paddy's at a Mexican bar called Dos Gringos. Ahsoon drove us there and it was fun, but Ahsoon left to go home since he wasn't drinking. I found some friends and had a few beers and shots, then called an Uber to go home. It was only 10 p.m., and I wasn't Dusty McAwesome on St. Paddy's. I was happy to go home to see my wife and show her I wasn't wasted on St. Paddy's.

I walked into the house and checked on the kids sleeping, then went to the bedroom to kiss my wife and found her sweating in her sleep.

"Are you ok?" I asked.

Jennie mumbled to me and I could not make out what she said.

"Ok, we're going to the hospital now," I said.

Then, very clearly, Jennie said, "No, I'm fine. I have court next week for the DUI and court with Colby for the kids."

"We have to go. I'm calling your mom to watch the kids."

"I made an appointment, Dustin. Please help me right now."

"I'll take you to the hospital."

"No! Just help me feel better."

"I can't, Jennie. Please, Jennie, let's just go."

"I can't miss court. That's what he wants. I'm fine, it's just a fever. After court I will do whatever you say. Please help me now, baby."

I went to the kitchen and opened the freezer and grabbed some ice packs I had for softball. I brought them to Jennie and placed them on her head and chest.

"I need to put you in an ice bath, babe."

"I don't want to move."

I went back to the freezer and got frozen peas and a bag of pizza bites and placed them on Jennie's naked body. It wasn't enough. I went back to the freezer and filled up bags we had for the kids' sandwiches with ice and brought them back to place on Jennie. I did this three times until her body was covered in ice. The ice was helping, but it was also melting, so I had to keep replacing the ice bags.

"Can I have a Sprite to drink?" Jennie asked.

"We don't have any, babe."

"Okay. I just really want one."

"I could drive to the gas station and get you one?"

"You were drinking at the bar—you shouldn't drive. It's St. Paddy's."

"I'll drive you to the hospital?"

"Drunk?"

"No, buzzed."

"No!"

I replaced her ice bags, then got on my beach cruiser and rode to the Circle K to get Jennie a Polar Pop Sprite. When I got to the gas station, there were three cop cars. I was happy I rode my bike. I got Jennie's Sprite, then rode home with one hand on the handlebars and the other holding the drink. I got home and left the bike in the front yard and rushed in to see Jennie. I could hear her moaning in pain.

"I have your Sprite," I said.

"You better not have driven."

"No, I rode my bike."

Jennie couldn't hold the cup, so I held the soda for her as she sipped from the straw. Jennie took a really long drink.

"That's so good," Jennie said as she finished her drink.

I kept replacing her ice bags and held her soda for her when asked. It was around 5 a.m. when the fever broke and Jennie went to sleep. I stayed up another hour watching her before I fell asleep next to her in the wet bed. I was awakened by Jennie handing me coffee around 7 a.m.

"Thank you for taking care of me," she said.

"Do you feel better?"

"Yes, thank you," Jennie said as she took two Tylenol and drank her coffee.

"Are you sure?" I asked.

"Moms don't get sick days, Dustin."

"Moms need to have a union then, babe!"

Jennie laughed, then got the kids off to school and said, "Wouldn't that be nice?"

I showed up to work and everyone thought I was hungover from St. Paddy's Day. I didn't want to explain why I was so tired, so I said, "Yes, I am." Also, I was scared.

I came home that night and watched Desperate Housewives in bed with Jennie. I hated the show, but I loved being in bed with my wife. After an hour,

I drove to the gas station to get Jennie a Polar Pop Sprite. I couldn't hold Jennie. She didn't like being touched lately. She wanted to touch me, so we fell asleep with our feet touching outside of the blankets.

Chapter 29
Jennie Elkin

We got through the weekend, and on Sunday I took the kids to church while Jennie stayed home to rest. She watched the service on her phone from bed. Brian took the boys to the jump park, and Jennie had told Sophie she would take her shopping—but Jennie wasn't feeling good and couldn't go.

"I will take Sophie shopping," I said.

"Would you? She was looking forward to it."

Jennie went to grab her purse.

"What are you doing?" I asked.

"Getting money for Sophie."

"They're not your kids anymore, they are ours. I got it."

"Thank you, baby."

"We'll set up a joint bank account this week, OK babe?"

"I have to go to the Social Security office to change my name to Elkin, and I have to go to court twice this week for the DUI and Colby wanting custody of the kids."

"We'll do it next week. I don't see any judge giving a dad who has never paid child support custody of the kids."

"He is representing himself, and I hired a lawyer. He just wants to waste my money."

"Our money?"

"He's ridiculous. I'm sorry. We'll never get rid of him. He has to bully someone."

"I don't want to talk about him. But Sophie? We are not shopping for over-the-shoulder boulder holders, are we?"

"No, she wants to go to thrift stores."

"Yes! I'm gonna pop some tags. I got $20 in my pocket."

"Thank you, Dustin."

"Get some rest, and I'll make dinner tonight when I get home, OK?"

"Can I do anything for you?"

"Can we not watch *Real Housewives* tonight?"

"*Beverly Hills 90210?*"

"Yes! I love Dylan McKay! He should have been with Kelly! Brenda was a bad choice."

"I really fucking love you, Dustin."

"I really fucking love you, Jennie. And Dylan McKay. He was the coolest!"

"Go have fun."

I yelled in the house, "Sophie, let's go shopping!"

From her room, I heard Sophie say, "Actually?"

"Yes, actually, let's go!"

I kissed Jennie on the forehead, and Sophie and I left to go thrifting at Goodwill and Savers.

Once Sophie and I got to the first store, Savers, I left her alone to look at clothes, and I looked at the toys and appliances. After an hour, she had three sweatshirts, two pairs of pants, and two shirts.

"How many can I get?" she asked.

I looked at the price tags and totaled them up in my head. It came out to $34.

"We can get them all," I said.

"Yes!"

I paid for the clothes, then we walked to the Goodwill in the same parking lot. She didn't find anything there, so we left, and I noticed her shoes—black Converse Chuck Taylors, worn out with too many rips.

"I know that's the style with your shoes, dude, but do you want to go to the mall and get some new ones?" I asked.

"Actually?"

"Yes, actually. Why do you keep saying 'actually,' dude?"

"Why do you keep saying dude?"

"Actually, I don't know, dude."

We drove to Superstition Mall a mile away, and we went to the Journeys shoe store. Sophie couldn't make up her mind on what color to get.

"Let's get black—they go with everything. And you have a birthday in a few weeks, so we can get you another pair in a different color if you want," I said.

"Bet."

"What are we betting?" I asked.

"No, bet! Like it's a deal?"

"Oh, OK."

We got the shoes, then went home. When we got home, Sophie rushed into our room to see her mom and show her everything she got. The two sat on the bed, and Sophie took everything out to show Jennie.

"New shoes too, Dustin?"

"She needed them, babe."

"Thank you, baby."

"Yeah, thanks, Dustin," Sophie said.

"Bet," I said.

"What are you guys betting?" Jennie asked.

Sophie and I laughed, then I went to the kitchen to make dinner. The boys were dropped off while I was making dinner, and they ran into the kitchen.

"What are you making, Dustin?" Max asked.

"Fettuccine Alfredo."

"I want mac and cheese," Noah said.

"It's the same thing," I said.

"It doesn't look the same," Max said.

"It's pasta with a cheese sauce. It's the same thing."

Both boys said, "I don't want it."

I thought about arguing with them, then decided I just wanted to feed them and watch TV with Jennie. So I made Kraft Mac and Cheese for the boys with dinosaur-shaped chicken nuggets, and for Sophie, I made noodles with butter. After I fed the kids, I brought Jennie's food into our bedroom. Jennie was sitting up and smiling.

"Are you ready for our 90210 date night?"

"Yes, and I brought you dinner in bed."

I brought two wine glasses into the room.

"I don't want to drink, baby."

I pulled out a two-liter bottle of Sprite.

"OK, that's my favorite," Jennie said.

The two of us watched *Beverly Hills 90210* in bed and had dinner and drank Sprite. Later, I tucked the kids in, then came back to bed and we watched more 90210 before falling asleep halfway through season four.

In the morning, I got the kids ready for school and let Jennie sleep in. She didn't have work because she had court for her DUI that day. Her mom went with her to court, and when they came back, Jennie had to serve a week in jail sometime in the future.

"I guess the kids can stay with your parents that week, and we can say it's our honeymoon?" I said.

"That's what I was thinking," Jennie said.

The next day was Tuesday and I had work. I came home on a break to see my family. Jennie was leaving as I pulled in.

"I'm going to Phoenix to the Social Security office to have my last name changed to Elkin."

"Jennie Elkin!"

"Yes, baby."

"How are you feeling?"

"Tired, but I want to do this."

"I'll get dinner tonight, babe."

"Oh, so we're having pizza again."

"You say that like it's a bad thing?"

"When I get better, I am cooking and we are all eating better."

"I love you, Mrs. Elkin."

"I love you, Mr. Elkin."

On Wednesday, Jennie had court with her ex-husband over custody of the kids. She called me at work to tell me the kids' dad had bluffed and, before court, tried to settle and give her full custody of the kids and sign over parental rights to get out of paying child support. Jennie told him no deal. She said she knew he would never pay but didn't want him ditching his kids. I said she should have taken it. The judge ordered him to pay sixty thousand in back pay and that he had to pay her $500 that day or be arrested. He paid the $500 and drove back to Utah to his other family.

I came home from work that night and found Jennie sweating in bed and the kids in their rooms. Sophie walked up to me and handed me her phone. It was her dad FaceTiming and wanting to talk to me. Max was asking me for waffles, and Jennie was asking me to go to the store to get her cortisone ointment. I tried not to talk to him.

He went on and on about how he wanted to co-parent and wanted to see his kids more, but Jennie wouldn't let him. Which was a lie, because he lived in Utah and chose to move there. He could have them anytime he wanted, but he lived in another state. While I was making Max waffles and trying to get off the phone with him, he said, "You don't have to tell Jennie we talked. This is between me and you." I hung up and walked into our bedroom.

"I just talked to Colby on the phone," I said.

"He called you?"

"No, he called Sophie and had her put me on the phone, then said I don't have to tell you we talked. Anyway, where do I get cortisone?"

"CVS."

"I'll be right back."

I went to the store and got the cortisone and brought it back to Jennie, then rubbed it on her where she told me to. After I put the kids to bed, I sat at the end of the bed and drank a beer while Jennie slept and I watched 90210.

The next morning was Thursday, and Jennie went to work and the kids went to school. I started work at 8 a.m., and when I got home at 2 p.m., I waited to take Jennie to her doctor appointment. Linda watched the kids for us, and I drove Jennie and me to the appointment. Jennie was weak, and I carried her purse for her into the doctor's office. I was happy we were finally there. We sat in the waiting room, then they called her, and she went back by herself. She came back thirty minutes later.

"They want to do blood work," she said.

"What does that mean?"

"They want to take samples of my blood to see what's wrong."

So we waited another thirty minutes before they called for her again. After the blood test, I ran to my car and drove it to the front so Jennie wouldn't have to walk so far. I helped Jennie into the car, then drove us home and helped Jennie change into sweats. Then I helped her into our bed.

The next day, Jennie went to school, but they sent her home for having a fever. I had to work at the salon until 9, but I took a break at 6 to bring Jennie and the kids Chick-fil-A for dinner since Jennie couldn't cook. When I got home that night, Jennie was in bed with a fever, so I put a cold, wet towel on her forehead and a couple of ice packs on her body. Sophie was at a friend's for a sleepover, so I took the boys with me to the Circle K to get Jennie a Polar Pop Sprite and let the boys pick out some snacks to eat while we had a boys' night and watched a movie.

We came home, and I walked into our room with the Sprite for Jennie and turned on the bedroom light.

"What the hell are you doing!" Jennie screamed at me.

"I got you a Sprite. I thought you might be thirsty?"

"Turn off the light! It hurts my eyes!"

"I'm just going to leave the Sprite here on the nightstand. Get it if you want it." I started to leave the room.

"Wait. I'm sorry, Dustin." Jennie started to cry. I sat on the bed next to her and gave her a hug. Her wet skin made her hair stick to her face.

"What's wrong?" I asked.

"I don't know! I'm sorry I'm being such a bitch."

"You said it, not me. How long until we get the blood work back from Banner?"

"They said maybe a week because they're really backed up."

I helped Jennie sit up and held her soda for her as she sipped it.

"Thank you, Dustin."

"It's okay if you yell at me. I won't get mad. We'll get through this, baby."

"I'm sorry."

"You don't have to say you're sorry. Okay? If you need anything, just holler. The boys and I are having a boys' night in the living room. We have snacks and are going to watch Rambo."

"Have fun," Jennie said.

Saturday morning, I took care of the kids until I left for work at 3. I came home after work, and it was the same thing. Every night that week was the same. I thought marriage was going to be easy. But I was doing a lot of work. I had a sick wife and three kids and was working. I loved taking care of them, though. It was nice to feel needed.

I came home from work at 2 on Thursday and took the hour I had alone to clean the house. Jennie still went to work at school every day, and she came home that day looking extra exhausted.

"Has Banner called yet?" I asked.

"No. I hope they do soon."

"Me too. You lay in bed. I got things covered."

"Okay, Mr. Mom. I bet you didn't think this was what married life would be like?"

"I was at Costco this week and I saw that they have mattresses in a little box, and you open it up and it grows into a full-size queen bed. Maybe I could get us one?"

"We don't need a new mattress. We need to save money to buy a house. This mattress is fine, Dustin."

"But this new mattress is like those little capsules you'd get as a kid that you leave in water and they grow into a dinosaur."

"No."

"Let's go for a bike ride on my tandem bike," I said.

"I don't feel like riding a bike."

"I just thought maybe some fresh air would help?"

"I will never ride with you on that stupid bike."

"Why not?"

"Because I've seen pictures on Facebook of you with other girls on that bike!"

"Before we dated, babe! Other girls? I've had this mattress for like fifteen years!"

Jennie sat up and got out of bed, grabbing the blanket and dragging it to the couch in the living room.

"Where are you going?" I asked.

"I'm not sleeping on that mattress ever again. Go get your stupid new mattress."

"Should I get dinner for us at Costco?"

"You better not bring home another pizza!" Jennie said.

I went to Costco and came back home with a new mattress and hot dogs. I set up our new bed with help from the kids, then we all helped Jennie back into bed, and the kids went to their rooms to go to sleep.

"You know, Jennie, it's been like two weeks since we've had sex, and this is a brand-new mattress we need to break in?" I said.

"You can't be serious."

"It's just the old Chinese proverb, babe."

"What Chinese proverb?"

"Confucius."

"You know Confucius' Chinese proverbs?"

"Yes. Confucius say: When get new mattress, if you fuck, get lots of luck."

Jennie threw a pillow at me, laughing. "I hate you," she said.

"That's why they call them 'throw pillows'? I love you, babe."

"I love you. Now get in bed and don't touch me."

I got in bed and went to sleep, then I felt Jennie's feet snuggling my feet.

"You said no touching."

"I can do whatever I want."

Chapter 30
April Fools Day

The next morning was Friday, April 1st. I woke up with everyone and went to make coffee. I came back into the room to hand Jennie her morning coffee. She stumbled as she was trying to put on her shoes.

"You can't go to work, Jennie. We need to go to the hospital!"

"They haven't called with my results yet."

"This is ridiculous! This is more than being sick! If you were just sick, wouldn't I have caught it by now? I've been in bed with you every night and changing the wet sheets after you go to work in the morning."

"What if it's bad, Dustin?"

"Then I can't fix it with ice bags, Tylenol, a wet towel, and Sprite!"

"I'll call the hospital today," she said.

"Are you ok to drive?"

"Yes."

"Okay, well I'm going to work for a staff meeting. You call me when they send you home for another fever, and I'm taking you to the hospital."

Jennie took a couple of Tylenol with her coffee. "I love you."

"I love you. I want my wife back."

"I'll get better."

Jennie left for work, and I got the kids off to school, then I went to my work meeting. About an hour later, I got a text from Jennie: "Can you pick me up at school?" I left the meeting and drove to Patterson Elementary and walked into the office.

"I'm here to pick up my wife," I told the woman working the front desk.

"One minute," the woman said and walked away. A short-haired woman wearing jeans came up to me and introduced herself as the principal and asked me into her office. I hadn't been in a principal's office in 30 years, and it still made me nervous.

"Where's my wife?"

"In the restroom."

"Why do I feel like I am picking up my kid that did something bad?"

"One of the other teachers said that Jennie seemed confused and disoriented and thinks she has been drinking."

"It's 9 a.m. I left her an hour ago," I said.

"We take these things very seriously, and there is a protocol we have to follow."

Jennie walked into the room clutching her bag and shaking. I held her trembling hand.

"What is the protocol?" I asked.

"Someone from the district is coming to give her a breathalyzer," the principal said.

"I want to go home, Dustin," Jennie said, looking confused.

"If she doesn't take it, she won't be allowed to work in Gilbert Public Schools again," the principal said.

"My wife is sick. You guys have sent her home twice for a fever."

Just then, an older man from the district building came into the room and introduced himself, then said, "We need to take Jennie to the district office to do the breathalyzer."

"The breathalyzer fits in your pocket. Why didn't you bring it? We've been waiting for you!"

"That's not how we do things," he said.

"And that's why charter schools have taken over Gilbert—your stupid protocol with everything. We are leaving. I'm taking my wife to the hospital."

"If you leave now and don't go with me, your wife will not be able to work for Gilbert Public Schools again."

"Fantastic. You guys are understaffed. She will go work for Mesa Public Schools or a charter school. Plenty of work for her once she gets better. Why don't you make yourself useful and go teach her class? You district guys get paid more and do less. Or do you have some important lunches to go to and take other teachers for breathalyzers? We're leaving."

"I strongly suggest you don't, sir."

"I strongly suggest you take better care of your teachers. You've sent her home twice for a fever in less than two weeks and let her back every day with a fever because you are understaffed and needed her."

I helped Jennie up and led her out of the office. She walked very slowly, and that made it hard to make a dramatic exit, so I stopped at the front desk and took a handful of hard candy they had in a bowl next to a small sign that said "take one." It was the only thing I could do in frustration. Jennie's mom taught at the school too, so I didn't want to swear at them or make a scene. I walked Jennie to my car and drove her home. Then I called the urgent care from my car and made an appointment for 1 p.m., the soonest I could get her in. I got Jennie in bed and under the covers, then I walked outside to have a cigarette. I was lost and scared and didn't know what to do.

At 12:30, I got Jennie out of bed to go across the street to the urgent care next to the Circle K I always go to. I was dressed in my work clothes because I had work at 3. I figured we'd take Jennie to get checked out by the doctor, then I'd pick up her prescription from CVS and take her home and put her in bed. Then I'd go to work for six hours and come home and take care of her and the kids.

We got to the parking lot of the urgent care and got out of the car. Jennie was sweating and looked disoriented.

"Are you ok, Jennie?"

"Mom! Mom!" Jennie called out to a random older woman that looked nothing like her mom.

"That's not your mom, Jennie."

"Of course it is. Mom! Mom!"

The woman didn't even turn her head. I took Jennie's purse and then led her by the hand inside the urgent care. I sat her down in a chair, then checked us in. When I came back to sit next to her, she looked worried.

"I left my water at home. I'm so thirsty. I need my water. Will you go get it, Dustin?"

"The gas station is next door. I'll run over and get you one. Don't move. I'll be right back."

I jogged across the parking lot to the gas station and grabbed a FIJI water bottle. While I was waiting to pay for it, I kept an eye on the urgent care and texted Jennie's mom.

"I have Jennie at the urgent care. Something is wrong. She was convinced this woman was you and she was calling out to her. Can you come down?"

"The urgent care by the house?"

"Yes."

"Ok, I'll be there."

I paid for the water and jogged back across the parking lot. Jennie was gripping her purse when I walked in.

"Where did you go, Dustin?"

"To get you water."

"How did you know I was so thirsty?"

"Just drink, babe."

I walked up to the receptionist and asked how much longer my wife would have to wait. She apologized to me for the wait but let me know that they were short-staffed. I walked back to Jennie and found her with an empty water bottle. She had drunk the whole thing.

"Do you want some more water, babe?"

"Yes, please."

I walked to the water fountain and filled up the empty bottle. I came back and sat next to Jennie and held her hand for an hour until we were called. We walked through a door and were led into a small room where I helped Jennie onto the examination table, and I took a seat in the corner. A nurse came in and started doing the standard tests. Then I heard her say something.

"That can't be right."

"What can't be right?" I asked.

"Let me try it again."

"Ok."

After another try, she said, "Sir, your wife's sodium levels are so low I don't know how she walked into the building. Let me go get the doctor."

Linda was calling my phone, so I answered.

"Where are you?" she asked.

"In the office. Ask the front to let you in. We are in the second room on the left."

Linda came back and took Jennie's hand, and I told her what the nurse had told me.

"I'm supposed to work at three. I'm going to call in."

"Go to work. I'll take care of Jennie."

"What about the kids?"

"I already called Brian, and he is going to watch them. I will call you and let you know anything they tell me."

I looked at Jennie and took her hands in mine. Then said very slowly, "I'm going to work for a little bit. Your mom is here with you. I love you, and I'll see you at home tonight, babe."

Jennie nodded her head to me, and I gave her a kiss goodbye.

"Thank you, Linda."

"Go. We'll be fine."

I drove to work and showed up five minutes late, and my client was waiting. I didn't tell anyone why I was late, just that I was sorry. I did my first two clients, then went to get my phone and call Linda to see how things were going. I had a missed call and a text message from Linda. The text message said, "Urgent care had me take Jennie to the emergency room. We're at Banner Gateway. Come here when you're off work."

I walked to the front desk and told them, "Cancel my appointments for the rest of the night. I'm leaving."

"Are you serious? You can't. You're booked all night," our receptionist said.

"My wife is in the emergency room. I'm leaving now."

I drove to the Banner Gateway emergency room and called Linda to let her know I was on my way. She met me in the parking lot and walked me to the room Jennie was in. Jennie was sleeping, and they had her sedated. A female nurse came into the room and told us they had gotten Jennie's bloodwork back and she had signs of Valley fever. Linda left so I could be alone with Jennie.

Before the nurse left, I asked her, "What is Valley fever?"

"It's an infection caused by a fungus or spore that's usually breathed in by dust. Two-thirds of the country's cases of Valley fever happen in Arizona—just usually not in someone as young as your wife."

"The Phoenix Suns just clinched the playoffs. 'Valley Fever' signs are all over the freeway. I didn't know it was a real thing?"

"I'm afraid it is."

"So you guys will just give us an antibiotic and I'll take her home?"

"The doctors want to keep her overnight."

"Ok."

The nurse left and Linda came back into the room, and we talked about everything the nurses had told us. Linda told me Brian had the kids at their house and they were going to spend the night. I spent about two hours in the room with Linda before the nurse said we should go home and rest, that there was nothing we could do and that Jennie was stable and we could come back at 10 a.m. to see Jennie in the ICU. I walked out with Linda and gave her a hug in the parking lot, and drove home.

I was trying to process everything that was happening. I had told my work I wouldn't be in the next day, and to cancel my clients. My in-laws had the kids for the night, so I stopped at the closest bar on the way home—that happened to be Fat Cats. I ordered a shot of Jameson and a tall IPA, then Googled Valley fever.

The results said it should last a few weeks to a few months. Some of the side effects were headache and altered mental status, which made sense as I thought back over the last few months. Valley fever also occasionally came with a rash, and that's why Jennie wanted the cortisone. Fatigue was also another sign of Valley fever.

I was sitting at the bar alone, then was grabbed from behind by some friends I used to work with. They had shown up to go bowling on a Friday night. They said congratulations on getting married, then asked how I was doing.

"I just left Jennie at Banner. She has Valley fever."

They didn't have a response.

"We're fine. I'm reading about it right now. I'm going to get her in the morning to bring her home."

Chapter 31

The Hospital

S aturday, I got to the hospital a little after 10 a.m. and checked in. I was sent to room 216. Linda was already in the room. Jennie was awake, looking better, and happy to see me.

"My mom beat you here."

"Well, I had to stop to get you a Sprite from QT." I gave her a sip.

"I love you so much."

A doctor walked into the room and introduced himself, then wrote his name on the dry erase board, much like a teacher does on the first day of school. His name I could not pronounce or spell. His last name looked like the chart they use for an eye exam at the eye doctor.

"You can call me Bob," he said.

Bob let us know they were going to keep Jennie over the weekend. She had a severe case of Valley fever and they wanted to run some more tests and monitor her. Then he left.

Linda left the room so Jennie and I could be alone. We immediately kissed long and hard like teenagers who were finally left alone in a room. Another doctor came into the room, and his name was even longer. He was a cardiologist. He looked at me, not Jennie, and spoke.

"Your wife is very sick and has been for a while," he said, as Jennie squeezed my hand.

"I'm right here!" Jennie said to him.

"Sorry, I thought you knew," he said, and left.

Jennie mimicked what I sounded like and said, "Babe, we haven't had sex in two weeks. Old Chinese proverb, Confucius say…"

"I'm sorry, I'll never ask for sex again."

"No, please do. I enjoy saying no."

"One of these days I'm going to say no to you for sex."

"Let's have sex right now."

"Ok."

"No."

I took the Sprite away from her.

"I can be mean too."

"No, you can't. Give me the Sprite," she said, and I handed it to her.

"I win," Jennie smiled as she drank her Sprite.

I told Jennie, "Do you remember my friend Ryan was flying in from Texas and I was going to meet him for a Spring Training game tomorrow?"

"Go to the game. I'm coming home Monday, babe."

"The game is not until 1:30, so I'll come here after church, then go to the game and come back after until they kick me out."

"You're going to show up to the hospital drunk after the baseball game?"

"No, buzzed."

Linda came back into the room.

"Dustin is ditching me for a baseball game tomorrow, Mom."

"Jennie!" I said.

"I'm joking."

"That sounds fun," Linda said.

The three of us hung out in the room for a couple of hours, and nurses came in and out to check on Jennie.

"Linda, if you're going to stay here, I'm going to go check on the kids. I'm sure Brian could use a break?"

"That sounds good, Dustin," Linda said.

"Jennie, I'll be back in a couple of hours."

We kissed, and I left to see the kids. The kids were not allowed in the ICU because of COVID rules—you had to be 13. The hospital was only two miles from our house, so it was very convenient to go back and forth. I saw the kids and let them know Mom was OK, then I took them to lunch and the batting cages. I came back to the hospital around 4 p.m. and Linda went home, and I stayed with Jennie.

Around 6 p.m., our male nurse, Nurse Rick, came in. He was a Filipino former Marine and the nicest guy. He told me visiting hours were over but he didn't care if I stayed in the room with Jennie. I had pulled a chair close to Jennie's hospital bed, and the two of us watched the TV show Friends for a few hours.

Around 7 p.m., Nurse Rick came back into the room to let us know he was leaving and that I needed to stay in the room because the other nurses would ask me to leave. We told him "Thank you."

Right at 8 p.m., a tall, masculine female nurse with her hair in a bun that was tighter than a sumo wrestler's came into the room and pointed at me.

"What are you doing here? You need to leave," she demanded.

"I think I need to go?" I told Jennie.

"Go home, baby. I'm tired. I'll see you tomorrow morning."

I kissed Jennie goodnight and tried to walk past the nurse through the door, but she wouldn't move. I think she was sizing me up.

"Excuse me?" I said.

"You're excused," she said and moved.

"Text me, Jennie, if you wake up or call me if you are bored."

I walked to the elevator and looked at my phone. I had a group text from three of my best friends from high school. We get together one or two times a year. We were supposed to hang out that night, but I had to cancel because Jennie was in the hospital. I told them I was leaving the hospital because I was kicked out, but Jennie was OK.

"Pick us up!" they replied. They were drunk.

"Where are you?"

I picked up my friends Jeff, Jared, and Doug. Doug's younger brother had passed away in December, and this was the first time since the funeral we were all hanging out. I drove us to the gas station by our old high school, Highland, where we used to use our fake IDs to get booze, and now older and in our 40s, they no longer carded us. I had my fake ID taken away there one night in high school after a soccer game. I scored two goals that night, and my dad gave me a $20 bill after the game for playing well. I tried buying beer at the gas station that night and forgot I was wearing my letterman jacket. The clerk asked if I was a 22-year-old sophomore, then kicked me out.

We grabbed beer and a bottle of Tito's vodka. I drove us to my house to hang out in the man cave.

Jeff's wife called while we were driving, and he made the mistake of answering the phone in the car surrounded by immature hooligans.

"Hey, honey," Jeff said.

"Get off the phone, these hookers charge by the hour," one of the guys in the back seat yelled.

"Are they even 18?" another voice shouted.

"No, honey, we are going to Dustin's to shoot pool," Jeff said.

"Yeah, shoot pool with hookers," a voice shouted from the back seat. I love my friends.

"You guys know she is going to make me come home now?" Jeff said.

We pulled up to my house and I opened the garage, and we played Golden Tee, pinball, and Cruis'n USA, using the pool table to hold our beers. The four of us drank vodka and lemonade that we chased with beers. We called each other bitches and other obscene things. The longer you know someone, the meaner you can be.

Jeff called an Uber and left first because his wife said she 'needed him.'

"She better be needing some dick," Doug said.

"You've been pussy whipped since prom," Jared said.

We all laughed and called Jeff a bitch, even though we loved him. Jeff took a hit of his vape pen, flipped us the bird, and got in his Uber.

The three of us finished the beers late into the night, then they passed out on the couch and La-Z-Boy, and I went to bed.

I woke up late and missed church, so I showered and went to the hospital. I told Jennie the boys came over and they said hi. We all grew up together.

"You slept in and missed church? What would your Pappy Earl say?" Jennie said.

"You got me, babe. When I hang out with those guys, we think we are 17 again. Good thing Jared and Doug live in North Phoenix, so I only see them twice a year."

"You guys are going to be 70 years old one day and acting the same, aren't you?"

"I hope so."

"Boys. What about your Sunday school group?"

"Jeff covered it. He went home early last night. His wife made him."

"I like Amanda."

"How are you feeling?"

"Better than you, Dustin."

"I believe it."

"But thank you for showing up."

"I'll always show up for you, babe."

I hung out at the hospital with Jennie until 1 p.m. Then Linda showed up, and I went to the Diamondbacks spring training game to meet my friend Ryan from Texas. It was good to see him, but I left early to go back to see Jennie. He didn't mind because he was having fun with some of his Marine friends he was staying with, and they were throwing beach balls they bought from the dollar store onto the field and into the stands. A cop came to stop them, but he was a former Marine and let it go.

I got back to the hospital around 4 p.m. and Linda went home. Then I laid on the couch in the room. Jennie was sleeping. She woke up.

"Hey baby, you came back."

"I told you I would."

"I thought Dusty McAwesome might come out."

"No. And I brought you some Carmex."

"That's why I keep you," Jennie said and put on the lip balm.

We watched Friends until 8 p.m., when I was asked to leave again by the big Amazonian nurse.

"See you tomorrow, babe," I said.

"I love you."

"I love you more."

I showed up the next morning with a Sprite for Jennie. It was Monday, so Linda was at work at school, and she would come over to the hospital when she got off. Then I would go meet the kids after school for a couple of hours before coming back to the hospital.

I had thought I would be taking Jennie home, but they wanted to run some more MRIs on her. They couldn't get the fever to drop. The hospital was monitoring Jennie's liquid intake, so the nurse told me no Sprite for her. As soon as the nurse left, I heard Jennie's voice.

"Ok, give me the Sprite."

"They said not to. I want you to get better."

"You're half Mexican. What did you say your mom gave you when you were sick as a kid?"

"7Up. You make a good point."

Jennie's lips were dry, and she licked them, looking at the QT cup dripping with condensation.

"One sip."

I put the straw to her lips and she drank and smiled at the same time. I looked over my shoulder so we wouldn't get caught. She stopped, and I pulled it away from her and took a seat in the chair next to her hospital bed.

"What did you bring me today?" Jennie asked.

I pulled from my backpack a can of Bed Head dry shampoo and her favorite hairbrush.

"My hair is so oily. Thank you, Dustin."

Jennie took the can and sprayed her head, then turned her back to me and I brushed her hair and put it back in a ponytail.

"Were you ok getting the kids ready by yourself today?"

"Piece of cake."

"I'm so hungry."

"Let's eat."

"I can't. They are monitoring that too. I just want to go home."

"I want you home too. I don't like sleeping without you. But we have to do what they say so we can get you better and back home."

"Ok," Jennie said.

"Before I left for the hospital today, I went to the bathroom to pee, and after I got to the bedroom door, I turned around to go put the toilet seat down."

"Your training is complete, but I do not grant you the rank of Jedi Master."

"Why not?"

"Because you still miss and hit the floor. Help me."

"Help you what?"

"Get up to pee."

Jennie had a lot of monitor wires attached to her that were hooked up to a machine on wheels next to the bed, but it was plugged into the wall. I helped Jennie up.

"What do you need me to do?" I asked.

"Just pull the machine to the bathroom for me."

Jennie took slow, small steps toward the bathroom and I pulled the machine until it ran out of cord.

"It won't go anymore, babe," I said.

"I need like two more inches!"

"That's what she said."

"Good one. I hate you."

Jennie was almost at the toilet.

"Babe, the cord's coming out of the socket."

"Don't let it come out, I'm almost there."

I slid to the wall to hold the plug in the socket.

"I can't hold it anymore, Dustin!"

"Me either, babe! Lift your leg and pee?"

She did, and just then Nurse Rick walked in to see Jennie holding the sink with one leg up, peeing into the toilet, and me on the ground holding the plug in the socket.

"What are you guys doing?" Nurse Rick asked.

"Peeing?" I said.

"You can unplug the machine and nothing will happen. It was just plugged in because it was charging."

"Oh, she won't die?" I asked.

"No, she's not on life support."

"Ok, I just thought, you know, don't pull the plug."

Nurse Rick got paged and said, "You guys ok?"

"Yes," we both said.

"Ok, I'll be back in a few."

I walked to the bathroom to help Jennie back to the bed.

"Babe, you said I miss the toilet when I pee? The toilet looks like it was sitting in the front row at a Gallagher show."

Jennie just gave me a look.

"I'll clean it up, babe."

I helped Jennie into bed, then went back and cleaned the toilet. When I was done, I took a seat in the chair next to the bed and we tried to find something to watch on TV.

Nurse Rick came back in the room and had to reconnect some of the cords that came loose on Jennie's chest that were monitoring her. The hospital gowns are loose and Jennie's boobs popped out.

"Now it's a party, boys," Jennie said.

Nurse Rick tried not to laugh.

"It's ok, she likes to make things awkward."

"I'm ready for my sponge bash," Jennie said, and I put one of the pillows over her face to make her stop. She took the pillow and hit me with it.

Nurse Rick finished up.

"Hey, I have good news—after your MRI today, they said you can order some food and eat," Nurse Rick said.

"All I had to do was show my boobs."

"Sounds like when you worked at Hooters in college."

Jennie hit me with the pillow again.

Chapter 32
My Friend Chad

Tuesday morning I went to the hospital and hung out with Jennie until I went to work. I used my lunch break to drive back to the hospital to spend 30 minutes with Jennie, then went back to work. Linda came to see Jennie when she was off work around 3 and spent time with her until they asked her to leave.

Wednesday was the same routine, only the doctors told us they wanted to do a spinal tap to check for meningitis. I thought Spinal Tap was a band. I found out it was a lumbar puncture in which a needle is inserted into the spinal canal to collect cerebrospinal fluid for diagnostic testing.

Jennie was scared.

"We need to do this, honey. We should have had you home by now. We'll get through this."

"Ok."

We agreed to the spinal tap.

I was off work at 2 on Thursday, and I drove to the hospital to visit Jennie. She was tired, but we talked and hugged and kissed. I only stayed for a couple of hours because I told the kids I would take them to see the movie Sonic the Hedgehog 2. Linda came to be with Jennie, and Jennie thanked me for taking the kids to have fun.

"Thank you, babe," I said to Jennie.

"For what?"

"Marrying me. I love you so much."

"I love you more."

I picked the kids up at their grandparents' and drove us to Fat Cats to see the movie in the recliner seats. I ordered a pizza for each of them that was brought to us in our seats during the movie. The movie was great, and we all laughed, and it was just what I needed—a little escape from reality for 90 minutes.

My phone was on silent, but I felt the buzz in my pocket, so I checked it. It was my friend Randy. He grew up in Runaway Bay with Jennie and me. He always invited me over to his parents' house to watch boxing fights. I ignored it.

Then he called again. And I ignored it again. I thought to myself, "Who is fighting this weekend?" My soda was empty, so I went to get a refill and took the kids' cups with me to get them refills, and I called Randy back when I was in the lobby.

"Dude, what's up, my man?" I said.

"Have you heard?"

"Heard what?"

"I'm sorry, Dustin. Chad passed away."

Chad. My friend who I've known for 25 years. Who I had just had a beer with last week at Fat Cats. Chad was at my Super Bowl party. I had to call him after the first quarter to see where he was at. Chad had looked sick for a few months. I'd ask if he was "ok" and he'd say "ya." So I believed him because I wanted to. But he didn't look good. He was quieter than usual and had a couple of cuts on his face that never seemed to heal. Chad had never done drugs. But a few months ago, he asked me to smoke some pot because he heard it's medicinal and makes pain go away. We smoked pot and ate two Tombstone pizzas. The pain didn't go away, but the pizzas vanished.

"What happened?" I asked.

"I don't know. The clubhouse sent him home to go to the hospital because he looked sick. He didn't go—he went home instead. And when he didn't show up for work, they had the police do a welfare check and found him dead in his apartment."

I couldn't speak.

"Are you there?" Randy asked.

"Ya, man. It's just too much. Can I call you later?"

"Ya, buddy."

"I love you, dude."

"I love you too, Dustin."

I threw my cup away, refilled the kids' cups, and went back into the movie and gave them their sodas. The kids were laughing and having a good time. I was trying not to cry. Their mom was in the hospital. They didn't need to see me cry.

We got out of the movie, and the kids asked if they could play some games, so I got them a $50 game card and let them play. I walked to the bar and ordered a Bud Light draft, Chad's favorite beer. I paid for it and left it on the counter in the corner spot where he always sat, and I leaned his chair on the bar like he'd be right back. Then I went to the kids.

That was the last beer I ever bought for my friend.

Chapter 33

Sophie's 13th Birthday

I left work early on Friday to visit Jennie at the hospital. The doctors had Jennie's test results back, and she had meningitis. The Valley fever had developed into meningitis, and they put Jennie on another antibiotic right away. I didn't know how serious this was. I felt safe because we were in the hospital.

"Jennie, I need to tell you something."

"I hope it's good news."

"Chad died."

"What? Why would you tell me that right now while I'm in the hospital and the doctors just told us that I'm sicker than we thought?"

"I don't know. When is it ever a good time to tell someone that someone died? I found out yesterday when I was with the kids at the movies," I said.

We sat there quietly for a few minutes.

"I'm sorry. Are you ok?" Jennie asked me.

"I don't know. Doesn't feel real. He has just always been there. It doesn't feel like I'm not going to see him again."

"Chad didn't look good at the Super Bowl party, Dustin."

"I know. I wish he had gone to the doctor then."

Jennie was holding a Care Bear stuffed animal.

"Where'd you get that?" I asked.

"My dad got it for me. He came to visit this morning."

"I think you got sick just to get out of Pat's Run and losing to your dad."

"I forgot about Pat's Run."

"We can walk it, babe."

"They want to keep me in over the weekend again." Jennie started to cry.

"It's ok," I told Jennie, and sat on the bed next to her and rubbed her head.

"I want to go home," she said.

"Chad died because he wouldn't go to the hospital. The doctors found out what's wrong with you, so we just have to wait for the medicine to start to work."

"I am really sorry about Chad. I know you guys were close."

I thought to myself about how Chad loved to gamble. He always knew the odds. I thought Jennie and I were going to be fine. What were the odds things could get any worse?

"I can't believe we've been in this hospital for one week already," I said.

"What a honeymoon," Jennie said.

"Well, we have a room for two with room service."

"It is nicer than the place you took me to in Flagstaff."

I pulled out the hospital food menu and handed it to Jennie.

"You order room service, and I'm going to walk to the gas station to get you one of those giant pickles, ok?"

I was walking to the elevator and noticed the people in the rooms next to Jennie's were all different from when we got here last week. I felt confident they would let Jennie go home with me on Monday.

On Saturday I went to the hospital before work and came back on my lunch break. That night I took Sophie and some of her friends to the

Starfighter arcade to celebrate her birthday since she was turning 13 on Wednesday. I took pictures and sent them to Jennie, who was stuck in the hospital bed. After a couple of hours, I took Sophie and her friends home. It was 11:30, and Jennie had gone to sleep, so after I dropped Sophie off at her grandparents', I stopped at the English bar Union Jacks for a shot and a beer. I sat by myself for fifteen minutes before the bartender came up to me and let me know they had already done the last call.

"You had your last call at an English pub before midnight on a Saturday?"

"Yes."

"God save the Queen," I said, and walked out.

I went home drinkless. I thought I really didn't need a drink because they usually led to more drinks, and I needed to go to church in the morning after missing the week before. I also realized I hated that bar and didn't know why I ever went back.

Sunday morning I went to church service, then class with my sixth graders after. I usually hung around and played basketball with the boys until their parents picked them up, but I had to get to the hospital to see Jennie, so I said we'd play next week.

The doctors were in the room when I got there, and they were talking about releasing Jennie on Monday but wanted her to go to a rehabilitation center for two weeks. Jennie refused. She just wanted to go home and be back in our bed. The doctors told me it would be better for Jennie to have 24/7 care as opposed to three visits a week. Jennie was having a slight problem with her speech and walking. A nurse came into the room to take Jennie for a walk down the hallway with a walker. Linda and I talked while Jennie was gone, and we both thought it would be better for her to be in a rehabilitation center. A good friend of mine happened to run one that was covered by Jennie's insurance and told me I could even spend the night there with Jennie.

Jennie came back into the room, and we told her we thought staying at the rehabilitation facility for two weeks was going to be the best for us. Jennie didn't want to miss Easter, which was the next weekend.

"The kids and I can spend Easter with you there."

"In the rehab center? Will they even let kids in there?"

"Yes, my friend runs it. Let's just focus on getting you better now while we're in the hospital and having you healthy for the Fourth of July."

"Ok. The Fourth of July is my favorite holiday," Jennie said.

"I know it is, babe, and I will get you the biggest firework they make. We'll light up all of Gilbert!"

"You were going to do that anyway, Dustin."

Jennie knew me so well.

On Monday morning I came to the hospital and stayed with Jennie until her mom got there. Then I went to see the kids for a couple of hours, and I came back around 5 p.m. Jennie was sleeping, and Linda went home. Jennie had ordered her dinner and ate most of it, so I picked up her tray and placed it by the sink. There was a piece of strawberry cake wrapped in cellophane. I didn't want it to go to waste, so I ate it. A male nurse came in and took the tray away, then Jennie woke up.

"Hey, baby," she said.

"Hey, gorgeous. I brought you some more dry shampoo since you killed the last can."

"Thank you," Jennie said and looked around the room for something.

"What are you looking for?"

"My cake? I saved it for when I woke up. Did the nurse take it?"

"Yes, he did. He just took the whole tray."

"I really wanted it. I was saving it. Stupid nurse."

Feeling guilty, I said, "I ate it. I'm sorry."

"Dustin, you eat my leftovers at home and when I'm in the hospital?"

"I'll go get you another one from the cafeteria?"

"No, they might not let you back in. It's almost 6."

"What do you want to do?" I asked.

"Just hold my hand and watch TV with me and tell me I'm pretty."

I took Jennie's hand, looked her in the eyes, and said, "I'm pretty."

"I hate you so much, Dustin!" Jennie said as she laughed, and we watched random sitcoms until I was asked to leave by the nurse.

Tuesday morning I came to the hospital before work, and Linda was there. She had called out of work to be with Jennie. I brought Jennie a Sprite from the QT, but the nurse said she couldn't have it because they were monitoring her fluids again and were going to do another MRI. When the nurse was gone, I let Jennie have a sip. Jennie had a cup of sponges on a stick soaked in water that she could have, but she hated them. I left for work and came back on my lunch break to see Jennie.

"Babe, we got married on Groundhog Day and now every day is the same. I guess you saw your shadow after you said 'I do,'" I told her.

The kids were staying at their grandparents', and the hospital visiting hours were done when I got off work that night, so I went to the movies alone to see Morbius. Jennie called me while I was in the theater, so I left to answer it. She sounded confused and disoriented, so I left to get in my car. Then she sounded fine.

"I love you, Dustin. You are my best friend."

"You're my best friend, babe!"

"Ok, I'm getting tired now. I'm going to go back to sleep."

"Ok. Call me if you wake up again."

"I love you, baby."

"I love you more."

We hung up, then I ran back into the movie theater to see the ending of the movie.

Wednesday was Sophie's 13th birthday, and she was now old enough to visit Jennie at the hospital. I stopped by the hospital before work, and then I came back on my lunch break. I met Linda and the kids at the check-in. The boys were too young to visit, and you could only have two visitors because of COVID, so Sophie and I went up to see Jennie. I had a bag with me.

"What's in the bag?" Sophie asked.

"Nothing," I said as we got in the elevator and went to room 216.

We walked into the room, and it was dark because the bright lights hurt Jennie's head from meningitis. Jennie was eating her dinner, and Sophie ran to her mom to give her a hug. Jennie was moving very slowly as she ate, and her lip quivered, but she tried to act normal in front of Sophie.

"You brought the present, Dustin?" Jennie asked me.

Then I threw the bag to Sophie.

"Happy birthday, kid."

"Is it for me?" Sophie asked.

"Well, it is your birthday," Jennie replied.

Sophie took a new Jansport backpack out of the bag and said thanks. She needed a new backpack since she broke hers a few weeks before.

"Thanks," she said.

"Open the backpack," I shouted. Sophie opened the backpack and found a new pair of green Chuck Taylor Converse.

"Thank you guys!" Sophie shouted.

Sophie gave her mom a long hug, then went to the couch and, like most teen girls, went on her phone. Jennie was sweating a lot. The doctors wouldn't let her go to the rehabilitation facility until the fever stopped. Jennie was taking the medicine for both Valley fever and meningitis. Neither was working.

The three of us sat in the room until around six when we were asked to leave. Jennie was very tired, so we left her to rest. She wasn't allowed to walk and had a catheter to pee. Sophie and I walked out to meet Linda and the boys. The boys were playing on a cement pole in the parking lot and seeing who could jump over it. I said goodbye and went back to work.

I didn't want to go to work. I wanted to be in the room with Jennie, but I wasn't allowed. I felt I had no control over my life. The only thing I had control over were my haircuts. So I went to work and gave the best haircuts I had ever given. Jennie wasn't going to be able to work for a while, and I needed money to take care of her and the kids.

Thursday I came by after work, but I had to stay late for a couple of clients. I had told Jennie I would bring her dinner—anything she wanted. She asked me for a turkey sub from Subway. I showed up with the sub sandwich, a footlong so we could share.

"I didn't think I was going to see you today, Dustin. You almost didn't make it on time."

"I haven't missed a day, babe."

"Thank you. I look forward to seeing you every day."

"You're the best part of my day, babe," I told Jennie.

We ate our turkey sub that was dry because the Subway employee forgot the mayo, but it was still good. I sat in the chair next to Jennie, held her hand, and we watched the TV show Friends until I was asked to leave.

Friday morning I came to the hospital, and Jennie was really tired—as was I. She slept most of the morning, and I did too on the couch in the hospital room until I had to go to work and Linda took my place. I kissed Jennie on the lips before I left and let it linger. She was so tired.

"I love you, babe."

"I know it's hard to go to work, baby. Thank you for doing it for the family."

"I'm going to get us a house even if you can't work."

"One without a Stormtrooper in the entry?"

"I forgot to show you." I took my phone out and showed Jennie that I had moved the Star Wars Stormtrooper from the entry to the garage and into the man cave.

"You do love me!" Jennie said.

"More than anything. I'll call you later." And I left for work.

I got off around 7 p.m. and texted Jennie, "I love you." She replied with, "I love you more."

I asked, "What are you having for dinner?"

She replied, "Chicken quesadilla."

"Mmmm, I miss you, babe!!! Please get better. I need you."

"Ok, baby."

I went home and went to sleep. I was awakened by a phone call from Banner hospital at around 5 a.m. I saw the caller I.D. and knew something was wrong. I didn't want to answer my phone, but I did.

"Mr. Elkin?"

"Yes."

"Your wife's heart stopped beating, and we resuscitated her. She is on a ventilator now. You can come see her."

I hung up the phone, then texted Linda. I was alone and took a shower. I was confused. I didn't know what was happening. I couldn't breathe. I sat back on the bed and passed out. I woke up and looked at my phone—it was 7 a.m.—and I drove to the hospital.

Chapter 34
Easter

They had moved Jennie from room 216 to room 203 in the ER. I looked lost walking around the floor, and a nice nurse noticed the confused look on my face and led me to Jennie's room. I walked into the room and couldn't see Jennie's face. There was a mask on her face to help her breathe. I talked briefly to Linda and held Jennie's foot at the end of the bed. Linda told me she was going home to get Sophie and bring her to the hospital. They were still only letting two people in the room at a time, so she would send Sophie up the elevator alone and I would meet her there.

I waited alone in the room, standing by Jennie's bed and holding her hand. I wanted to kiss her, but the mask was covering her face. A nurse came in and told me they were going to transfer Jennie to another hospital on Power Road. They said Banner Baywood would be better at handling Jennie's situation. I had a friend who was a nurse at Baywood, so I texted her that we were getting transferred there.

The nurse in the room was talking to me, but I didn't understand anything she said. It was like the adults in Charlie Brown were talking. Two words she said stood out from the rest. She said "life support."

"Life support? What do you mean, life support?" I asked.

"Your wife is on life support."

"I thought she was on a ventilator?"

"That's what life support is, sir. I'm sorry."

I started to pray. I didn't know where to start. I didn't know what to ask

289

God for. He had already given me everything I ever wanted. Why would He take it back?

There was a knock at the door. It was the hospital chaplain.

"Hello, son. Would you like me to pray with you?" the chaplain said.

"I was just trying to talk to your boss. I guess He sent you?"

"If you believe in Christ, He's your boss too."

"I do."

The chaplain held Jennie's and my hands and prayed for us. He was a soft-spoken older man, and his words and tone were comforting and gentle. He asked the Lord God to heal Jennie and comfort her family during this time. He prayed for the nurses and doctors. Then finished in, "In Jesus Christ's name, amen."

Some more nurses came into the room to check on Jennie's ventilator, and I tried to stay out of the way. The ER room wasn't comfortable like the ICU room. There was one small plastic and metal chair, the kind you find in a school cafeteria. I sat in it in the corner of the room, watching the nurses work on Jennie.

The nurses asked me if I could leave the room for ten minutes. They had to do something to Jennie, and I couldn't be there. I walked out of the room and got a call from Linda. Sophie was on her way up the elevator. I went to meet her. I told her we had to wait a few minutes.

"Did you eat breakfast?" I asked Sophie.

Sophie shook her head "no," so I led her to the vending machines where she got a Kit Kat bar, and I got a Twix. We sat quietly in the waiting area, eating our candy bars. To break the silence, I said, "I don't know why Twix are called candy bars. They're more of a cookie."

Sophie nodded her head in agreement with me.

"Did Nana explain to you about your mom?"

Sophie nodded again.

"Mom's going to be fine, but she looks different today than she did on

Wednesday. She has a mask on that's helping her breathe."

A nurse came into the waiting area and told us they were done and we could go back in the room. I led Sophie into the room and next to the bed. Sophie grabbed her mom's hand to hold, but Jennie couldn't grab back. After a minute, Sophie let go of her mother's hand and took the lone seat in the corner of the room and looked at her phone to escape, I'm sure. I stayed standing next to the bed and held Jennie's right hand in my right hand and checked her forehead with my left. She was still hot. She still had the fever. I stayed in the room for an hour, then called Linda and told her to switch with me. She should be in the room with Jennie and Sophie. I met Linda at the elevator.

"They're going to be moving Jennie to another hospital in a bit," I told Linda.

"Ok."

"I'm going to run to the store and get the kids' Easter stuff for tomorrow, and I'll meet you at the other hospital."

"Ok, are you going to work today?"

"No, not today."

I drove to the Walmart by our house to get Easter things for the kids. I picked up baseball gloves for the kids that I was going to use as Easter baskets. I took the kids to the batting cages a lot, but they didn't have any gloves to play catch. I picked up 50 empty plastic eggs and Easter candy to fill the gloves. When I got home, I grabbed a stack of one-dollar bills I had been saving to put in the plastic eggs. You can't hide chocolate in the eggs in Arizona in April because it melts. In one yellow egg, I placed a twenty-dollar bill. That was the golden egg.

I called my work to say I wouldn't be in today, then I called the owner of the salon, Lethan—one of my best friends—to say why I wasn't coming in. He didn't have much to say. What can you say when your friend tells you something like this?

Jennie and I only told a few friends that she was in the hospital. We never posted anything on social media about her being in the hospital. I needed help. I posted on Facebook that Jennie had been in the hospital for the last two weeks with Valley fever, and today she was placed on life support. If they could take a moment to pray for Jennie, we would really appreciate it.

I took out the kids' new baseball gloves and filled them with fake plastic green grass, and I fit as much candy as I could in each one. Then I laid on the couch and stared at the ceiling fan going around and around and around until I got a call from Linda telling me Jennie was at the Baywood hospital now. I got up and kissed Chichi, then gave her some cheese, and I left for the hospital.

I stopped at the Quick Trip for a Sprite and a black coffee for Linda. I got to the hospital and checked in at the front desk, and they gave me my name tag. Then I walked to the elevator and took it to the second floor and walked to room 203.

We were back in the ICU and in a much more comfortable room than the ER. I handed Linda her coffee, then held onto the Sprite for Jennie in case she woke up. Jennie was hooked up to the ventilator, but she looked peaceful. A nice blonde female nurse with tattoos came into the room and talked to us. She let us know she was taking care of Jennie overnight and that she was going to get this mama better to go home to her kids.

I texted my friend Beth, who was working at the hospital, and told her what room we were in. Beth showed up not too long after, and she was friends with the nurse who was taking care of Jennie. Beth looked over Jennie's paperwork.

"She's really sick, Dustin," Beth told me.

"I know."

Beth was going out of town with her husband and kids for a few days but told me to call her if I needed anything. Linda laughed.

"Boy, you and Jennie know everyone in town, don't you?" Linda said.

Jennie and I grew up in the East Valley and still lived and worked there. The two of us made friends with everyone we met. We couldn't go out to eat or to the store without one of us running into someone we knew.

I told Beth thanks. Then the tattooed nurse said that Jennie was sedated and wouldn't be waking up anytime soon. She said that we should go home and rest—there was nothing we could do there—and to come back in the morning. We took her advice and went home.

The kids were with their grandparents—the best place they could be. Their grandparents' house was home. They had lived there for five years and at my house for only two months. Max was only six; his grandparents' house was all he knew. I saw the kids for a little, then told them I'd be back to pick them up in the morning to go to church for Easter.

I got home, and I was alone. My friends were calling me and trying to hang out with me, but I didn't want to be cheered up. How could I be cheered up? I sat on my couch staring at the TV that wasn't turned on. I looked at my Bible sitting on the coffee table, but I didn't feel like reading. Then I looked at the bottle of Buffalo Trace bourbon sitting on my bar and poured a heavy glass that I drank in two drinks. Then I poured another. I just wanted to sleep.

I woke up in the morning on my couch next to an empty bottle of Buffalo Trace. I picked up the kids for church and drove us there, then checked the boys into their Sunday school classes. Sophie's junior high class was canceled so they could go to the adult service. I was supposed to lead my sixth-grade boys group, but thankfully I had Jeff there and he covered the class for me. Then I went to the adult service with Sophie.

I've always loved Easter service at church. There were many years when that was the only day I went to church. But my head wasn't there that day. My thoughts were on my wife in the ICU. I closed my eyes during the service and prayed for Jennie.

After church, I took the kids back to their grandparents, and we celebrated Easter together. Linda had cooked an Easter ham while we were at church. After the kids were in the house, I hid the eggs at the park across the street from their house, then I brought in their Easter basket baseball gloves from the back of my car and gave them to the kids. We went out to the park for the Easter egg hunt, and I filled up water balloons. We let the kids start the Easter egg hunt, and Brian and I threw water balloons at the kids as they searched for eggs. Brian's dog, Ruby, was out and getting excited. She got free from Brian and ran to Noah and took his basket, then shook it furiously, throwing the eggs everywhere. We thought Max walked up to help his brother, but Max was putting the eggs into his basket.

"Max, those aren't your eggs," I said.

"I know—it's Easter. They're the Lord's eggs."

"Stop doing the Lord's work and give them back to Noah."

The kids walked back into the house wet and ready to count their money. Max found the golden egg. We had our Easter meal around their table, then I left first to see Jennie. Linda gave me some pink marshmallow Peeps as I walked out.

"Happy Easter, Dustin."

I got to the hospital and walked to the room holding my Peeps. Jennie was stable. I gazed at her and thought, How could you be so sick and look so beautiful at the same time? I pulled the recliner chair up to Jennie's bed. She was unconscious, but I told her about Easter with the kids—how Ruby took Noah's basket and Sophie was mad she got hit with a water balloon in the head and ruined her hair. Then I turned the TV on and ate my pink marshmallow Peeps.

Chapter 35
Keep Swinging

On Monday, when I got to the hospital, the doctors said the Valley fever had spread all over Jennie's body. The only thing we could do was wait for the antibiotics to work. Later that day, they were going to give Jennie another MRI to see where we were at with the meningitis. Linda was at the hospital with me. She decided to retire from teaching to be at the hospital with Jennie.

I left to get the kids when they got home from school, and Brian went to the hospital to be with Jennie and Linda. Sophie was going to go to a friend's house, so it was just me and the boys. The three of us decided to go to Freestone Park to swing in the batting cages and break in their new baseball gloves. The boys asked if we could have Chick-fil-A for dinner.

"Chick-fil-A is for winners," I said.

"We are winners!" both boys said.

"Okay, if one of you hits six baseballs in a row, we get Chick-fil-A. If not, we get McDonald's."

"But we like both," Noah said.

"It's called a win-win, boys," I said.

"I want Chick-fil-A though," Max said.

"Then hit six in a row!" I said.

We got to Freestone Park, and I got the boys a cup full of tokens for the batting cages. We went to the slow pitch softball. Noah went first. He didn't hit six in a row. Then Max went into the cage, and he barely hit two out of the twenty. I stood outside the cage, hanging on the chain-link fence, and yelled to them to keep their elbow up. I started to daydream about when I took Jennie to the batting cages when we first started dating.

Jennie liked to go to the batting cages. She told me she would go by herself sometimes when she was mad at her ex-husband, just so she could hit something. She would pretend she was swinging at him. One time, Jennie was with me and swinging too low and missing, so I yelled, "You're swinging too low, babe!" and she smiled at me with her batting helmet on and said, "No I'm not. I'm aiming for his balls!"

The boys were running out of tokens, and Max was next. He asked me, "I just have to hit six balls in a row?"

"Yeah, but they have to come from the pitching machine, Max." I thought this smart kid might pick up some loose balls to hit.

"Yeah, I got it," Max said and walked into the cage.

Max put his two tokens in the slot and waited for his first pitch. He missed the first three and hit his bat on the ground after the last strike. Then he did something I've never seen. Max stood on home plate, squared up with the pitching machine, and lifted his bat over his head like he was going to chop wood.

"Max, what are you doing!" I yelled. "The ball will hit you if you miss!"

The slow softball pitch came, and Max tomahawk chopped it. He got a hit.

"Max, get out of there!" I said, and another pitch came—and Max got another hit.

"Max, stop! You're going to get hurt!" I yelled.

"No, I won't. That's why they make you wear a helmet, Dustin."

Another pitch came, and Max got another hit with his tomahawk chop. Other dads with their sons were looking at us and laughing. But I was laughing too. Another pitch came—another hit.

"That's four, Dustin!"

"I'm counting!"

Another pitch came, followed by another hit by Max. We waited for the next pitch. The pitch came with another tomahawk chop hit by Max! Max threw his bat, and Noah and I cheered for Max.

"Chick-fil-A, Dustin!" Max said as he pointed at me while standing on home plate. Another pitch came and hit Max in the helmet, and he fell—but he didn't cry.

"Max, that was only ten pitches. You get twenty, buddy!"

Max scrambled to get his bat, then stepped into the batter's box to take a few regular swings. He hit three.

Noah was upset that his little brother won the Chick-fil-A for them.

"You guys both won, bro. Baseball is about playing. As long as you play, you win," I said.

"But I want to win! What if I get a hit in the fast pitch cage?"

"The 60 miles an hour cage? Get one hit, and we get froyo."

"Bet," Noah said and walked to the fast pitch cages. He stepped into the cage and shut the gate, then put his two tokens into the slot and stood in the batter's box, waiting for his pitch. The first one came and brushed him off the plate. He looked scared.

"Just swing, buddy. It doesn't matter if you miss. Just swing," I said.

Noah swung at the next pitch and missed. Then another pitch came, and he swung and missed. Then another pitch came—and he hit the ball right back at the pitching machine!

I screamed, "Yes!" in excitement, and Noah stood in the same place with his body shaking from the hit. Noah walked out of the cage and told me, "Froyo!" Another pitch went by, and Max walked into the cage and stood in the batter's box. The pitch came and zoomed past Max, and he said, "That's too fast," and walked out of the cage. I gave the boys a hug.

"Good job, guys. Life's like baseball. You have to swing at everything life throws at you. And when you miss, you stand back in the batter's box and keep swinging!"

The boys looked confused at what I said, so I said, "Let's eat." We walked back to the car and got in. Both of the kids got in the back seat like I was their Uber driver. I looked in the rearview mirror before backing up and noticed Max still wearing a rental batting helmet on his head.

"Max, what's on your head?"

Max touched his head and felt the helmet.

"Oops, I forgot. I'll be right back." Max got out of the car and ran back to the batting cages shack to return his helmet. The helmet was too big for him, and it bounced around as he ran. Little body with a big helmet—he looked like a real-life bobblehead.

"Where are we at, Dustin?" Noah asked.

"The batting cages."

"What ones?"

"The only ones we ever go to. Why?"

"My dad is texting me and asking."

"We are at Freestone Park," I said and thought, Why did his dad in Utah want to know what batting cages they were at?

Max got back in the car, and I took the boys to Chick-fil-A and then for some froyo. I didn't eat because I was running low on money. I had been missing a lot of work to see Jennie. I had food at home, so I was fine. This was for them.

During froyo, the boys asked when they could see Mom.

"I don't know, guys. Soon, I hope."

"Are you going to see her tomorrow, Dustin?" Max asked.

"Yes, I am."

"Will you tell Mom I love her?" Max said.

"Me too, Dustin. Will you tell Mom I love her?" Noah said.

"Of course I will, guys. But your mom already knows you love her. I'll still tell her—I know she likes to hear it."

298

Chapter 36
Sleeping Beauty

Tuesday morning, I got to the hospital and brought a Sprite in case Jennie woke up, and a black coffee for Linda. Linda and Jennie both took their coffee the same way. It was nice bringing Linda coffee—it felt like I was bringing Jennie her morning coffee.

I loved having morning coffee with Jennie. When Jennie still lived with her parents, she would bring me my coffee with a splash of milk into her room. I'd be half awake while she talked and not really listening. I'd take a sip of the coffee, then place it on her desk and lay back down while she got the kids ready for school. Her mom would leave for school, then her dad would walk the boys to the bus stop with Ruby. After the boys got on the bus, Brian and Ruby would go for their morning walk. Sophie would leave after them to her bus stop. Jennie would come back to bed and hand me my coffee again, then I'd sit up and drink it. Jennie was still just tutoring then, so we'd lay in bed for a few hours until I left for work. I missed those mornings that now seemed so meaningless at the time.

It had been over two weeks since I slept next to Jennie in bed, and I missed her feet touching mine.

The doctors told us everything was the same. I left Linda with Jennie and left for work. I took a two-hour lunch break that day to go back to the hospital to see Jennie. I stopped at In-N-Out to get a cheeseburger. I had gotten cash tips that day and asked how many cheeseburgers they could fit in a box. They told me eight, so I ordered nine—one for me and eight for the nurses. The nurses had been so nice to us, I wanted to do something nice for them. When I got to the hospital, I gave a nurse the box of In-N-Out cheeseburgers, then

299

walked into Jennie's room. Linda left to get lunch, and I felt bad I didn't get her one. Several of the nurses stopped by our room to say thank you.

I turned on the TV in the room to watch SpongeBob SquarePants next to my silent wife. I held Jennie's hand and rubbed it with my thumb. I would tap with my thumb like a Morse code to say "I love you." It was something she showed me that she did with the kids.

I left for work, and the nurses thanked me again for the cheeseburgers. I finished my clients' hair that night and didn't tell any of them about Jennie. I just told them stories about the kids and how everything was great. Then I went home and tried to sleep but just stared at the ceiling fan all night until I fell asleep.

Wednesday was a replay of Tuesday.

Thursday, I went to see Jennie after work for a few hours, and her condition was the same. I left the hospital that night and went to take the kids to dinner. Sophie said her stomach hurt and didn't want to go.

I drove Max and Noah to Organ Stop Pizza.

Organ Stop Pizza is family fun, but not a family fun center. The pizza is okay, but the atmosphere is like nothing else. An organ comes up from below the stage with a person playing it. Every note is connected to an object in the room, so while the organ player plays, the room becomes alive.

While we were driving there in the car, UB40 came on the radio. It was their cover of the Elvis Presley song "Can't Help Falling in Love," our wedding song. Earlier that day, I had heard another version of the song by the band Yellowcard. The boys tried to change the radio station.

"No, leave it. This is your mom and my song. We danced to it in the cabin the night we got married."

"I want to listen to Drake," Noah said.

"Well, you're a good girl and you know it."

"Dustin called you a girl," Max said.

"But Drake's cool!" Noah said.

"Drake is cool, Noah, but I need this, okay, buddy?"

Noah moaned, and we pulled into the parking lot of Organ Stop Pizza. We walked inside, ordered a pepperoni pizza, and walked upstairs to sit down and wait for our pizza. The organ player wasn't playing yet.

Noah asked me, "Where are we?"

"Dude, it's pizza. Why do you care where we are?" I said.

"My dad is asking."

I thought, Why does he care? He wanted to sign over custody of the kids three weeks ago, and now he cares where they hit baseballs and eat pizza?

"Organ Stop in Mesa."

"Thanks," Noah said.

Music started to play, and Max said, "Look!"

The organ player was coming up from the stage, and the walls were moving.

"It's your song again, Dustin!" Max shouted.

The song was "Can't Help Falling in Love," played on a giant organ.

Our pizza was ready, but I waited for the song to finish before I went to get it. I heard our song three times in one day—all different versions.

I went and picked up the pizza, and me and the boys enjoyed the show. We saved a few slices of pizza for Sophie and went home. I felt good from hearing that song. I felt like Jennie was communicating with me somehow.

It was ten minutes to eight when we got in the car, so I asked the boys if they wanted to stop at Water and Ice for a snack. Of course, they said yes. I pulled in front of the store two minutes before they closed, and we ran in.

"Hurry, guys. You only have two minutes," I said.

"Take your time, no hurry," the store owner said.

"Thank you," I told the owner, then went to help the boys pick.

Noah grabbed a bag of Doritos. I took them away from him.

"No, Noah. You have those at home." He was always so difficult in stores at choosing something. That was just Noah.

Max settled on an old-fashioned rock candy, which was just sugar on a stick, and Noah got some sour ooze that came out of a toy-sized fire extinguisher. We went home to their grandparents', and I walked the boys inside. Brian noticed Max had the rock candy out of the plastic wrapper and in his mouth.

"It's bedtime. Why don't you save that for tomorrow, Max?" Brian said.

I took it out of his hand because Max would have never given it up willingly and placed it on a small plate on the kitchen island. I walked the boys upstairs to brush their teeth, then I went home to sleep.

Friday morning was the same. I went to see Jennie for a few hours before work and brought Linda her black coffee and Jennie a Sprite. I got to work and blocked out a lunch hour to go back to the hospital. After I finished my 3 o'clock client, I checked my phone and I had several missed calls and text messages from Brian.

Brian had gone to meet the boys at the bus stop, and they never got off. He was calling me to see if maybe they forgot what day it was and walked to my house. Then Sophie didn't get off her bus, and none of the kids were answering their phones. A panic and anger swept over my body. Were the kids kidnapped? I told work I was leaving and left the salon. I got to the parking lot, and Brian called me back.

"Colby took the kids," Brian said.

"Of course he did. Jennie's on life support. He's the kind of guy to hit you when you're down."

The kids' dad had driven down from Utah and not told us. He went to the courts and got temporary custody of the kids since Jennie was unable to take care of them at the time. Then he took the kids out of school early and drove back to Utah with only the belongings they had on them at the time.

He was the kids' father, and there was nothing we could do. He could have told us his plan, and at least we could have had their belongings packed for them. The kids only had three weeks left of school. It didn't make any sense to take them away. He wasn't looking out for the kids' well-being. He was looking for attention.

I drove to the Sadusky house and walked into the kitchen and found Max's rock candy waiting for him on the kitchen island that he was never going to eat.

Brian, Linda, and I stood around the kitchen island talking. We decided we wouldn't say anything about the kids being taken around Jennie. There was a chance she could hear us while on the ventilator, and we didn't want to upset her.

Saturday morning, the doctors told me they wanted to perform a tracheotomy on Jennie to get her off the ventilator. I had to ask what a "tracheotomy" was. The doctor told me it was a procedure to help air and oxygen reach the lungs by creating an opening outside the neck, and a tube would be inserted into the opening. I signed off on the procedure to be done with Linda in the room. Linda let me know that she had talked to the kids' dad but not the kids yet. I left for work.

I had no control over anything in my life. I prayed to God, but it felt like He forgot about me or was too busy. Jennie was on life support, the kids were taken, and I had Chad's funeral to go to on Wednesday. I was quiet with my clients that day. I blamed it on my allergies and just focused on my haircuts. I got lost from the world in my haircuts, and they kept me from thinking about everything else going on in my life.

When work was done and there were no more heads to cut for me to focus on, no kids to entertain, or a wife to talk to, I drove home and got drunk by myself. I showed up to church at 9 a.m. hungover. But I made it. I stayed for the 10:30 class with my sixth graders, then left for the hospital to see Jennie. The doctors let me know they would be performing the tracheotomy Monday morning.

I stayed all day in the hospital watching TV with Jennie. The Godfather was on. Watching the movie, I remembered in high school I had some friends that sold ecstasy for Sammy the Bull. I thought about those friends and if they still had connections and what if they could make the kids' dad an offer he couldn't refuse. But it was just a tough guy daydream, and I switched the TV to a baseball game to daydream about the Dodgers winning the World Series.

I'd occasionally hold Jennie's hand and pray to God. It reminded me of the two of us holding hands and saying prayers before bed.

I went home that night and looked through some mail on the counter. One letter was addressed to Jennie from the Gilbert Municipal Courts. I opened it and read it. Jennie had a probation violation from her DUI for not signing up for alcohol classes that were court-ordered. Jennie being in the hospital the last three weeks, it had slipped our minds. The court date was for the next day, Monday, April 25th. I decided I'd go and explain to the judge our situation.

I came back in the morning to the hospital with Linda's black coffee and Jennie's Sprite, and we sat in the empty room as they wheeled Jennie's bed away for the tracheostomy procedure.

Instead of waiting around, I went to the Gilbert courts. I tried to see a judge early or just have it rescheduled, but they said I had to go to the courtroom at my appointed time. I went home and changed into nicer court clothes, then came back two hours later. When I got into the courtroom, I had to wait more. I had been in the hospital so much with not much to do, so I started watching the Johnny Depp vs. Amber Heard court case on TV, and now I was in real court. Even though I wasn't in any trouble, having to go before a judge made me nervous. Like when a cop pulls you over and you haven't done anything wrong, but you're nervous.

The judge finally called for Jennie, and I took the stand.

I said, "I am her husband. My wife has been in the ICU since April 1st and on a ventilator since the 15th. I just opened this letter yesterday, and Jennie is currently getting a tracheostomy done." The courtroom was silent.

The judge spoke and said, "I am sorry for your situation, and I will postpone the classes for two months."

I said, "Jennie is supposed to do a week in jail next month for her DUI."

"Yes, would you like to postpone that too?" the judge asked.

"No, I was hoping we could do the time now while she was in the hospital so when she wakes up, I can say, 'Congratulations, you already served your week in jail while you were sleeping.'"

"I'm sorry, that's not how it works," he said. But it was worth a try.

When I returned, I found Jennie back in the room with the ventilator gone. Her lips were so chapped, and I kissed them.

"Jennie, I'll bring you some Carmex tomorrow, babe."

"Everything went fine, Dustin. The doctors told me we just have to wait for the anesthesia to wear off and for Jennie to wake up," Linda said.

Finally, some good news.

My friend Frank had reached out to me that day. He was a respiratory therapist and living in Boise, Idaho, as a traveling nurse. He used to work in the hospital we were in. I told him Jennie was off the ventilator and the tracheostomy went well. He gave me some advice. Frank knew I was spending a lot of time in the ICU and warned me not to get lost in there. That every day is the same, and you can get lost in your own head. That time seems to stand still in the ICU. Days turn to a week, and weeks turn to months.

He reminded me that while time seemed to be standing still, there was a real world going on with or without me. Frank compared it to the classic movie Bill and Ted's Excellent Adventure. He told me to remember to wind my watch and keep it set on San Dimas time. That while it was fun to time travel through the memories I have with my wife lying unconscious next to me in the hospital bed, when I left the hospital each day, I shouldn't forget to live and take care of myself. That it's okay to smile and do something fun.

I told Frank thanks for the advice and that we needed to get a beer when he got back in town.

The doctors told me it would take a day or two for Jennie to wake up. I looked at the calendar, and it was April 26th. I couldn't believe we had been in the ICU for 26 days now. It didn't feel like that long.

Jennie's friend Mary came with letters friends had written to Jennie to get well, and she read them all to her out loud.

The next day was Tuesday, and I passed a taco shop called Tijuana Taco. Jennie told me it was her favorite, but we hadn't gone there together yet. I thought about that first night with her when we made tacos together. I hadn't brought Jennie food to the hospital to eat since the dry sub from Subway almost two weeks ago. I was happy Jennie would be waking up soon, and it being Taco Tuesday, I went into the taco shop and got a dozen tacos for the nurses to say thank you. I couldn't feed my wife, but I could at least feed the people taking care of her.

Wednesday morning, I went to visit Jennie. I brought her a Sprite, but she wasn't awake yet. I left for work around 11:30 and wouldn't be back later to visit because I had Chad's celebration of life that evening at the Val Vista Lakes clubhouse. I quietly did my clients' hair and enjoyed my job. I never thought work would be an escape for me.

I left work early for Chad's service at 6 p.m. I went home, showered, and changed. Then my friend Derick picked me up, and we drove to the clubhouse. The parking lot was full, so we had to park across the street at the condos where my brother lived. We drank a few beers in the parking lot. It felt right to tailgate for Chad's celebration of life.

We started to walk to the building, and I looked at my phone to see the score of the Dodgers vs. Diamondbacks game. The D'Backs won 3–1. Chad always gave me a hard time for being a Dodgers fan because he was a die-hard Diamondbacks fan. I smiled with my sunglasses on, walking into the building and saw a picture of him, and I said, "You son of a bitch."

I made eye contact with my brother and nodded. He was sitting with my nephew Jaxson. Justin and I were talking again. Chad was one of Justin's best friends as well. My brother and I shared a lot of best friends over the years. If you were friends with one of us, you were bound to be friends with the other sooner or later.

They were getting ready to start the service and there was no place to sit, so I stood off to the side with a few of my friends. I looked around the room. They were having the service in the reception hall where they have weddings. Jennie and I were talking about renting the room out for a party in August to celebrate our wedding with friends on the one-year anniversary of the first night we kissed—that was 25 years in the making.

I thought about how I had told Jennie that Chad died just a few days before going on life support. I thought, I can't believe this is my third funeral since December. My friend Doug's little brother passed away in December, as well as an ex-girlfriend, Traci. Coincidentally, we all went to Highland High School. I thought, Jennie is going to be fine, because things always seem to come in threes. She's probably going to open her eyes tonight and Linda will call me. Just as I thought that in my head, my phone—on silent—began to buzz in my pocket.

I looked at my phone to see the number. I didn't recognize it, so I ignored it. Something about that number just made me angry. I'd never seen it before, but I knew I didn't like it. My phone vibrated again with a text message notification, so I looked.

"This is Colby. Please call me when you have a chance."

My gut feeling was right. I was standing in the back, so I texted him back: "Not today. I'm at a friend's funeral."

Of course, he immediately responded with, "The kids wanted to know the condition or prognosis of their mother."

I turned my phone off. Linda had talked to Sophie earlier that morning—the kids knew how Jennie was. I had no idea what he was up to, and I didn't care. This was Chad's time.

A woman started to talk on stage who was Chad's boss for several years back when I was in high school. I recognized her because she kicked me out of the clubhouse many times. Once she suspended me from the clubhouse for a whole month for being asked to leave after mouthing off at the front desk. I thought that woman deserved to slap the hell out of me for what I was like as a 16-year-old. I had my sunglasses on still and hoped she didn't recognize me.

When she was done talking, they played a video of Chad from when he was a baby, growing into an adult, with the last picture of him taken last year at a Diamondbacks game. After the video, people went up one by one to share stories of Chad. Chad was such a private person—I knew he would have hated that. I didn't go up to talk; I thought I would keep our stories private. But really, I was physically in the room, and my mind was on Jennie back in the hospital.

I turned away from the person speaking and looked out the windows to the lake, where there was a pontoon boat docked. Chad and I used to break into the clubhouse after hours with an 18-pack of beer and take the boat joyriding. This wasn't in our 20s. The last time we did it was just before Jennie and I started dating. It never felt like we were breaking in since Chad had the keys to the boat and to the side gate that we took to avoid the security cameras.

I turned back around and there was a new speaker saying they were naming the boat the Chad Morrisey. I smiled because I knew he would have hated that too. Then they showed an 8x10 picture of Chad that they were going to hang near the entrance along with a plaque. My friends and I all laughed and knew that he really hated that. I used to tease him that he had worked there so long that when he retired they were going to put up a plaque or a statue of him. And they did!

After the service, there was only one thing left to do: drink. We drove to Fat Cats since it was close and one of Chad's favorite spots. There was a good group of people there. We all told stories about Chad and talked about how loyal and reliable he was. With each compliment to Chad came another round of shots and cheers. My friend Jeff's mom, Shirlee, even showed up for a drink and ended up giving me a ride home. She had known Chad just as long as me from him working at the clubhouse, and he always helped her out. Chad always helped everyone out. To sum up Chad best is to simply say he was a good dude.

I showed up late to work the next day. I didn't sleep in—I had work at eight in the morning, and for some reason, I woke up at 6:30 wide awake. I just laid there and didn't move, just staring out my bedroom window until after 8, then I got out of bed and got ready for work.

I got to work and no one said anything about me being late. I was coming and going as needed. Work was slow, so I left for the hospital. Jennie's condition stayed the same. Her lips were dry and chapped, so I put some Carmex on them. I sat in the room staring at Jennie, thinking how she looked like Sleeping Beauty, so I gave her a kiss to see if that woke her up. It didn't. That kind of thing only happens in movies.

I sat in the room most of the day until the nurse came in to let me know visiting hours were over but that I could have a few more minutes. Then she left us alone. I didn't see what a few more minutes would do, so I just grabbed my backpack and left. I was frustrated.

Tomorrow would be the same: I'd wake up and go to the hospital, then to work, then back to the hospital, then back to work, then go home and drink to fall asleep—then wake up and go to the hospital, then to work, then to the hospital, then back to work, then home to drink to fall asleep.

I got to the hospital Friday morning with Jennie's Sprite and Linda's black coffee. Linda was stepping outside to make a phone call but told me on her way out that the doctors wanted to put Jennie on dialysis because her kidneys were not functioning correctly and causing her body to swell. Linda told me the doctors would be back to explain to me what was going to happen and have me sign the papers for Jennie to go on dialysis.

I was alone in the room with Jennie when a redheaded male nurse came into the room to check the machine Jennie was hooked to. I had no idea how to read what the machine said, despite spending 29 days now in the ICU staring at it. It looked like it was detecting earthquakes.

I was sitting in the recliner reading a *Deadpool* comic book I had brought with me when, out of nowhere and very coldly, the nurse said, "If the dialysis doesn't work, it's going to be time to make the final steps."

"Final steps? Listen—Dr. Kevorkian, is it? No—Nurse Kevorkian, my bad. Can we wait and see if the dialysis works before you start talking about pulling the plug on my wife? The doctors haven't even talked to me about the dialysis yet and now I'm getting the news from you?"

He was a little taken aback by my response and left the room. He knew he messed up. It wasn't his place to tell me that. I stayed for a few hours and signed the paperwork for the permission to do the dialysis, then I went home to get ready for work. On my way home, the thought of losing Jennie hit me hard and I had to pull over into a parking lot. For the first time, I thought that there was a chance I wasn't going to be bringing Jennie home—ever.

I called work and said to cancel my appointments. I just couldn't fake it today. I went to pull out of the parking lot and head back to the hospital, but I stopped. I saw a Chinese food place Jennie and I loved—Grace Gardens. It was Friday. I had just been paid, and I had paid rent early the day before, so I thought I would get the nurses some Chinese food. I walked into the restaurant and waited to order. Then I remembered the last time I was there.

It was back in February. I was about to go to the gym and Jennie asked me if I'd pick up a to-go order from Grace Garden for her and the kids because it's on the way.

"Sure, call the order in 30 minutes and I'll pick it up on the way home."

"It's ready now, baby. It's on your way?"

"It's also on my way home. So you want me to go drive halfway to the gym, then stop and turn around and come home, then go back to the gym? That's not on the way—that's out of the way, babe."

Jennie gave me that stare only a wife can give you when you are completely right and they are wrong. It means you're wrong.

"Ok, I'll go," I said, and Jennie handed me a handful of cash and I drove to Grace Gardens. When I arrived, my order was waiting for me. The total was $35.27. I started to count the cash, and Jennie had only given me $33. I reached for my wallet but I didn't have it because I thought I was going to the gym.

"I'll be right back," I told the cashier.

I drove back home and walked inside, and all three kids came running up to me. They were hungry and thought I had food.

"Where's the food, Dustin?" Jennie asked.

"You didn't give me enough."

"Yes I did!"

"No, you didn't." I walked past Jennie and handed her the money back, then grabbed my wallet off the table and drove back to get the food. I came back home this time with food and gave Jennie a kiss.

"You're not mad?" Jennie asked.

"No, I'm hungry. Let's eat."

"So you're not going to the gym?"

"Heck no! You will eat all the Chinese spare ribs like you did last time!"

I missed her.

I ordered food for the nurses, then drove back to the hospital and gave it to them. I stole a fortune cookie out of the bag and walked in to see Jennie. I opened the fortune cookie and told Jennie, "It says we should have had sex on the new mattress. I'm kidding—remember when we went to Pei Wei and I lied and said my fortune cookie said I'm going to marry you? Get better, babe. I really need you."

The redheaded male nurse came into the room and asked, "Did you get us Chinese food from Grace Gardens?"

"Yes."

"Thank you. It's my favorite."

"Thank you for taking care of my wife."

Saturday morning I went to the hospital to see Jennie, then went to work. I left work early at 5 to go see Jennie before visiting hours were done. I got in the room and Linda was there knitting. She picked up her things and let me be alone with Jennie for the last hour. I sat next to her bed, holding her hand, until I was told visiting hours were over. I gathered my things and went to give my wife a kiss goodnight. I closed my eyes and kissed her lips—then I opened my eyes, and Jennie's beautiful blue eyes were staring back at me!

I screamed in excitement, "Babe! Jennie! I love you!"

Some nurses came rushing into the room to see if everything was okay.

"Jennie opened her eyes!" I told them.

The redheaded nurse came by the room.

"Let's not start planning any final steps yet, bro!"

I hugged the female nurse and slapped the male respiratory therapist on the ass.

I thought when I married Jennie that was the happiest moment of my life—but this was the happiest moment of my life. To stare at Jennie's face for two weeks and finally have her open her eyes and look back at me. It was a happiness and excitement I'd never felt before.

I stayed in the room for another hour talking to Jennie. Jennie couldn't talk; she just stared at me. She looked lost and confused, like the day I picked her up from school. Her eyes slowly closed back shut and didn't open back up. The nurses said she was resting and if she was responsive or talked, they would call me.

I prayed to God and thanked Him, then I walked out of the hospital and high-fived several nurses on my way out. We weren't out of hot water yet, but at least now we were swimming.

Chapter 37
The Long Shot

I went to church Sunday morning and was congratulated by friends who had heard the news of Jennie opening her eyes. At 10:30, I went to lead my 6th grade boys group. I was feeling great, so after church I played basketball with the kids and beat them in a game of 21. I didn't give them a rematch that day because I was excited to go to the hospital to see Jennie.

When I got to the hospital, Linda was there staring at Jennie. Jennie's eyes were open. The dialysis was working, and Jennie's body wasn't looking swollen. She looked good—like she was resting.

Linda left me alone with Jennie, and I stared into her blue eyes. They looked like the ocean after a storm: blue, calm, and peaceful. Looking into her eyes, I remembered how I had a hard time sleeping at Jennie's when we first started dating because I was a night owl. Jennie would play the sound of the ocean on her phone for me, and I'd drift off to sleep. Staring into her eyes and thinking of the ocean, I grew tired, so I sat in the chair next to the hospital bed and leaned over to rest my head on Jennie's chest.

Monday morning I had to drop off Jennie's Jeep to have a breathalyzer installed, as ordered by the courts. Then I had to drop my Pap's truck off at Best Buy to have a CD player installed. I had made the appointment and paid for it back in March. I was planning on taking Jennie home in the truck when she got better. When I got to the hospital, Jennie's feet were out from the blankets. Jennie hated her feet to be touched, so I squeezed them and she pushed back.

"Wake up, babe! I'm going to keep touching your feet until you do."

I squeezed her feet a few more times and she pushed back, then I covered her feet with the blanket.

Tuesday morning I showed up to the hospital with Linda's coffee and a Sprite for Jennie.

"Babe, I got you a Sprite. If you wake up, you can drink the whole thing. I don't care what the nurse says."

Jennie lay in bed with her eyes closed. Linda told me they were open earlier. I missed it. Jennie should have been awake already.

Wednesday was the same. My life was stuck in limbo.

Two of Jennie's best friends, Margo and Ashley, flew into town to see her with Marry. I left for work early so the four of them could be together.

As I walked away, I thought, "Maybe she would wake up for them."

Jennie didn't.

Thursday was May 5th. I thought about how on St. Paddy's Day I was with Jennie and thought she would be good by now and how the two of us would be celebrating Cinco de Mayo. I decided to still celebrate it. After work, I brought the nurses tacos from Backyard Taco. This time I brought Linda some too.

Friday I showed up to the hospital and Brian and Linda were there. The doctors asked the three of us if we could go talk to them in another room.

Two doctors walked us into a room that looked like it was for board meetings, then they started to talk. Nothing they said was good.

A neurologist came into the room to show us Jennie's MRIs. They were showing very low brain activity. They compared them to the ones from when Jennie checked into their hospital after being on the ventilator, and the meningitis was shutting down Jennie's brain activity. To add to everything, the Valley fever was still going strong in her body. The doctors talked to us about taking the last steps.

They said Jennie was being kept alive by the machines—that she would never be able to live without them and that, at the very least, she needed a kidney transplant.

Jennie's father, Brian, immediately offered his. Then I said, "You're old, she can have mine."

"It needs to be a match, Dustin."

We all sat quietly.

"Even if we do a transplant, Jennie will spend the rest of her life on machines. Have you talked about this with your wife, Dustin? What would she want?" one of the doctors asked me.

"She told me if she was ever in the hospital to make sure her eyebrows and hair looked good," I said.

"We don't have to make a decision now, do we?" Brian asked the doctors.

"No, we're just here to let you know what you may have to do," the doctors said.

"So we see how the weekend goes. Jennie still has a shot?" I said.

"Of course," one of the doctors responded.

The doctors left the room and the three of us talked—but not much.

"Jennie wouldn't want to live like this," I said.

"No, she wouldn't," Linda said.

The three of us sat quietly.

"Well, we still have the weekend," I said and walked out after hugging them. I stopped at Jennie's room and gave her a kiss.

"Get better, babe. We are running out of time. I'm going to work. When you wake up I know we'll have bills, and you want to buy a house. So rest, babe. I'll take care of it." Then I went to work.

Saturday I went to the hospital before work to kiss my wife. I didn't stay long. I got to work and heard about the Kentucky Derby.

The long shot Rich Strike won. I remembered Jennie betting the long shots when I was at Santa Anita. Rich Strike came from behind to win the Kentucky Derby. I raced back to the hospital to tell Jennie.

"The long shot won, babe! You are the long shot, and you are a winner!

315

Babe, you are going to win this! I know it!"

Jennie lay in bed, sleeping with the sound of the machines helping her breathe, and I left back to work. I was happy—this was a sign.

I got off work early and met Brian, Linda, Matt, and Cameron, who had come into town to see Jennie. The five of us went out for sushi to celebrate Mother's Day a day early with Linda. I got Linda some flowers from my friend Dana's flower shop.

After dinner, some friends wanted me to go to a reggae show at Dos Gringos. I didn't want to go, but I remembered what my friend Frank said about staying in San Dimas time. I picked up my brother and we went to meet our friends.

My brother wasn't there for me at my wedding, but he was there for me now when I needed him. The two of us took shots of tequila and sang and danced while hugging each other and high-fiving. I held my little brother tight that night and I felt like everything was going to be alright.

Sunday I went to church, then the hospital. The nurses had written "Happy Mother's Day" on Jennie's window in dry-erase markers. Things hadn't improved with Jennie. I spent all day with my wife, thinking about the Mother's Day cards the kids would have drawn for her—and if we were home, how I'd bring her coffee and breakfast in bed. Mostly, though, I just stared at her. She was so beautiful.

Chapter 38
Last Kiss

Monday, the doctors had Linda, Brian, Matt, and me in a room and talked to us about taking Jennie off of life support. Pulling the plug.

Matt had a lot of questions for the doctors, but I wasn't listening. I couldn't comprehend what was happening. I was silent. We decided we would take Jennie off life support on Wednesday, May 11th—her brother Matt's birthday.

I went to work on Tuesday. I was in denial. I wasn't going to lose my wife. In between clients, I went to the bathroom to cry. After the tears, I would splash water on my face and blame my mood on allergies to my clients and coworkers. My haircuts were great that day. I focused on them. Cutting hair took me away from reality. I got to make people feel good when I felt bad.

I took a lunch break and went home to take a nap. I was exhausted. I grabbed the book Jennie gave me for Valentine's Day and held it tight, then I slept on my couch for 30 minutes and drove back to work. I was pulling into the parking lot when I got a phone call from the hospital, so I answered it.

"Hello," I said.

"Yes, Mr. Elkin, were you going to be coming by today to sign the papers for tomorrow?"

"Oh, it's really happening?"

"I'm sorry."

"Yes, I'm on my way."

I hung up and parked, then walked into the shop. My client Phil was waiting, and I cut his hair. I don't know why I did. I felt like I was on autopilot. Then I left for the hospital. Nothing seemed real. I felt like I was in a dream and waiting to wake up.

I got to the hospital as Linda and Matt were leaving.

"Go, Dustin, you still have time," Linda said to me.

I was holding the book Jennie gave me for Valentine's Day—*The Missing Piece* by Shel Silverstein.

The room was dark when I walked in, and I put the book on the counter. The only sound in the room was the beeping of the machines. Then I spoke after a long silence.

"This is it, babe. You have to wake up! Everyone has given up, but I haven't. You need to wake up! Fucking wake up, Jennie! I need you! You can't leave me, babe! You are the strongest person I know! Wake up! Colby took the kids! If you don't wake up, he gets them. I'm sorry we didn't tell you, but this is it, babe. Please wake up! You've got to fucking wake up!"

A nurse walked in the room.

"I'm sorry. I know this is hard," she said.

I ignored her and said, "Wake up, babe."

"I've seen her MRIs. This really is best," the nurse said.

"She opened her eyes and looked at me," I said.

"I'm so sorry. I know this isn't easy. She is not responsive. When she opens her eyes…"

"The lights are on, but no one's home," I said.

"Yes. I'm so sorry."

"Can I have some time with my wife, please?"

"Of course," and the nurse left the room.

I took the book from the counter and opened it and began to read it to Jennie out loud.

"It was a missing piece, and it was not happy… so it set off in search of its missing piece."

I read the whole book to Jennie word for word. Then I put it on the counter and kissed her lips. I played music from my phone for her—Willie Nelson's song *Just Breathe*. Then I played Sublime's *What I Got*.

"I'm so proud of you, Jennie. You were so strong. It's okay to rest now, babe. I'll be okay, and I promise I will find a way to take care of the kids. They are ours. I fucking love you, babe." I kissed Jennie's lips and tucked her in with the hospital blanket, then gave her one more kiss on the forehead. Then I walked out of the hospital and drove home.

I sat alone in my house. I had prayed to God so much over the last five weeks and He didn't help me. So I spoke out loud to Him.

"I prayed to you, Father, on my knees as my God, and you didn't answer me. I'm asking you now to be my friend. If you wouldn't get me out of this, then can you please get me through this?"

I walked into my room with no answer from God. Then I saw Jennie's Bible that I got her by the bed. I opened it. There was a bookmark to John 11:35: *Jesus wept* was highlighted, and Jennie had written at the top, *Blessed are those who mourn*.

It got me thinking about Jesus and how He had to be human to feel our pain. Jesus was 100% God and 100% human. The night before His crucifixion, He begged God, His Father, if there was any other way out of this—but there wasn't. He had to bear our pain. To be human is to suffer, but He got through it.

There was my answer from God.

I climbed in bed with my work clothes still on and picked up Chichi and put her in bed with me. I stared at the ceiling until daylight broke, rubbing my little dog's head and ears. Chichi was a good girl. Then I walked around the house in a daze, waiting to go back to the hospital one last time.

I showered, then I stared into my closet. What do I wear to watch my wife die?

I grabbed a t-shirt that I loved, then I put it back. I grabbed a blue Dixxon button-up and put it on with a pair of black shorts. Then I had to pick my shoes. I chose a blue Adidas box. I remembered the day they came in the mail and Jennie telling me, "Why did you get another pair of shoes?"

I told her, "I've wanted a pair of Adidas Gazelles since junior high."

"You can't get everything you ever wanted in junior high, Dustin."

"I got you, didn't I?"

I put the shoes on and walked outside and drove to the hospital. When I walked into the hospital, the receptionist already had my I.D. badge ready. She didn't say a word to me, but her eyes said, "I'm sorry." I took the badge and went to the elevator and took it to the second floor. When I walked into the ICU, the nurses who were always so happy to see me didn't make eye contact with me, and I appreciated it. They had done all they could. What could they say? I wished I had brought them more tacos.

I walked into Jennie's room and Brian, Linda, Matt, and Cameron were already in there. Brian pointed to the book I left in Jennie's room.

"Shel Silverstein, *The Missing Piece*. That was one of Jennie's favorites," Brian said.

"Yeah, Jennie gave it to me for Valentine's Day, and I read it to her last night." The two of us shook hands firmly, then I hugged everyone in the room, and I took a seat next to the hospital bed and held Jennie's left hand.

A nurse came in with a tray of sodas and sandwiches and left them on the counter for us. We all sat quietly. The nurse let us know that the pastor that was coming to pray for us was running behind and asked if he could do it on the phone.

No one was angry. What could this pastor do? Even if it was the great Billy Graham, my wife was leaving us. So the pastor called and we put him on speakerphone and he prayed for us. Next, a doctor came in and gave Jennie a shot and let us know it was for pain and that Jennie wouldn't feel anything. Then they took Jennie off of life support.

Marry and her husband came into the room and Marry kissed Jennie. They stayed for a few minutes, then left crying. I wasn't crying. I wanted to. But I couldn't.

Jennie's heart rate dropped slowly and I held her hand. The family and

I would talk and I would make a joke to lighten the situation. Then Brian would tell a story of Jennie when she was young and Matt would bring us back to reality and say how much her heart rate had dropped.

Once her heartbeat dropped below 100, we watched the monitor like a time clock to doomsday. Everyone was silent.

Her heart rate went below 50 and I kissed Jennie softly on the lips.

"I love you so much, babe."

Jennie's heart rate dropped below 10, then to zero, and she let out a gasp.

I was holding her hand. The machine said she was dead. But I still felt her presence.

The room was silent. Then Jennie let out a second gasp, and I didn't feel her anymore. Jennie was gone. It was the scariest and most beautiful thing I had ever seen. A human soul leaving this world. My human's soul was leaving this world.

The nurse came into the room, and everyone wept. We all hugged, and I walked to the window to look out and wept. Then I grabbed a diet soda from the tray.

Linda was holding Jennie's hand and staring at her daughter's face. I remembered Jennie telling me that when she left her ex-husband and moved home to her parents' house with the kids, she would crawl in bed with her mother because it felt safe. She loved her mother so much. Jennie felt safe now.

The nurse came into the room to let us know we had an hour, then they had to take her body.

Linda and Brian lost their daughter, Matt lost his sister, the kids lost their mom, and I lost my wife. So much loss in one room.

I went back to hold Jennie's hand, but it was cold. My wife wasn't there.

When Jennie's soul left her body, her head leaned to the left, and now her face was bruised on that side. There was no more blood circulation. The room began to smell different.

I grabbed the book from the counter, then I hugged and kissed Linda on the cheek.

"I'm leaving," I said.

"Are you okay?" Linda said.

"I'm okay."

I hugged Matt and Cameron, then went to shake Brian's hand, and he pulled me in for a hug.

"Where are you going, Dustin?" Brian asked.

"I don't know. I just have to go."

"Well, come by the house later, Dustin. We're family."

"I'll come by later. Thanks."

I kissed Jennie's cold lips, then I put on my sunglasses and left the room and walked to the elevator. Everything was silent and gray. I handed my hospital badge to the receptionist. I wanted to say thank you, but no words could come out. I got to my car and started driving. I didn't know where I was going, but I drove. I ended up on the freeway and passed the hospital Jennie was at the last time I talked to her. I don't know if music was playing on my car radio, but I didn't hear anything. I just drove until my car stopped.

I ended up back in Val Vista Lakes, parked by the lake. I got out of my car and walked to the grass as several Canadian geese hollered at me, then fled to the water. I sat down staring at the lake with the book in my hands. Jennie and I had our first kiss here. I looked at the million-dollar homes on the lake and remembered Jennie and I picking what house we wanted to live in. Staring at these big, beautiful homes with palm trees and pools on the lake, I remembered Jennie saying we could never afford to live there—not unless we won the lottery. I realized then that wealth wasn't the size of your house or whether it was on a lake; it was who you shared the house with that made you rich. And for a moment, Jennie and I were the richest people in Val Vista Lakes.

I opened the book and read it again. This time the ending spoke to me.

The Pac-Man-shaped thing had found its missing piece, but he had to let it go.

I read the ending out loud: "So it stopped rolling … and let the piece down gently … and slowly rolled away."

The book had extra pages with nothing written on them. Jennie had asked me if I would write the rest for her—about us.

I remembered then, staring at the still water of the lake, that Jennie told me she always wanted to write a book.

So I wrote it for her. This is her book.

I love you more, Jennie.

Epilogue

I had just seen my wife cross a bridge that I wasn't meant to cross yet. My wife was in heaven, but I was stuck in some place between heaven and hell called Earth. I wanted to sleep. I wanted to sleep forever.

I came home from the lake and turned my phone off so I wouldn't be bothered. I laid down on my brown couch and cuddled with my Chichi. Chichi looked sad. I told her, "Jennie went to a big farm up north, and she's chasing rabbits." Chichi looked excited and then burrowed her head into my side. I stared at the ceiling fan spinning around and around until I fell asleep. Sleep. Sleep was all I wanted. Maybe I'd be lucky and not wake up. I didn't want to die, but I didn't care about living much either. Sleep was all I wanted. I wanted to sleep my life away.

There was a loud knock at my door. More of a pounding. It woke me up.

"Fuck! Who is it?" I got up and walked to the door. It was my friend Derrick.

"Dude, you're not answering your phone?"

"I turned it off because I didn't want to talk to anyone."

"You text me Jennie's gone. Then you don't respond to my texts or phone calls!"

"What else is there to say?" I went back to my couch and threw my Batman blanket over myself and tried to go back to sleep.

"Do I need to take your guns, Dustin?"

"No, Derrick. I'll see Jennie again, but not today—and not that way."

"Do you want to get a drink?"

"I'm not getting rid of you, am I?"

"Nope."

"You're buying."

We drove to the English bar I hated for some Guinness and Jameson. I hated this bar, but I also hated this day, so it made sense. I had three shots of Jameson for every Guinness. I had two Guinnesses. I didn't feel drunk, even though I was trying to feel drunk. I was trying to feel anything. Derrick and I didn't talk much. I just sat there spinning my wedding ring on the old oak bar.

I woke up the next morning and reached for Jennie in bed to wake her and tell her about the nightmare I just had. She wasn't there. It wasn't a nightmare—it was my life. I laid in bed for a few minutes, then got dressed and headed to church. I had to plan Jennie's funeral. I had to plan Jennie's funeral before I could plan our honeymoon. I drove slowly to the church. I did everything slowly now. I had nothing worth hurrying to anymore.

After church, I got home and looked at Jennie's Bible. I was afraid to talk to God after Jennie passed away. I had asked Him to heal her, take me instead of her. I felt like a dog that was smacked by his master for begging. So I stayed quiet now.

About 300-plus people showed up for Jennie's celebration of life. It was held at our church, Mission Community. The kids' father had brought them back to Arizona from Utah for the service. He didn't let their grandparents or me see them except for a few minutes when they came by my house to get some of their things.

I spoke at Jennie's celebration of life along with her father and her three best friends: Mary, Margo, and Ashley. After the service, we were walking outside to let balloons go when Colby got on the stage and took the microphone from the pastor and started talking. He made the kids come on stage and made them talk. The kids just cried. They didn't want to be there. Once again, Colby was going to make this about him. He said, "You have no idea what it was like to have to tell my children that their mother was dead…" He sobbed like a corrupt televangelist trying to get your money. I was angry and started walking to the stage to make him get off. But as I walked, I noticed the look on everyone's face in the church. He disgusted all of them.

You don't have to make bad people look bad. They do it themselves if you give them time. After the service, he lingered around and people ignored him like a man with leprosy in biblical times.

I didn't see the kids again after the service. I sent them care packages and their birthday presents marked from Mom and Dustin. I text them, and they text me.

I spent the next months drunk. Every day was the same. After five weeks, I had to get my life back together. It was time to go back to work. My friend Joe reached out to me. His grandpa owned a body shop in Phoenix. He said we could use the shop to paint my truck. I just had to pay for the paint. I had something to look forward to.

On Sundays, Joe and I would work on my truck for a few hours in the Arizona heat in a garage near Sky Harbor Airport. We removed the decals and sanded the paint off and fixed small dings, prepping it for paint. The prepping was the hard part and took the most time.

Going back to work was hard. So many of my clients I hadn't seen since before the wedding. So when they asked how the wedding was, I had to tell them, "The wedding was small, but the funeral was big."

Months went by, and I was still wearing my wedding ring. One day at work, while shampooing a client, I noticed it was not on my finger. I looked in the drain for it and couldn't find it. On my lunch break, I went home to see if it had fallen off in my bed. Jennie once lost her wedding ring in our bed. I found her ring for her while she was at work and I was making the bed.

I walked to my car, and there was a piece of paper on the mirror. In pink cursive writing, it said Ecclesiastes 3:1. I put it in my pocket and drove home.

I looked in my bed for the ring and did not find it. Then I looked on the floor and in my bathroom sink. I could not find it. Then I saw Jennie's Bible and I opened it to Ecclesiastes 3:1. And it read:

There is a time for everything,

And a season for every activity under the heavens:

A time to be born and a time to die,

A time to plant and a time to uproot,

A time to kill and a time to heal,

A time to tear down and a time to rebuild,

A time to weep and a time to laugh,

A time to mourn and a time to dance,

A time to scatter stones and a time to gather them.

I put the Bible down. It was time to stop wearing the ring. I still wanted it, though. Jennie gave it to me. But I understood it was time. So I went back to work.

That weekend, my nephew Jaxson was over while his father and I watched football. Jaxson was shooting lizards in the backyard with a suction-tipped bow and arrow he won at Fat Cats. He found something shiny in the rocks that the sun was hitting. He brought it to me. It was my wedding ring. I was so happy I took Jaxson to Fat Cats and let him spend all of my tickets I had saved—about 30,000 to be exact.

I didn't trust the ring on my finger anymore, so I put it on my necklace with my cross. It reminded me Jennie was in heaven with Jesus.

Time went on, and Joe and I worked on the truck on Sundays after church. But we hit a few stumps. Joe got COVID, and a few times we were both too hungover to work on the truck.

It was December now. The holidays. It didn't feel like the holidays. I thought about Jennie and me, where we were the previous Christmas. It seemed not long ago.

Then I got the best news ever—the kids were coming to visit! Linda had bought them tickets to come out before New Year's. I missed them so much. All three of the kids had Jennie's blue eyes. I couldn't wait to look into them.

But the tickets were booked during the 2022 Southwest Airlines crisis, known as the Southwest meltdown. All flights were canceled. I was so close to being happy.

But Linda found another flight later in the week—January 5th. The kids would come out for two nights. January 5th was when we would have Christmas.

Brian, Linda, and I drove to the airport in Brian's Ford Flex. We got there so early that I disappeared to get a beer at the Chili's airport bar.

Linda went back to meet the kids as they got off the airplane. Brian and I waited at the terminal. Funny thing, a client of mine was waiting there for his wife. She was on the same flight. Only I hadn't done his hair in two years and he had a fresh haircut. I had done his hair for ten years.

"Hey Peter," I said. He looked surprised to see me, like I caught him cheating on me.

"Hello, Dustin."

We had small talk. Peter was from Germany, and my father-in-law spoke some German, so they talked for a minute. Then the kids came down the runway.

Their smiles, their blue eyes. We all hugged—the five of us. I found my missing pieces. I felt whole again for the first time since Jennie had passed away.

Noah's hair was long and he wore it in a man bun. Max looked the same—innocent and full of life. And Sophie looked mature. She was growing into a woman. She looked beautiful. We all walked to the baggage claim with our arms around each other. We were a family again.

The kids were excited because it was their second Christmas. We still had the tree up at my in-laws' with their presents under it. Christmas doesn't have to be on December 25th. Christmas is with your family. And I had my family back.

We ordered pizza, and the kids grew anxious waiting, so we started opening presents. The kids were so excited—Max most of all.

Noah opened his present from Jennie and me—a Nintendo DS. He gave me the biggest hug.

"Thanks, Dustin."

"It's from your mom and me."

The next day, I went to work but got off early to see the kids. We went bowling at Fat Cats and played miniature golf. Life was good again.

I realized then the meaning of life. It was kids. Life's about kids. It's such a short part of your life, being a kid. Make it a good one.

The last night came, and I had gotten some Chinese lanterns for us to light. I told the kids they were going to send these to heaven to tell Mom hello.

Before we got to do that, Sophie had told her dad she wasn't coming back. The boys heard what Sophie said and they said they didn't want to go back either. They wanted to stay with us. I wanted the kids to stay so much. I thought there was no way their dad would let them. But he did.

And just like that, the kids were back in my life. They lived with their grandparents, but I got to see them all the time. That night we lit the Chinese lanterns and sent them into the sky and the heavens. I thought to myself, "I told you, Jennie, I would take care of the kids."

Jennie and my one-year wedding anniversary came, and I went alone to Tombstone to spread some of her ashes. I waited until sunset to spread her ashes at the OK Corral. The saying in Tombstone is "The town too tough to die." Well, Jennie and I had a love too tough to die. I guess that's why we got married there.

I bought a $20 scratcher that day in Tombstone. I didn't scratch it until I got home. I won $500.

I had told Jennie I wanted to get a 75-inch TV for the house after we got married, and she said the TV we had was fine. I heard in my head—maybe my soul—"Go get your stupid TV." So I did.

I spread Jennie's ashes all over Arizona, to all the places we went to together.

I put some of her ashes in a small bag and taped it to a mortar firework, then sent it into the heavens with a loud bang and beautiful green lights.

I spread her ashes in Pinetop at her parents' cabin with the kids. We all dug small holes with a spoon from the kitchen and placed Jennie's ashes in the holes with sunflower seeds. Sunflowers were Jennie's favorite flower.

I drove home that day with Max and Jaxson in the backseat. We hit some bad traffic coming home. It was Labor Day weekend. Traffic was at a standstill. The boys were restless. But I was calm. As my car was stopped, I looked out of my car window and saw sunflowers as far as the eye could see. I was happy.

After the traffic broke up and we were on our way home, we passed a small town I had never noticed. I had driven past maybe a hundred times. The town's name was Sunflower.

Sunflower. It made me think of the night I asked Jennie to marry me at the Van Gogh experience.

Sunflowers.